For David Monagan, born in Connecticut to a staunch Irish-American family, a lifelong interest in Ireland was perhaps inescapable. David studied literature at Dublin's Trinity College in 1973 and '74, and he became captivated by the country. After enjoying many visits in the intervening years, in 2000 David and his family relocated from the U.S. to Cork, Republic of Ireland. David has written for numerous publications, including the *Irish Times*, *Sunday Independent*, and *Irish Examiner*, and in his wide travels has developed a keen eye for things baffling and marvelous, such as he finds everywhere around him in modern-day Ireland.

JAYWALKING WITH THE IRISH

DAVID MONAGAN

LONELY PLANET PUBLICATIONS
Melbourne • Oakland • London • Paris

Jaywalking with the Irish

Published by Lonely Planet Publications

Head Office:
90 Maribyrnong Street, Footscray, Vic 3011, Australia
Locked Bag 1, Footscray, Vic 3011, Australia

Branches:
150 Linden Street, Oakland CA 94607, USA
72–82 Rosebery Ave, Clerkenwell, London EC1R 4RW, UK

Published 2004, reprinted 2005
Printed through The Bookmaker International Ltd
Printed in China

Edited by Meaghan Amor
Designed by Nic Lehman

National Library of Australia Cataloguing-in-Publication entry

Jaywalking with the Irish

ISBN 1 74059 597 1.

1. Ireland – Description and travel. 2. Ireland – Guidebooks.
3. Ireland – Social life and customs.
I. Title. II. Title : Jay walking with the Irish

914.15

Text © David Monagan 2004
Maps © Lonely Planet Publications 2004

LONELY PLANET and the Lonely Planet logo are trade marks of
Lonely Planet Publications Pty. Ltd.

For Jamie and three eager young wayfarers
on distant shores

IRELAND

SCOTLAND

N
W E
S

0 — 50 km
0 — 30 mi

ATLANTIC
OCEAN

DONEGAL

DERRY

ANTRIM

NORTHERN
IRELAND

TYRONE

Lough
Neagh

☆ BELFAST

River Blackwater

FERMANAGH

ARMAGH

DOWN

SLIGO

LEITRIM

MONAGHAN

MAYO

CAVAN

LOUTH

ROSCOMMON

LONGFORD

IRISH
SEA

MEATH

REPUBLIC
OF
IRELAND

WEST
MEATH

GALWAY

Galway

River Shannon

OFFALY

River Liffey

DUBLIN

☆ DUBLIN

Galway
Bay

KILDARE

Wicklow Mountains

Aran
Islands

The Burren

LAOIS

WICKLOW

CLARE

CARLOW

Limerick

Mouth of the
Shannon

LIMERICK

TIPPERARY

KILKENNY

WEXFORD

KERRY

WATERFORD

CORK

Cork

CELTIC SEA

ATLANTIC
OCEAN

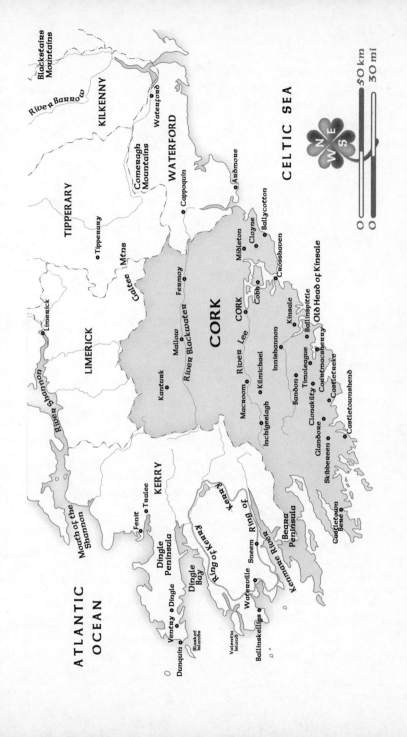

Chapter 1

For Ireland, the morning sky was a strange canvas of blue peace, the day before the most fateful September 11 in history, and the world felt at once fresh and familiar as I entered the Turkish barber on Cork's MacCurtain Street.

A swarthy fellow with a long black ponytail and hefty gold neckchains motioned me into the chair. He tucked a bib under my chin and began clacking his scissors.

"What's your name?" I asked companionably, looking out at the pedestrians ambling on the street named after a lord mayor who was shot dead by British irregulars eighty years earlier.

"Ahmad, I am called. And you, you are not from here?"

"No. The States."

"America?" he asked, clipping and chopping with a vengeance.

"Yes. And yourself?"

"I am from Iraq." Pause. Snip. His scissors suddenly flew into overdrive. "We are at war."

Gulp. Being trapped in a foreign barber's chair before a hulking figure who deems you his blood enemy is not reassuring, especially when the man in charge has a variety of razors at his fingertips and is commencing blade work close to the jugular. Psychologists refer to the "Stockholm syndrome" when captives develop an inordinate desire to befriend those in control of their fate. I embraced it.

"But we are not at war. It is our governments that are butting heads, and the Iraqi people don't exactly love Saddam Hussein either, do they?" I tried, scarcely imagining what engines of destruction were wheeling forward at that moment.

"Saddam a great man," Ahmad insisted, curling a length of string into a curious noose-like configuration.

I considered bolting out the door then and there with the bib hanging pathetically from my neck. But then, any rash movement could have proved terminal. So I instead meekly asked, "Have you been here long?"

"Two years," he said, his fingers ominously tightening the looped string. I nodded, having just commenced a second one in the Irish bedevilment boot camp myself. Weren't we merely fellow sojourners in the end?

"Is your family still in Iraq?"

"Yes, my father a pilot," Ahmad fairly spat as he leaned over my straightjacketed self. Without warning, he cinched his miniature noose around a stray facial hair and yanked the ends with all his considerable might, sending the errant follicle flying in the general direction of Baghdad. It hurt.

"Oh, he flies an airliner?" I struggled for composure.

Whoosh went another hair.

"No, a fighter jet. He is captain in Iraqi air force."

This was getting bad. Friends of my deceased fighter-pilot brother had probably lined Ahmad's dad up in their sights more than once. Dim recollections of UN sanctions and jump-jet-enforced no-fly zones burst into my head. Better not mention the brother, I decided, as the Barber of Baghdad dipped a Q-Tip into a jar of oil. This he set on fire.

"Do you like Ireland?" I tried, then watched openmouthed as he drove the tiny torch into my ears, ostensibly to burn off more errant hair there, or maybe just to keep me in line for an official Baath Party stiletto knife tucked in his apron.

Ahmad, eyes going adamantine, had the look of a man gleefully at one with his work. "It is far better than America."

At that point, I shut up. Happy to get out unmaimed, I in fact tipped Ahmad generously and limped off, nursing a head full of questions. Outside, the incongruous contrasts of Irish life lay rampant – purveyors of tin whistles, curry and "free poppadum," New Age potions, Baptist bible services, adult entertainment, country house heirlooms, and black stout stood side by side, while a pig farmer I'd once met began his day's lurch toward a dark den favored by local musicians and poets. Here lay the curious sweep of the Republic's second-largest city or, more accurately, the biggest village in Ireland, about to be celebrated as the European Capital of Culture for 2005. But could it ever be home? The security implied by that humble term was poised to go up in flames. And, at least temporarily, countless American transplants on foreign shores were destined to lose their deepest bearings, whether in plumbing the Irish end of the rainbow, or any other Shangri-la the globe offers.

But at that naive moment, all I knew was that the simple act of getting a haircut had grown at once sinister and comic. Ahmad had seemed a pro. Knowing Cork as I do now, I'd consider betting a tenner he was simply winding me up. But the story must begin at the start, with a fascination with Ireland that reached back through decades.

"I'm not going!" our six-year-old son, Owen, shouted when, eighteen months earlier, we had announced our plans to drop everything and move to Ireland. Then he crawled under a coffee-table, squeezed sheets of newspaper into balls, and furiously flung them out in all directions. His parents, the people he trusted more than all others, were destroying everything he treasured, so he now barricaded his small fortress with cushions from the couch.

Why a comfortable family should suddenly pack off across the seas to a rain-lashed chimera in the Atlantic is a question that confounds us still, as does the very essence of this brooding island that inspires, baffles, and wounds with equal sport. For nearly thirty years, wanderings to Hibernia had been a peculiar constant in my life, with the wife led by the hand through more than half of them. The place's siren call captured her spirit as well.

We had hit that time in life when an inventory of achievements, possessions, and responsibilities revealed that certain intangibles had gone missing, ingredients like adventure and renewal. So, crooked roads being the paths of genius, we would take the family off for the biggest expedition in our lives, a safari to Ireland.

"You'll love Cork City," Jamie promised, which was a stretch, because she'd been there for only a couple of hours once. But the compact bustle of the place had grabbed us at first sight, just as the wild beauty of West Cork had done, when we had recently visited at length; Dublin, on the other hand, felt like exactly the kind of frantic sprawl we had spent years avoiding. "You won't have to be alone so much because we'll be surrounded by other houses with all kinds of new kids to play with right outside our door."

At this point, two pillows parted and Owen's blue eyes glowered suspiciously from the floor. The next thing I knew, a fresh wad of newspaper went flying over my head. Then the wall of cushions closed again.

Jamie, on her knees now, kept searching for words of solace. "It will only be a year," she whispered. "I promise we'll make it fun. You know how much you love trains? They've got them all over the place there. And lakes and waterfalls and . . ."

Myself, I started passing photographs into the sarcophagus, showing Owen grinning on glorious Irish beaches, on boats and mountaintops, all of these from a vacation a year and a half before. Then Jamie slipped a plate of cookies through a gradually widening gap in the pillows. Suddenly, a shriek of hysterical laughter erupted from within, Owen's nature being far too sunny to carry the protest on any longer.

The ten- and eleven-year-olds, Harris and Laura, looked at us as if we'd flipped our lids. And perhaps we had.

When my father was my age he'd gone off and, without telling anyone, purchased a yellow convertible – which I eventually drove into a creek. My mother's father, on the other hand, had dropped everything to buy a pair of steeds and a pistol to ride off to the Yucatán for a go at silver mining with my grandmother.

"You're moving where?" asked our mothers, their faces drooping in dismay. They knew something about Ireland. Its quicksilver was in their genes, its hot and cold running emotions and doomed aspirations and pirouettes of talk and dream were handed down to them in buckets by their forebears and passed around in endless measure by their husbands now dead. Ireland to them had another simpler identity – it was the starting point for a flight to a better life elsewhere. Inexplicably, their offspring were turning straight back into the vortex, heading the wrong way down history's highway.

It was no help that thousands of seekers from all over the world had recently done the same, and lived to tell the tale.

It had all started in May of 1973, as I prepared to study at Trinity College in Dublin, after having dabbled at similar pursuits for the previous year in London. In search of experience, I took a train to Holyhead in Wales and the ferry across the Irish Sea.

Cement-stained laborers milled about in tweed caps and ill-fitting coats, invariably smartened by a threadbare but neatly knotted tie, a hand-me-down tradition perhaps from the English aristocracy who had ruled Ireland for all but five decades of the last eight hundred years and now employed the scorned Paddies on every British building site. With fascination, I listened to my fellow passengers' soft murmurs and watched their faces brighten as the burden of exile lifted. Through the night of that sea crossing, I drank dark pints with country folk from Galway and Tipperary, with returning masons' helpers and a poet and a priest. The language was the same English I had always spoken, but suddenly it had run wild, with twisted weeds and gorgeous orchids blooming in the midst of what should have been ordinary sentences. Sleep was unthinkable.

In the course of a life one sees countless dawns – and forgets most of them. But my first vision of Ireland will never be forgotten. The rising sun over Dun Laoghaire was only a whisper behind the haze, a vapor above dark mountains. The ship's passengers surged toward the rails, anticipating the embrace of their waiting loved ones. Ireland's lost daughters and sons, its no-hoper husbands banished to the factories and sewerage schemes of London, Manchester, and Birmingham, its arthritic old men, its reeling alcoholics, and eager nannies and virtuous nuns – they were all leaning forward, almost hurrying the ship's pace with the pulse of their quickening hearts. Down the gangplank they stumbled, clutching battered suitcases, satchels of presents, and above all their nostalgic vision of a place that was to them as boundless as legend. Their heartfelt embraces, their sobs of joy, and excited outbursts cast a magnetic circle of emotion around that pier. I was transfixed.

In that first Irish year, the lines between fantasy and reality blurred. Mountains caressed by mist, farmers who would put down a hoe and talk about the soul as if it were a moth struggling to fly from the wet grass, a Dublin full of bearded rogues who looked as if they had slept on a park bench and had pints and tobacco-wheezing laughter for breakfast – the island became raveled in my soul. Hashish would have been safer.

Onward flew the years, and I built a respectable life in the straightforward world of America, transmuting the instability of the freelance writer's life into a career producing specialty publications; marriage, children, and houses followed, as if one was punching in all the requisite points on life's time card. Yet plans for the Great Irish Escape continued. Jamie's grandfather was born in Roscommon, giving her an innate connection to the country as well as direct access to Irish citizenship. She passed a number of test visits, including our sublime month with the children in West Cork in 1998 when daughter Laura and I stood along scalloped coasts and, when luck was with us, hauled mackerel in one by one, each glistening catch landing like a sign. With the right lures, it seemed one could alter time.

At dinner parties in the U.S., everybody talked about wanting to cast aside their dreary obligations and do something fresh with their lives. Middle-aged couples indulge themselves similarly everywhere. Yes, yes, pass the wine. Well, we were two fools who actually decided to do it. People said Ireland had the best educational system in the world, that the pace remained slower, the life richer, the society ideal for raising children. Why not find out? Why not muster one great adventure before we were worn down with age or savaged by school tuition bills?

"You're so brave, we envy you," people in our tight-lipped little town of Cornwall, Connecticut, began to offer when it became clear that our scheme would actually happen. Some even swore they'd soon be doing something similar themselves, just wait and see, but they really thought we were nuts.

We planned and we packed. I had a regular feature column

and wrote for a corporate-backed publication, and both felt like they could be produced from anywhere, so why not find out? And didn't Ireland hold the promise of new tales for the writing?

Meanwhile, Jamie, restless after ten years of full-time motherhood, wanted to see if the fabled explosion of Celtic Tiger wealth might bless her with a colorful new career. Ireland's economy had supposedly become one of the fastest growing in the world; the place felt like it might offer new business ventures to be explored, for us both. So what did we have to lose? Pack the nets and the dreams, and there was no telling what one might catch in that summer of 2000.

Goodbye lunches, farewell dinners, and "when will you ever get out of here" parties were followed by tears and protestations of love as we said goodbye to our friends and families, wondering which one of the older generation would die in our absence. On the plane, there was much hand-holding, in the upraised fashion of prayer, or of roller-coaster riders hanging on for dear life.

We soon discovered that Cork's airport has some unusual features, including typhoon gusts from the North Atlantic that toss arriving planes around like confetti, and tractors that are kept on call to plough lakes of torrential rain off its runways. Calming tablets should be dispensed as arrivals thump down in the gales and suddenly confront the confusion of a country straddling two eras, with cows munching serenely in the fields to one side and cranes hefting together an antiseptic concrete and glass business park on the other.

With thirteen suitcases and five human beings crammed into two taxis, our new lives commenced. We parked before the Victorian house we had rented sight unseen on the north side of Cork City. The place was located in Bellevue Park, a cul-de-sac with a row of ivy-clad stone terrace houses to the right, and two lanes breaking left, the first a narrow passage mottled with shade.

Down that lane our future waited beyond a green gate. The house, a brooding relic of red brick and gray pebbledash, boasted pretty stained-glass windows on either side of its front door. Inside, a pair of sofa-ridden high-ceilinged sitting rooms gave way to an airy modern kitchen, which opened onto a slate patio. Beyond, tall hedges and small trees wreathed a tennis-court-sized rectangle of lawn.

Upstairs, on what's called a "first floor" (as opposed to the "floor zero" below), waited three bedrooms and a study, bifurcated by more steps and landings leading to a top floor. From there, downtown Cork could be seen tucked in between the twin branches of the River Lee, with squat freighters docked at grain silos almost close enough to be hit with a flung stone. Cathedral steeples soared like exclamation points over the warrens of the small metropolis, and sent the eye searching over the byways that fanned out around them. The beginnings of Cork's great bay gleamed silver to our left, while an amphitheater of green hills rolled lazily into the shadows of peaks leaning off toward the Kerry border. So far, so very good.

I led Jamie out onto a flat square of roof, and waved at the panoramic visions under the floating clouds.

"It's fantastic," she squeezed my hand, breathing in the enormity of our changed lives. "The town is so compact, and yet everything stretches out into the imagination. It all looks so interesting and new. Plus, this house is superb. I love it. That you found it the way you did is incredible. The kitchen is so big and bright, and the garden so perfect and private for the kids. Can you imagine the parties we could have here? This is exactly what we needed!" With that, Jamie, high on a roof at the absolute top perch over our new town, closed her arms around me.

Well, now, ahem. A guy could get used to this kind of thing. And Jamie, with Cork's bay gleaming behind her, looked as gorgeous as the day we met: her blue eyes radiant, her high cheekbones freckled and her blond hair glistening in the wonderfully beneficent light. I felt there was only rightness between us now, and that our marriage would be stronger for this journey.

I stepped back and pointed toward things discovered on my reconnaissance trip a few months earlier, when I had found us a real-estate agent and told him exactly what kind of house we dreamed of. Past a leafy park to a glassy edifice to the west lay what is known as "the tallest building in Ireland," and this was flanked just across the river by "the longest building in Ireland," a granite former lunatic asylum that has been transformed into luxury apartments for the beneficiaries of the country's new wealth. Between these points lay what is known as "the straightest road in Ireland," and this in due course leads into Irish-speaking regions where locals congregate on a nearby mountaintop at what is known as "the highest pub in Ireland." A mean little bar down the road, I'd heard, is sometimes disparaged as "the lowest pub in Ireland." Taking all this in, with my wife appreciatively at my side, I was, for a moment, the happiest man in Ireland.

Not for long. A horrible screeching erupted from somewhere in our perfect house, and we hurriedly climbed back through the top bedroom's window.

"It's not yours, Harris!" That was redheaded Laura with a shrillness in her voice that flooded the labyrinths of our new abode's stairs and inflicted agony on all eardrums within its reach.

"I'm not sleeping in a pink room! I've never had my own room. You've always had your own room!" screamed Harris. Then Owen flaunted his impressive lung power. Friends sitting at a tranquil candlelit dinner party on the deck outside our house in the States once heard a similar outbreak of hideous screaming and alternating demented laughter from our miniature threesome inside, and remarked that it sounded like a mad chamber from the Marquis de Sade. Racing down the stairs, I could picture our little darlings' nearly pure Irish blood flushing their freckled cheeks as scarlet as the hue sometimes glimpsed in those of their deceased grandfathers, Bill Donnelly and Jake Monagan – the latter surname being a bastardization of a flinty line of dirt-poor Monaghans who emigrated to Lowell, Massachusetts, to card wool at the beginnings of the Famine's ravages in the mid-1840s. Deasy and McDermott, Butler and McKeon – even the grandmothers' sides of the family were ridden with Irish blood.

Poor Harris was our biggest worry. Only yesterday he had been living in the woods, prowling for his beloved snakes, salamanders, and frogs. He knew there were no snakes and few frogs in Ireland,

and that his world had been turned upside down. Laura, the ready adventurer, had embraced the scheme more easily – until now.

"I'm not sleeping in the same room as Laura!" Egging on the fray was moppy, blond Owen, who would follow Harris off the edge of a cliff, would do anything to be at his brother's side. Owen is a boy who refers to the early summer months as Julune. A perfect name for an Irish summer, that.

So it was the children who began searching for their new senses of identity – with all-out warfare, and shrieks to the neighbors announcing that the Yanks had arrived.

In an effort to find peace we decided to walk into town. The vertiginous Military Hill, with its Ambassador Hotel formerly known as "the hospital for the incurables," and its St. Patrick's Hospital and Chapel of the Holy Ghost, led us to the shady descent of Wellington Road, and then the San Francisco-steep St. Patrick's Hill spilling down to the balustraded St. Patrick's Bridge over the Lee to greet St. Patrick's Street and its many Pats, Patricks, Paddies, and Padraigs waiting on the other side.

Wishful thinkers like to dub Cork "the Venice of the North" because the downtown is but an anvil-shaped island between two branches of the Lee. A few hundred years ago half the lanes in the place oozed water and several avenues hosted boats, before being drained and filled in to make streets. Were Cork hot enough to breed mosquitoes, great numbers of its 220,000 residents might contract malaria, which would help explain the behavior of certain of its more peculiar citizens. The original name, Corcaigh, means marshy place, and engineers say that the town's tallest buildings have no right to stand upon their foundations in the enduring subterranean mud.

Today, the main branch of the Lee runs so deep that oceangoing ships dock at the city's southern end. A bustle of modern commerce is everywhere visible from that point, with shop-crowded quays sweeping toward stately Georgian and Italianate facades and the Romanesque colonnaded St. Mary's of the Dominicans spliced between a boxy mishmash of modern theaters, department stores, and car "parks."

Above this tableau, on Shandon Street, the 150-year-old St. Anne's Cathedral's "liar's tower" thrusts its four clock faces, each of which was once said to tell a different time, before tapering into a spire crowned by an incongruous salmon. Although two thousand or more of that wild species somehow make it through the alluvium below to cleaner waters upstream, the lower reaches of the Lee are more commonly inhabited by gangs of mullet, which lounge beside effluent pipes discharging the city's wastes. These scavengers recently attracted a hungry pod of killer whales whose five-foot dorsal fins struck wonder into drinkers attempting to separate themselves from certain quayside Cork taverns at closing time.

Elated and curious, we crossed St. Patrick's Bridge toward the outstretched arm of a soot-black bronze monument – dubbed De Statue – of Father Theobald Mathew, a charismatic nineteenth-century advocate of temperance, now spending eternity urging ever more indifferent sojourners onward toward deliverance. Today, de poor fella's right arm held some prankster's recently emptied can of Guinness. "De smell off Patrick's Bridge is wicked. How do Father Mathew stick it?" goes one local ballad.

Great clots of people thronged the main thoroughfare, yakking with a blithe animation. An amazing percentage, some only ten or eleven years old, simultaneously chatted on mobile phones, a device the nonstop talking Irish have adopted with a unique mania, as evidenced by the presence of shops selling phones on nearly every block. The ambience was festive, sauntering and laughing with summer ease, and also chaotic with young and old cutting across traffic whenever and wherever they felt like crossing the street. The way everyone ambled before onrushing vehicles, like matadors fighting the modern age, was impressive. Young mothers shoved prams before buses, school girls giggled between accelerating cars – yet drivers never blasted a horn. The anarchy seemed to be governed by secret rules.

At the next corner a hunched-over Jimmy Durante look-alike was tap dancing on brass-studded shoes to jigs and reels creaking out of his tinny boom box. A teddy bear sat inexplicably beside him, pensively eyeing hordes of skimpily dressed teenage girls in platform shoes and push-up bras with earrings stuck into their exposed belly buttons: Britney Spears appeared to be a shoo-in for Irish sainthood. All her young devotees seemed to be smoking, puffing heedlessly without so much as a disapproving glance tossed their way. For years, I had told my wife what a moral and protective place Catholic Ireland would be for raising our children. Doubts were already creeping in.

Farther along, a wan individual sat on a stool, working a bent saw with a violin bow. The thing released ethereal, mesmerizing versions of "Moon River" and "When You Wish Upon a Star;" one wondered what the man could do with a hammer and nails. On the next block, four gaudily shirted Romanian Gypsies played trumpet harmonies from Herb Alpert's 1960s' Tijuana Brass.

"The place feels like an audition studio for dreamers," said Jamie, and I suddenly felt Owen squeezing my hand with excitement. Harris, his eyes roving in wonderment, was holding my wife's, and suddenly even Laura, just turned twelve and growing standoffish, was leaning tenderly against my shoulder.

A friend had predicted that the best thing about our adventure wouldn't be the sights savored but how permanently the experience would pull our family together. This was wisdom, I thought, as a redheaded midget in a plaid jacket and blue tie tottered forward, steadying himself from one parked car to the next. He turned out to be called Small Denis, and was famous all over town for the way he scaled certain bar stools and, after a mere pint, disintegrated into bouts of uncontrollable laughter over jokes only he heard. But then raucous laughter is never rare in Cork.

We found our way to a side street that housed the irresistibly named Cronin's Gentlemen's Outfitters, Jamie being overcome with a desire to ask about school uniforms that might be needed in, oh, another four weeks. The proprietor poured on his loquaciousness the instant he understood her quest. "Your sons are attending Christian Brothers? Why that's a fine choice for a school. Very strong."

"My husband was impressed," replied Jamie, referring to the whirlwind trip I had undertaken earlier to arrange our affairs. "And we're both thrilled with the idea of the boys wearing blazers and ties after the baggy pants and ripped T-shirts you see in American schools. Every day you get a new clothing fight back there."

"I can imagine. But you should understand that Christian's uniform has some particularities that give it a special class. Look carefully here," the proprietor said, pulling a black blazer off a rack. "You see the piping on the sleeve, the gold braid? The stuff is not come by like snuff at a wedding, that I can tell you. Why, there are only two manufacturers who still make it, and they might as well own Fort Knox. A shoebox of that material costs £900. Madness! Why, you couldn't even be leaving it overnight with a tailor if you wanted to see it again!"

Fearing the conversation was only beginning, and sensing that the boom was about to lower on the price of this guy's golden jackets, I slipped outside. A shadowy half-open door across the road boasted a gnomic sign, saying Hi-B.

"Hi-C and -D, too," I thought.

The dark stairs, with the first landing resembling a Giant's Causeway of beer kegs, looked dirty enough to harbor specimens of interest to bacteriologists. Painted in a sickly maroon, it was straight out of the dour old Ireland of decades past. But some unusual aura beckoned and I vowed to investigate another time.

For now I turned my back on the place, returned to collect the family, and we continued to wander the streets of our new home. The high, scrubbed northern light shimmered a soft magic on every edifice. From a recent sea-brilliant month in West Cork, from a honeymoon foray into Kerry's mountain fastnesses, and from other visits, the cool tranquillity of this light had lodged indelibly in my memory, as transfixing as a scent suddenly recalled from decades past. I asked myself whether it was right to have moved us all to Ireland, and replied "Yes." Definitely, yes.

How could one not love the place's unceasing oddness? On Oliver Plunkett Street – named after the saint whose pickled head now stares out of a glass case in a church in Drogheda north of Dublin, while one of his arms reposes in Cork's North Cathedral – shopfronts shouted of glassy and chromium modernity. Mannequins preened in skimpy tight skirts and shocking lingerie – one shop was even called Undies – that not long ago would have set passersby to making disapproving signs of the cross. In fact, an earlier Cork bishop decreed that, to prevent lustful thoughts, curtains must be drawn over shop windows when mannequins were undergoing a change of clothes.

Clearly, the world had changed. There were bookshops and boutiques and flash cafés exuding aromatic coffee smells. Coffee? That was a rare luxury in Ireland a couple of decades ago, when pots of loose-leaf tea were protected against the chill by wool caps known as "cosies," and the road crews employed a specialist in a tin hut who kept the brew fresh for work breaks that recurred all day long.

The tea brigades had long vanished, departed forever along with the thatched cottages, donkey carts, and quiet roads where old geezers on bicycles pedaled timelessly, with blue curls of smoke wandering out of their ancient pipes.

What kind of place, I wondered then, was this modern Cork City – or for that matter, this jumped-up new Ireland? Was the country the one I imagined that I understood?

Or was ours a journey into nostalgia, an indulgence a hundred times worse than purchasing a yellow convertible? The question worried me. No priests or nuns negotiated the sidewalks. The Cork grannies with black shawls had given way to fifty-somethings in bright American tracksuits, and stylish young women with carefully tended manes, gaudy jewelry and glittering Irish eyes flashing seduction in a glance. Here and there one saw old men with time-worn Irish faces and tweed caps tapping canes on the sidewalk, still seeming to have all the time in the world. They looked like people who held the ancestral memory of their race in their eyes. What would happen when they were gone?

I kept eyeing the stampede of Cork's jaywalking whimsy. People of all ages were cavorting in the traffic, dipping and diving into its flow like surfers probing waves. A sign said "Live Traffic Ahead" and I wondered if this place had dead traffic, too. A laborer strode between a truck and a bright red sedan, called a "saloon car," as opposed to a station wagon, which is called an "estate" and never mind that a modest housing development is known as an estate also. The Gypsy trumpets echoed and people ambled with a remarkable nonchalance. The weight of years began to slip off my shoulders. There was laughter in the air and loud shouts of "How ar' ya dere boy." No, it was not America yet, hardly. Not like any city I'd ever known.

We entered a quiet pub and ordered a round of toasted "specials," which turned out to be ham, cheese, and tomato, the same as every other toasted "special" in Ireland. Customers may ask for any kind of sandwich they wish to be toasted, but these other mutant varieties will never be billed as "special." The pubs always serve a soup of the day, questions about which are pointless. "It's veg." But the stuff is invariably fresh and delicious, so we ordered that too and savored our every drop, while listening to the conversation close by.

"Did you know that the sun is a nuclear weapon?"

"I never heard that, no."

"Well, it is, and if you are against nuclear power, you are then against the sun, and therefore you want to be dead."

"The only time I want to be dead is when I am listening to you."

"In fact, if you think about it, there are all kinds of people with nuclear energy radiating around their heads now, because they use the microwave so much and the mobile phones are dripping with it too."

"Radioactive Irishmen?"

"Yes, just like yourself."

As spellbound as the children were by this mad talk, it was time to put their jet-lagged bones to bed. A long row of cabs awaited fresh fares from a halting lane in the middle of the broad Patrick Street, but we noticed that, for some reason, no one ever approached the first taxi in the queue. Some hopped in the sixth or the seventh or even the eleventh, but not a soul ever progressed the few feet toward the first. Wanting to join in with the local spirit, we jaywalked across the street, dodged a bus marked "No. 1 Orbital," and climbed into a taxi at the end of the line.

"Is there a system here?" Jamie asked naively.

The elderly driver cackled in disbelief. "Would this be your first visit to Cork?"

Chapter 2

His travel-exhausted mother and siblings had collapsed into their new beds, but Owen refused to sleep and instead followed me into the lane outside our house. Everything was quiet, even the birdsong had grown melancholy as the clouds thickened. I wondered about the scores of people who lived in the terrace houses across the way, and the transformations awaiting us after leaving a neighborless life deep in the Connecticut woods.

A boy on a bicycle appeared, then slowly pedaled away and returned, three times. There seemed to be an Alice in Wonderland aspect to whatever was happening – illusions and dreams that could take us down any wishing well into which we happened to peer. The boys locked into their mutual sizing up.

"Time to start making new friends," I whispered to Owen.

"I don't need more friends. I already have Myles," he said of the soul mate with whom he had shared complete comfort and happiness, and the severance from whom broke his heart.

"Well, you can never have too many," I replied and asked the scrutinizing kid his name.

Thirty or forty seconds passed and the two boys slipped into our garden. There they kicked a ball. Then other children – two, three, and now a fourth – began to materialize like young deer out of the shadows.

The father of one of these introduced himself. He was in his early thirties, dark-haired and slender, more Corsican than Celtic-looking, just as are a great number of Corkonians, thanks to the genetic contributions of so many invading Normans, shipwrecked Spanish sailors, and Moorish pirates washing up on the southwestern Irish coasts. His head had been nearly shaved to the scalp, in a ubiquitous style inspired by the county's revered soccer star Roy

Keane of Manchester United fame (who would later walk out on Ireland's World Cup team in a classic Irish tantrum). But he smiled in that slightly canny way Cork people have, as if forever dwelling over the unspoken next thought.

He was called Diarmuid.

Dermot?

Diarmuid.

Once, people in Ireland were called James or Mary, Francis or Margaret. But the man's son was Feidhlim, and a girl in the garden below was Aoife (pronounced "Eeefa") – the most popular Irish girl's name at the moment – and the simple "Michael" is often pronounced the Irish way as "Me-hall," while Rory has reverted to Ruairi. The native Irish tongue – spoken by 90 percent of Corkonians 150 years ago – may be dying out, but people from Dublin to Donegal are christening their kids and pets with phonics-defying concoctions of vowel disorders. There are Aoifes beyond counting, and Ann has morphed into Aíne. How Aodhagan is pronounced is anyone's guess. Perhaps to help people figure such things out, dozens of schools have cropped up where all instruction is conducted in Irish, even though almost no graduates will speak it in their daily lives. Diarmuid's children attend one of those. In fact, all Irish children study their ancestral ancient tongue for twelve years and develop some appreciation for the irreducible poetry of Gaelic, although most rarely utter a word of it afterward, despite the fact the government spends countless millions duplicating forms and signage in a hopeless dream of reviving the country's dying native language.

"Did you just get in, like?" asked Diarmuid.

Our past connections and fresh hopes were described.

"Ye have moved to an excellent park," he said, using the peculiar Irish-English expression for culs-de-sac. "You'll find no trouble here. It's very safe, and there are heaps of kids who get along just grand, like."

It sounded too good to be true – would in time prove far too good to be true – but it was what I wanted to hear, because surrounding the children with a web of reassuring intimacy was our first goal.

Diarmuid went on to explain that the sizable terrace houses in Bellevue Park were built for ascot-wreathed army officers who once were deployed in keeping ever-defiant Cork, the Rebel City, under the imperial English thumb. Field Marshal Montgomery, who would become famous for vanquishing Rommel's panzer divisions in North Africa and leading the Allies' northern pincer into Germany, began his military career there, as did Lord Percival who presided over the ignominious fall of 130,000 British and Allied troops to the Japanese in Singapore.

"Twenty-one bullet holes are lodged into these houses from one skirmish with the Irish Republican Army," my new neighbor told me. In minutes, because Diarmuid is a talker, I learned that history's ghosts lay all around.

A thousand feet up Military Hill from where we stood, the rank-and-file occupation troops had been housed in a sprawling barracks that has since been renamed after Michael Collins, the charismatic leader of the 1920–21 War of Independence. As the rebellion intensified, the British filled the place with hit squads of roving irregulars, including a thug-like group known as the "Black and Tans." In one brutal episode, a drunken Tan shot a sixty-five-year-old Cork priest through the forehead. His mates also murdered Thomas MacCurtain, the first duly elected lord mayor of Cork (and a commandant in the Irish Republican Army). The replacement mayor, Terence MacSweeney, was duly arrested and promptly went on a seventy-four-day hunger strike, culminating in his death in October 1920.

IRA guerrillas got even by tossing a petrol bomb into a car full of Black and Tans outside the barracks, killing one and wounding several others. The next night, December 11, the Tans undertook a booze-soaked rampage, burning nearby houses before proceeding into the city center where they torched half of St. Patrick Street, the public library, and the town hall, beating pedestrians, kicking priests, killing two men in their beds, looting, and destroying shops by the dozen.

A disgusted participant wrote his mother in England shortly afterwards:

In all my life I have never experienced such orgies of murder, arson, and looting as I have witnessed during the past sixteen days with the RIC Auxiliaries. It baffles description . . . Many who have witnessed similar scenes in France and Flanders [during World War I] say that nothing they had experienced was comparable to the punishment meted out to Cork.

Suddenly a shout arose from the children playing on our newly rented lawn, and a soccer ball went careering past our heads.

"Notice that your garden there is a perfect rectangle," Diarmuid observed. "That's because it once served as a tennis court for Montgomery and the other Brit scoundrels. But, ah sure, no one will hold that against ye."

My new friend laughed and walked off with a smile, but I wondered.

The next morning boasted an astonishing display, for Ireland, of brilliant sun. I found the boys fast asleep in their bunk beds, with their treasured blankets from infancy lovingly tucked by their sides. At the top of the ladder to Owen's perch, a favorite stuffed bear, handmade by a friend, kept a tender guard. At the bottom rung, two pairs of slippers waited, toes out in perfect symmetry, while photographs from earlier good times stood reassuringly on their dresser. Already, Jamie's protective touch of order had transformed their new room. It would clearly not take her long to cast an aura of belonging over our new home.

Feeling blessed, I walked to the top of our lane where another neighbor quickly put out his hand, introducing himself as Pat O'Neill. Not Paddy, but Pat.

He had keen blue eyes and a gaze that left the recipient nowhere to hide. It became apparent that Pat O'Neill had watched our arrival closely. He said he had worked in New York and California and loved America, thought it was the best country in the world. Really? In Ireland, one tends to take such grand statements, in fact assertions of every kind, with a grain of salt. This is because many times a cheerful pronouncement actually is but a lure to draw a person out. Pat next warned us to watch ourselves because it was very different in Cork, that everybody minds each other's business constantly.

"They call it the valley of the squinting windows," he explained, as children not seen the day before began lingering curiously outside our green gate.

Another neighbor introduced himself as Shaun Higgins and, with a barely concealed smile, asked if I was a journalist.

And was he a bloody espionage agent? True, the *Irish Times* had just published a humor piece I had penned from the U.S. about certain peculiar Anglo-Irish expressions, and I planned on doing more magazine and newspaper writing about our adventures. But I hardly thought the whole country would be placed on red alert with my first offering, much less peg me on sight.

"I saw ye get out of the taxi yesterday and couldn't help wondering if ye might be the person who wrote the newspaper article about moving from America to Cork, and I don't mean to be forward, but I was just curious, because it was funny. Ye don't have to tell me of course."

Like hell I didn't. In Ireland, they can still coax information from your pores, can charm and entice typically overly frank newcomers into revealing all manner of things. In Ireland, fresh information is treasured like pearls plucked from an oyster. One man may have a wallet choking with fifty pound notes, another a slick new car, but he who has collected the most secrets will in some way feel the richest at the end of the day. Pat O'Neill pretended to be refinishing his iron fence – he never stopped chipping away at that thing as the months passed – but he was listening to every word, not wanting Shaun Higgins to mine the fresh ore before he did.

After spending thirty-five years as a ballet dancer, a few early ones as a boxer, and working the stage in Dublin and on Broadway, Shaun had a gift for fast conversational footwork. A great character, he was born at the other end of the terrace from where he now runs a bed-and-breakfast with his equally engaging wife, Breda, at that moment eyeing us from behind a curtain. Running a B&B seemed like an occupation from Ireland's earlier era of modest expectations. But hold on, it turned out that Shaun and Breda pocketed enough from all those rasher, tomato, blood pudding, and egg plates, to holiday for four months every winter in Florida or Australia, or both. Did they need an assistant?

"Well, I wish ye the very best here with us, and if there is any way we can help, please ask," Shaun offered warmly. It felt as if we were being welcomed into a village, rather than some anonymous foreign city.

In search of food, I found my way to a prodigious supermarket whose offerings would have once filled a hundred corner shops. In fact, it was about ninety times larger than an early Irish prototype I used to visit on Dublin's north side, back when such emporia were as exotic to the island as string bikinis. That sleepy bazaar had proffered such delicacies as dirty spuds, burly cabbages, and fatty mince, along with tinned kippers, tinned steak and kidney pies, and tinned tongue, the latter foodstuffs having virtually disappeared since. Back in 1973, food was not something with which the Irish pampered themselves, nor was much of anything else. The ancestral memory of the Famine still hung over the land.

But behold now. A shivering chill pervaded this cavernous new supermarket, and the engines of its refrigeration systems rumbled as if a Boeing 747 might be advancing down aisle eight or nine. Gauntlets of frozen dinners and pizzas gave way to seemingly infinite varieties of potato chips, called "crisps." Plain, cheese and onion, salt and vinegar, smoky bacon, barbecue, steak sauce, garlic, pickle, sour cream, prawn cocktail, cracked pepper, pizza: endless fantasy flavors beckoned in the place of the kettles of boiling spuds that once graced every hob and hearth in the land. The adult Irish clearly still adore their spuds – only the trendiest restaurants would think of serving a meal without heaps of them, one fried or mashed and the other baked and saturated in some form of goo. Potato skins, potato wedges, potato salad sandwiches, potato pancakes and soup – all are freely available too. Yet Irish chip shops now import all their spuds, and a dinner partner would soon bemoan that his children were losing track of the potatoes in their souls. "There was no pasta in this county when I was a boy. Pasta is not Irish. Rice is not Irish. But that's what the kids want now. Who knows where this country is headed?"

In any event, the aisles of crisps gave way to walls hung with plastic garden chairs, cappuccino machines, and black brassieres of a shocking scantiness. Another department offered choice single malt whiskies; Finnish vodkas; Hungarian, New Zealand, Chilean, South African, and even Lebanese wines – wine from about every sun-blasted country on earth. In the 1970s, a person asking for wine in Ireland would have been regarded as a boarding-school prat. But now people in a working-class suburb were tickling their tongues at delicate tastes from free sample bottles.

With a groaning cart, I proceeded to the cash register and an object lesson that Ireland, despite its eager strides into the "never-never," as they used to call a life built upon debt, can still entail curious time travels. As my purchases were added up, a frown settled upon the cashier's face. "I'm afraid your total comes to £117. We have to clear all credit-card charges over £100 with our central office," she said in a somnambulant tone that suggested this drill was repeated often. "Won't be a sec'."

People back in the queue, evidently long inured to the practice, began to sag their heads and age visibly as the clock ticked. And ticked. Finally the clerk returned from the far ends of the store.

"I'm very sorry, sir, but you have a foreign credit card and it won't go through. Credit cards are meant to be used in their country of origin."

Was this a signal to drop one's spuds on the floor and head for home? I had told our friends I knew Ireland inside out, but I suddenly didn't know where I had brought my family at all. Clueless, I pulled out another equally foreign credit card, whispered hocus-pocus, and jettisoned some nonessentials – the bottle of Bordeaux hurt – to bring the total under 100 punts. Voila!

After sharing a fine lunch with the awakening family, I set to other organizational vicissitudes. And here came another rendez-vous with Oddness Abroad. In addition to the usual government bureaucracies, a newcomer to Ireland must cope with several huge and Byzantine monopolies that might as well be called One and Only Electric, Amalgamated Phones, and Go Away Insurance. None, I'd been warned, would talk to potential customers unless they had first established a checking account, which sounds simple enough until one discovers that, on this logic-defying island, this is about as difficult as wresting top-secret clearance from the CIA or MI5.

An accountant's son, I imagined I had prepared for every mundane exigency required. So later that afternoon, I entered a branch of one of the most powerful banks in the country, and, after the appropriate introductions, confidently dropped a quarter-inch sheaf of financial documents on the desk of a prim middle manager, explaining my quest.

"It's a checking account you'd like, is it?" she responded in that peculiar way that Irish people have of tediously restating what somebody asked clear as day, turning the simple communication into a question, and looking out at the idea in dazzled wonder, while they buy time to arrange their secret thoughts.

"That's it."

Mousy-eyed and purse-lipped, she proceeded to eye our bona fides with a drawn-out fascination that made me think she was savoring the pleasure of divining and memorizing for later conversation every last detail of our family's financial secrets, just as Pat O'Neill had warned.

"You have a valuable house."

"Yes, a fine house."

"And two cars and some savings."

"Yes, yes."

"Very good." Flip went some more pages, then she sighed. "It's an unusual situation."

Day Two of our brave adventure and my palms were sweating before the task of pleading for a checkbook. Some explorer.

Finally, the bank clerk fluffed out her white sleeves and leaned closer. "Although our normal policy is not to issue check-writing privileges until a customer has been with us for nine months, perhaps we might be able to bend things a bit in your case, and authorize this in six months if your transactions prove to be orderly."

"But I've had a checking account since I was sixteen."

"I'm sure you have," she replied coolly. "But none of your

records specifically pertain here. Not to cause any offense, but how can we possibly know that you are who you say you are until six months have passed?"

The odd truth is that this was in some ways a fair question, considering we had uprooted everything that makes for a person's identity – a career, a community, a home, friends and family all left behind. Why? I didn't have the words to make her understand. I kept insisting that I still had a contract to produce one of the lucrative newsletters that I had researched and written for fifteen years, a worldwide publication for cardiologists, not realizing that ace in the hole would unexpectedly lose its corporate backing and vanish in another four weeks.

She knew what she knew and we just didn't make sense. We had thrown off the most enviable stability any parents can give their family, and why? For the vague quest to make one's life new at the dubious age of forty-seven, and in Jamie's much better preserved case, forty-two. Not checking-account material then.

Our spacious (and newly rented out) house in Connecticut was located at the end of a third-of-a-mile-long driveway into a sanctuary of five hundred acres of woods. Our town was a picture-book place with white-steepled churches, a red clapboard-covered bridge over a trout-filled river, and eight hundred full-time residents, most of who knew each other well – too well. At night we could hear coyotes yowl, and wild turkeys giving up the ghost to feasting great horned owls and bobcats. Harris was enthralled with the life in that forest. He, Owen, and Laura would happily idle away their summer days on the lake five minutes down the path from the door we never locked. After school in winter, they hurtled down the slopes of the nearby family-run ski area and were whisked back home in time for hot chocolate and supper. Neighboring parents would look after each other's children without a second's thought. It was about as perfect a place as modern-day America offers for raising kids.

And yet, after twelve years of impersonating model parents, we were itchy. People in North America's endless suburbs and smaller towns have withdrawn into hermetically sealed worlds. They buy their groceries, pick up their mail, fetch their children from school, and are never otherwise seen again, unless they participate in some ruthlessly organized activity like the drill teams of children's sports named U.S.A. Hockey, or U.S.A. Little League, or U.S.A. Pick-Up Sticks, each with a dozen pages of officially sanctioned U.S.A. Rules and boards of governors to look after the behavior of each U.S.A. Child.

The creature comforts and automobile to-and-fro of modern life swallow entire families into oblivion. Televisions offer two hundred channels, video shops two thousand movies, and the Internet connects people to previously unimaginable distractions from all over the globe – but not to their neighbors. The thralls of easy celebration that united previous generations have all but vanished. Americans have become ever more serious and efficient, and increasingly antisocial, thanks to men and women slaving in equal measure, both being too exhausted and time-starved at the end of the day to pause for a social drink or street-corner chat. This guardedness may reach its worst extreme in a historically reserved New England community like Cornwall, Connecticut, where the preening of six hundred or so weekenders arriving every Friday from New York City adds an extra measure of status to set against mixing too freely. But the art of free and easy conversation is dying, and isolation is a peculiar by-product of modern affluence everywhere.

For a long while we remained patient, sure that things would change. They did and they didn't. Friends were made and rites of passage shared. But undercurrents rippled through our town that looked so ideal to outsiders. Here and there, the circles of sociability began to implode. Yesterday's glowing young mothers latched onto desperate schemes for self-improvement in the battle against growing ennui and lengthening crow's feet, while their husbands grew more distant or clouded with self-doubt. Barbs between dinner guests grew sharper, and one day we looked around and realized that things would not likely improve. One after another, couples were bitterly breaking up and sometimes reconfiguring in awkward new arrangements. Meanwhile, Jamie and I were getting restless ourselves, and older.

Ireland had always promised a separate reality, a place where we could let down our guard and slide into the amble of conversation, both feeling like we somehow just fit. This conceit may have been no more than a holiday-steeped dream, but its sway held. We contemplated moving to certain seashore towns closer to home, but they seemed too similar to what we already had, promising more of the same dull earnestness and fastidiously programmed lives that we wanted to escape, if only for one more fling at youth or freedom before it was too late. One night in March we looked at each other and said let's finally do it; let's embrace one great adventure before the children grow any older and our next rendezvous with excitement will have to be postponed to our denture days.

The decision was not easy. Our fathers were newly deceased; our widowed mothers were aging visibly; beloved uncles and aunts were reeling from one disease to another; my wife's sister had been paralyzed from a car crash for years. Were we heartless, or selfish, or brave? Or screaming fools?

"How can we possibly know that you are who you say you are until six months have passed?" asked the bank lady. My, but she had a point.

Chapter 3

"Jamie, come here!" I shouted. Pottering about in the front room, I had just discovered a photograph on an alcove wall that jabbed shivers down my spine. It was of a stone cottage in a sheep-studded greensward bordered by a Kerry "beehive" – one of those conical, shoulder-high stone formations thought to have been erected for hermetic monks to sit in for weeks at a time while they meditated on the Lord or cursed the infernal rain. The foreground revealed a six-foot-long stone slab lifted high on three standing stones – the configuration imitating that of the ancient dolmens that pagan Celts may have used as altars for praying or sacrificing choice cows or irritating daughters. Nobody rightly knows, because these mysterious structures were built one to three thousand years before writing came to Ireland.

"I didn't pack this – did you?" I demanded, certain that we had left a nearly identical photograph on the wall of our study in Connecticut. Having been on hand at the creation of these particular monoliths, I had taken that picture.

"No, absolutely not."

Bizarre. The cottage, dolmen, and beehive were the handiwork of a dear friend of mine named Bun. In the monsoon-wracked winter of 1975, I joined him to muck around with troughs of cement at the end of Kerry's magnificent Dingle Peninsula, between an English-speaking village called Ventry and an Irish-speaking one called Dunquin and the celebrated Blasket Islands beyond. The winds howled and a mad shepherd screamed while we troweled stones purloined from the recently dismantled movie set for *Ryan's Daughter* into the slowly rising walls of the very cottage in the photograph – this strange hieroglyph to my own past.

Journeys are said to often assume the shape of a circle, but this was too much. Beyond uncanny, it breathed over the house like a talisman. Bun Wilkinson had been a beloved figure in my life, and his spirit had forever beckoned us back to Ireland.

In September 1973 I had rented a gate lodge on the Hill of Howth on an isthmus north of Dublin, a clapboard bungalow at the entrance to a nineteenth-century estate that was ringed by cliffs and elaborate gardens lazing above the capital's vast bay. The address, ten miles from the Trinity College I was meant to be attending, was half country at the time. Alas, Ireland's gaudier classes are now paying one and two million pounds for digs in the vicinity, which their parents could have purchased for a song. Back then, the shady Ceanchor Road and its neighboring lanes whispered refuge. Cows swatted flies across the lane and the post office was a dark parlor in an old lady's gloomy house. On the long lawns of the Stella Maris Convent a thousand feet away, Joyce's Leopold Bloom enjoyed his celebrated frolic with Molly, which was reenacted there in Joseph Strick's film of *Ulysses*.

The cliffs ranged in a mile-long crescent to the unicorn-white tower of the Baily Lighthouse, whose young keepers used to invite me up for late-night bottles of porter. Their foghorn moaned through winter nights so damp that one could have scooped glasses of water from the air. Like a monk in a Kerry beehive, I read constantly – above all, Brian O'Nolan who is better known by his pseudonyms of Flann O'Brien and Myles na Gopaleen. His fabulous characters leaned so long into their bicycles that they became half-bicycle themselves, and were stalked by noncorporeal beings with names like De Selby and Joe. Flann O'Brien celebrated a world only partially awakened from dream, one that was still prone to roll back to sleep if that strategy would make life's demands go away. He drank himself to ruination.

But what a mark did Flann leave:

> Having placed in my mouth sufficient bread for three minutes' chewing, I withdrew my powers of sensual perception and retired into the privacy of my mind, my eyes and face assuming a vacant and preoccupied expression. I reflected on the subject of my spare-time

literary activities. One beginning and one ending for a
book was a thing I did not agree with . . .

Examples of three separate openings – the first: The
Pooka MacPhellimey, a member of the devil class, sat
in his hut in the middle of a firwood meditating on the
nature of the numerals and segregating in his mind the
odd ones from the even. He was seated at his diptych or
ancient two-leaved hinged writing-table with inner sides
waxed. His rough long-nailed fingers toyed with a snuff-
box of perfect rotundity and through a gap in his teeth he
whistled a civil cavatina . . .

The second opening: There was nothing unusual in the
appearance of Mr. John Furriskey but actually he had one
distinction that is rarely encountered – he was born at the
age of twenty-five and entered the world with a memory
but without a personal experience to account for it . . .
His knowledge of physics was moderate and extended to
Boyle's Law and the Parallelogram of Forces . . .

The third? Buy the book. You either have a taste for such toying
with reality, or, lacking Irish ancestors, you don't. In any case,
mothers should warn their sons against reading *At Swim-Two-
Birds*, or any other works by Ireland's most famous hallucinator.
Alas, mine didn't know better.

Ireland in the early 1970s was still a Flann O'Brien world, a place
where bicyclists inscribed slow circles on misty back roads, and the
night's last buses erupted with raucous song, often with the driver
joining in. Of course, just when things seemed idyllic, the IRA
would detonate a horrendous bomb in London or Dublin, while
in Northern Ireland, only eighty miles from my Howth refuge,
masked avengers from both sides of the sectarian divide would
shoot out each other's knees. The grim reaper meanwhile was kept
infinitely busier on the killing fields of Vietnam.

I knew all this, but could gaze endlessly at Dublin's ever-changing
bay and the Wicklow Mountains listing through purple clouds to
the south, and think of Ireland as a romantic haven, perfect for an
apprentice at ignoring responsibilities.

Farm fields clambered up the hill behind my cottage to a dense rhododendron forest beside Howth Castle, where a massive dolmen spoke back through the ages. Beyond lay what was then still a fishing village, while doubling as a yachting playground for young Irish movers and shakers like Charles Haughey, later to become the most notoriously underhanded and high-living prime minister (called a *Taoiseach*, or "chief of the leader") in the country's history: Tricky Dick with a wink.

Bun, three decades older than myself, was looking after the semi-abandoned estate that included my gate lodge beside the cliffs. A widower, he had recently nurtured the owner through her cancerous final demise. Like me, Bun was at a crossroads, though he well hid whatever anxiety he felt.

He offered me tea the first time we met. Three hours later I stood up, in wonder at the richness of his conversation and the refrains of laughter that he tossed around like bouquets. I would have rented that gate lodge if it had three walls, because he filled the place with grace. I can still picture him walking up the dirt driveway to greet me in weather bleak or kind, bounding with the exuberance that was his gift, and whistling, always whistling – he was whistling me forward.

I would shuffle around the cottage in the morning, perhaps frying fresh herrings bought at Howth's pier, with the door thrown open to the light and, by mid-February, a sea of daffodils waving outside. Under an archway of woven vines, the same small robin, infinitely tamer than the heftier, redder-breasted North American version, waited patiently. I'd sit down to breakfast and the robin would skitter in. Merely pushing my chair back a foot was a signal for the robin to hop onto the table. Then this preternatural little bird sidled onto my plate, claiming the crumbs of brown bread and fish. It happened nearly every day. Sometimes an auburn-haired German girlfriend would read me poetry as we lay back in the grass. Trinity? Trinity was my secret joke. The place had no idea what I was doing.

Not once did I ever hear my father whistling; not once did I ever see him walk with Bun's buoyant gait; and it lifted my spirits to have a man so much older than myself finally fill my life with encouragement and the idea that the world could remain full of vibrant color as one grew older. Those mornings still seem close, when there would be that cheerful whistling sounding through the hedges whenever Bun arrived with his baskets of hot bread or scones from the oven, or vegetables plucked from the extensive walled gardens he tended by the main house below.

"Good man yourself," Bun would say, his blue eyes beaming above his long sloping cheeks and craggy chin. Although tall and powerfully shouldered, he moved with a lax ranginess, a lack of physical self-consciousness that is rarely found in an adult. His son Paddy, now in his mid-fifties and my friend for nearly thirty years, moves the same way.

The kettle would be fired up, and rambling dialogues would ensue on just about any subject under the sun. At night there were trips to Gaffney's pub at the top of the hill, then a country place, where the owners, spellbound by Bun's talk, slipped us into the back room for more wild storytelling after closing time. Whatever I read or thought was reviewed and enriched by Bun, rather than the Trinity College lecturers to whom I was a passing shadow.

Drummed out of pre-law studies for which he was thoroughly ill-suited, Bun dabbled briefly for a time at acting. He in due time followed his older brothers into farming outside Dublin, just as his Anglo-Irish planter family had been tilling Ireland's soil for three hundred years. Eventually selling his farm, Bun came to Howth in the late 1960s to set up a wood-carving shop. Then he taught himself to chisel fantastical figures in stone. What he carved best were stories, and parades of daily visitors – lorry drivers, lawyers, jewelers, and fishermen – showed up in hopes of losing themselves in his magical tales. Whether we were having tea in the conservatory of the run-down main house where he tended grapes, or smashing croquet balls around the ballustraded lower garden by the bay, or hiding in closets to escape unwanted visitors, laughter ruled. On weekends, he hosted trips to every curious and beloved Irish place he knew. Through visits to ancient monasteries, the wilds of Connemara, or mad parties until dawn at his brother Dick's Wicklow cattle farm, Bun made a gift of the Ireland he treasured and introduced me to every last person he'd met. Often we traveled to a Tipperary village called Terryglass, to help with his son Paddy's exquisite pub restoration. The singing there, with Bun on the squeezebox, was mighty.

A demon for making wine, Bun regularly dispatched me to gather for his concoctions wild dandelions and rose petals, and to scour Moore Street's bawling, open-air vegetable stalls for the most leathery carrots that could be found. One absurd night, a friend in the Irish Communist Party and I scaled the walls of an army barracks in order to nip a bushel of military carrots that we had spotted in the yard. "Bun had better be happy now," shouted my friend as we jumped onto his dodgy motor scooter, our sack of purloined provender safe between us. Fortunately, no bullets penetrated our derrieres.

"Ambrosia and nectar" is the way Bun described the resultant elixir, which he called carrot whiskey, proffering it with a rolling hand motion and diabolical glint to his eyes.

"It's only enough to kill a hardened sinner. Drink deep."

I did, and drank in the essence of an Ireland I had come to love. With Bun, every day was an inspiration. All it took was for one of us to start a sentence and the talk would flow for hours. He was a soul mate, such as one rarely finds a second time in this life. When the year finally played out, Bun and I parted with tears. Neither one of us knew what we would do next, only that we had shared a unique interlude in which two ages of life crossed in a way that is rarely available to fathers and sons.

A year later, Bun invited me to Dingle to help with that cottage, his testament in stone, whose picture would ineffably materialize in our newly rented house in Cork. He had started this project with his latest young love (women fell for Bun constantly), but that affair had played out, leading to the bugle call my way. There was laughter alright after arriving there, especially when we stole saplings for replanting from the local convent, or hurtled over the roads smashing crab claws – offered from an admirer in town – on the Renault's floor for instant snacks. But, alas, all was not perfect this time. Dingle's panoramas drop jaws in summer, but the winter weather proved unspeakable. The gales lashed off the Atlantic, and the quarters in Bun's building-site trailer, or "caravan," were cold, cramped, and too close. Our joyous equilibrium of the year before became tainted by some of reality's heaviness. Both of us had the weight of uncertainty on our shoulders, our private anxieties mounting about what lay ahead.

We parted reluctantly at the end of 1975. If only I had known then that I was saying goodbye for the last time. Letters crisscrossed constantly, Bun's lengthy, eloquent missives keeping my alternate Irish reality ever vivid. Bun and his son Paddy occupied themselves in restoring stone buildings around the Irish countryside. Meanwhile, back in America, I struggled to piece together a living, but never stopped thinking of my old friend. Suddenly, on a dark November day in 1982, I received word that Bun, now in his sixties, was dead. The loss never healed, and here I was called back again under his sign, trying to ease my entire family into a country that was now ineradicably changed.

Chapter 4

Earlier explorers of distant lands often returned with spectacular tales of having to hack their way through dense jungles, climb hoary mountains, or traverse wild seas in order to reach their El Dorados. Our family's first tasks, after arriving in Cork City, kept leaning toward the tedious. Arrangements for a new phone line were attempted with at least eleven different help lines at Eircom, the privatized national phone monopoly that seduced 400,000 Irish people, most of whom had never purchased a sheaf of stock in their lives, to buy shares that became worthless overnight. And no wonder, because none of the cheerful operators at Eircom had the slightest ability to connect with their colleagues at the next desk.

"We have a comprehensive basic service for thirty-two punts per month, or in your area you might wish to consider installation of a special ISDN Internet-access line."

"How much will that cost?"

Silence. Crackle. Dead phone.

Twenty more calls and still nobody has the answer.

"Do you want a split line?"

"I'm not sure . . . Wait a minute. Wait just a minute."

Crackle. Gone.

Cork's Department of Motor Vehicle Taxation recently came up with the perfect bureaucratic solution – announcing that, due to unmanageable volumes of calls seeking personal assistance, they were henceforth suspending all answers to that line.

Nevertheless, we solved each tedious logistical challenge in its turn, and even landed a checking account from a bank manager who evidently bet his vault's holdings on dark horses. Meanwhile, our boys kept recruiting one friend after another, while rapidly maturing Laura steeped herself in books about Ireland, and gingerly tested the waters with a couple of slightly younger neighborhood girls. Jamie, attempting to stake her claim in an unfamiliar world, nested with a vengeance. Armed with a block of "Fairy" soap, she organized every corner of the house, from drawer to shining drawer, and began to make sense of mysterious Irish household entities such as the hob and "hot press," the linen closet that also houses the hot-water tank, invariably controlled by mysterious electrical timers. In fact, everything in this house seemed to be controlled by a network of these things, which turned washing machines, dryers, and furnaces on and off at their whim.

One afternoon, I found Jamie muttering in the laundry cubicle, which we had been told housed "the most advanced American appliances."

"What's the matter?" I asked, seeing her scowl.

Thereupon, she produced in either hand a formerly adult shirt, now shrunk by the most advanced imported American appliances to miniature elfin sizes. Until very recently, the Irish used to believe that the missing sock problem was explained by fairy mischief, which suddenly seemed plausible to me.

"Just right for a leprechaun who fancies Marks and Spencer," she growled.

Women of course possess a knack for establishing networks that could cement kingdoms over problems just like this. So hassles small and large became fodder for constant visits with the neighbors. For a while, it seemed that every time I turned around, gregarious spirits like Breda Higgins, on the day shift, or the hilarious Belfast-born Mary Lynch, who preferred to stop in after 10 p.m., appeared in our kitchen to transform conversations about their favorite "cling film" or the mysteries of Gas Mark 6 on the cooker into weightier discussions, often ending in peals of laughter, about Ireland and America, restaurants, shops, movies, novels, and the like, before digressing into the more personal stuff of passions, memories, and dreams. Thus was our web of new connectedness woven, with Jamie dispensing tea or wine as was called for, and mixing as freely as if she had been in Ireland all her life. The idea had been that we'd just settle in for a sabbatical of renewal for one year or maybe two. But watching my wife and kids embrace their changed lives, forever seemed possible too.

David Monagan

Me, I manfully procured four wheels by buying a small "estate" car, or station wagon, that had a sign in its front window two hundred feet from our house. Something's not clicking? Take your clicker out of your pocket and click it, said the avant-garde composer John Cage. The kindly Welsh owner, whose name sounded something like Brynbrrryn, handed over the keys three days before being paid, which was very trusting indeed for a locksmith. Click. A celebration seemed in order, and I instinctively thought of that curious upstairs pub I had espied on our first walk about town, the Hi-B.

"Wigs for Hire," a wiggy sign said on the floor just above it, but never mind. In no time at all, I climbed those dingy stairs to the linoleum landing, and then opened a black door to an aria blast such as emitted by Mahler in one of his more bellicose moods. Behind a crescent-shaped bar, a man with flying wisps of white hair stood waving an imaginary baton beside shelves thick with whiskey, his pupils rapturously dilated. He was singing something that went – dee, Dee, DEE! It definitely was not B.

Before the maestro, a number of curious-looking individuals hunkered over cylindrical columns of black stout. One had an unruly beard whose tendrils looked as if they might store months of famine-resistant nutrition. Another with a goatee expelled the heavyweight word "procrustean," albeit garbled in the Urdu-like thickness of West Cork speech. Beaming at him was a dark-haired woman with a puppy at that moment raising a hind leg as if contemplating releasing a benediction on the floor.

I found a free stool and gazed about in wonder. The proprietor, who I quickly learned was named Brian O'Donnell, offered some fleeting curiosity my way as he fussed with his Coke-bottle-thick eyeglasses.

"That's a sad light tonight," he pronounced about an element not much of which looked to have ever touched his milky white skin.

"Drive a man to seek refuge," I tried, not realizing that our interchange could have long-term consequences.

"I take it you are from America. Americans are not often intimate with the word 'refuge.' Nothing personal, but I am just

44

thinking, isn't vocabulary diminishing everywhere?" Brian said and turned away. His voice was peculiarly shrill and his attention span short. He lost himself for a while in fishing through a stack of papers with a manner not unlike that of an eccentric collector of antiquarian books. My kind of man, I thought, while mentioning that I was from Connecticut.

"Ah, the Constitution State, I believe," Brian countered with that astonishingly pinpoint knowledge that the Irish often manifest about places halfway around the globe.

"That's amazing! Most Americans don't even know that's what it's called."

Here, my interlocutor produced a self-pleased smile. "Ah, ah now, I do know a thing or two about the world. And I had a particular friend from a period when I was in medical school who ventured that way, a certain Michael Buckley from my, ah, shall we say, salad days."

Gasp. "You've got to be kidding. He's a friend of my parents!" Serendipity being my guiding Irish star, it soon developed that Brian had spent some of his riotous youth with the self-same Cork-born doctor I knew in Connecticut, a retired friend of my parents.

"My, I'm just saying now, isn't it a small world?" said Brian, amiably squinting through his nearly opaque glasses.

Seizing on the connection, I dealt forth a quirky story which involved my posing, in 1974, as a young American psychiatrist beside a real Irish one – a friend of Bun's named James O'Brien – in a Dublin schizophrenia ward. At Gaffney's I had badgered James with questions from my recent readings about the intersection between creativity and madness until he finally invited me to come and see for myself as he made rounds. The first patient on our tour was a diminutive man who called himself Daft Jimmy. DJ promptly held out his hand, demanding, "Cut off these four, Doc, and I'll be okay." Jimmy explained that if he had but one finger, he wouldn't be troubled anymore by thoughts of strangling innocent pals. "If you can do it, Doc," Daft Jimmy beamed my way, "I'll invite you to me house for a spot a' tay."

Brian drummed his fingers on the bar, wondering where I was

heading. Somehow, I felt compelled to demonstrate that I could spin a tale with the best of them. I hurried on, "So Daft Jimmy is there chuckling when who walked in but the hospital's chief."

"Sticky," Brian said.

I explained that James O'Brien quickly introduced me as "Doc Monagan from the States."

"Where in the States?" asked the arch-browed chief.

"Connecticut."

"Connecticut, is it? Where exactly?"

"Why, Waterbury," I had said.

"Isn't that remarkable! I worked there myself. In which hospital do you practice?" chortled the major domo.

"St. Mary's," I had groaned like a cornered rodent, having been born in that one.

"Then you must know Dr. Buckley? How's his wife, Hylda?"

"Who?" I had gulped.

"So in other words you were a stuck pig?" laughed Brian, grasping that this tale was all about the serendipity that stalks through Ireland, in this case nearly thirty years ago and now newly repeated between him and me.

"Exactly." I told how James O'Brien yanked me away by the elbow, thus ending one of my first object lessons in the need to watch one's every move in the improbably interconnected warp and weave of Irish life.

"Extraordinary," Brian clucked, making me feel as if I had just passed a challenging entrance examination for acceptance to the Hi-B. "And to think that this is the same Mick Buckley I knew so well. I have great time for that man."

A rambunctious punch of Wagner muscled forth, and Brian began introducing me to various figures inhabiting neighboring stools.

"Would you mind if I had a cup of coffee?" one asked, a civilized-looking sort with neatly parted brown hair and tortoiseshell glasses such as university lecturers wear.

An inexplicable darkness spread across the Hi-B owner's face. His voice assumed an oddly mincing quality and his hands began to tremble as if confronting a shocking transgression. "Would ye know what a public house is for, fella? Well, you ought to after all the time you have warmed that stool. We do not serve buttered scones and coffee, as you well know. Or perhaps ye intended to call into a sandwich shop?"

Men up and down the bar began sniggering into their pints, knowing the Hi-B's ways intimately. Brian, looking pleased, topped off his already plenteous cognac, as the would-be customer poodled away in a huff. "Summertime, and the living is queasy," he began singing for no particular reason, and then abruptly stopped to point out a nearby pencil sketch he had drawn of the great Gershwin. There were a dozen similar portraits on the walls, likenesses of famous composers, movie stars, and authors he had sketched with fair talent, back in the days when he cared to pursue that kind of thing.

People came and left, conversation eddied and flowered, then Brian's face suddenly contorted at the sight of some fresh affront in the back precincts of his small pub.

"It is as distasteful as eating chips in a bar," he blurted toward whatever was bothering him. The regulars sniffed trouble, knowing (as I later learned) that Brian once took such a visceral disliking to the bright colors of a customer's tie that he surged forth from the bar with a pair of scissors and severed it at the knot. He then abruptly shoved the shorn ends into the man's pocket and said, "Now you've got a hanky to match." Another time, a lady in a hat rejected one of his bawdy overtures so indelicately that for the next three months he refused to serve drink to any haberdashery-crowned customer who ventured into the Hi-B.

"Ye would not eat chips in a bar, would ye?" Brian now demanded over my shoulders, his eyes bulging like those of a foraging fish. "That is enough!"

My curiosity was itching. Were the marauders behind us smoking grass? Drooling? Picking their noses?

"I think ye had better leave! And don't come back too soon!" Brian suddenly yelled as a young woman and her tall male friend sheepishly exited in confusion.

"Would you mind my asking what they were doing?" I asked.

Brian moved closer. "*Osculating*," he cackled.

"How horrible,' I said, knowing this peculiar Latinate word for kissing.

Someone with a red beard saw me chuckling. A shopkeeper with a penchant for placing hefty sums on the races (a weakness shared by about every fourth male in Ireland), he warned that Brian's mood swings were not the only thing to worry about in this vicinity, because when the moon was full and the tidal conditions unfavorable, many lanes in downtown Cork could gorge with rising waters from the Lee.

"It hasn't been too bad lately, though," he offered, as I began to wonder if anybody in this place or this town or country talked straight. "And you should have no danger of drowning here, thanks to the protection of the stairs. Plus you appear to be lucky in general," this penetratingly eyed creature, who turned out to be an immediate neighbor, continued.

"Why do you say that?"

"Because the place where you have chosen to reside is the best park in Cork, because you have just found the best bar in Ireland, and because Brian seems to like you, which is not always or even often the case and which could of course change."

"I like it here," I said, thinking this was all gorgeous theater, just what had been missing in the careful coordinates of our pre-Irish days.

"You should. Even to have found a stool is like a *pishogue*."

"A what?"

"That's a word for a kind of superstition. Like a foxy lady."

"Who?"

"If a fisherman sees a foxy lady on the pier, he knows he will drown and so he does not on that day go to sea. There are good *pishogues* and bad ones, various classes that we might call *pisheens*. It is a good sign to have found a stool here, because in doing so you have assumed a seat in the senate, the Roman senate. Here we sit and judge the world, while the plebeians sit at our backs."

Some might say this was madness. But the scene was resplendent to me, and suggested that a life of vibrant color, unpredictable and spontaneous, was ours now for the taking. If only I could collect all these impressions in a jar and get them home safely, I thought as I sipped, the wife will love me, and our adventure will be blessed with hilarity. Okay, I was already tipsy.

"We all must contribute something," offered Brian, helping his glass to a fresh dose of rocket fuel. "This is not a pub in the ordinary sense. It is a contributory to the great river of words. A club of a peculiar sort."

Nod.

A swarthy man in his late forties made it plain that he'd been eavesdropping. He had sensitive brown eyes and a Scottish accent softened by many years spent in London and now Cork. We exchanged pleasantries. "The thing you need to know about Cork is that this is not like any other place you've likely ever been, at least not in Europe or America. This isn't Europe; Cork's not even Ireland really. It's altogether strange. In other places people are valued for being organized, for being predictable and reliable and straightforward. That is the worst way you can possibly behave here. In Cork, people are valued for being unpredictable, for being chancers and dreamers and misfits, and above all for being characters. If you are odd here, you might fit in."

Just what my wife wants to hear, I thought.

Chapter 5

The true symbol of Ireland is a circle, and the country's dull tri-colored modern flag does not fit the bill. Runic whorls and spirals speaking of a cosmos without end are inscribed on the walls of countless caves and prehistoric passage-tombs and repeated on ancient Celtic crosses in hidden cemeteries: the circle is Ireland's talismanic shape.

The country remains a place where one never stops reconnecting with that which has been encountered before. Two years after Bun's death, Jamie and I ventured to Ireland on our honeymoon. We ranged the west, and I even had time to catch a couple of spring-run salmon in County Mayo, while my watchful ghillie nestled with a collection of beer cans into a sheep hollow and celebrated my casts with burps. Then we visited Paddy and his wife, Anne, at the timber house they had built in Carlow's Blackstairs Mountains, where they were struggling at tending beehives and renovating canal barges on the River Barrow, after selling their pub in Tipperary's Terryglass, which had become quite famous since my last visit. That wasn't the only noticeable change. Their daughter Gwen, a toddler at our last meeting, had become a gangly beanstalk. "No one can replace the relationship you had with my father, but I will always be your friend," said Paddy.

We also visited an odd nearby pub called Mary Osborne's. The proprietor had wild shocks of gray hair and eyes as inscrutable as a cat's. You could travel far in those. The back wall of her dingy establishment was lined with wooden drawers into which Mary randomly deposited bills and coins in a way that suggested a more likely future as mouse bedding than circulating currency. A grandfather clock by the door picked its way through the hours. Old farmers shambled in with threadbare tweed jackets and twine-cinched trousers caked with sheep's wool and manure. The customers nodded between sips and eyed us as if we were strange beings indeed. Mary's brother occasionally retreated into a back room with Guinness cream dripping from his nearly toothless mouth. After a while, his screechy serenades on an ancient accordion – better known as a "squeeze-box" – began to filter through his lair's open door. Old men sang through yellowed teeth, their noses exhaling sour jets of smoke.

For honeymoons, other grooms accompany their gorgeous brides to the pleasure palaces of the azure Caribbean, for romantic larks in Paris, Rome, or Bali; but, no, I had delivered mine to Mary Osborne's.

"Where's the ladies'?" Jamie asked.

Mary's slate gray eyes fluttered. "Cross the street and open the gate there and you'll be sorted."

My blond bride soon discovered that she had been sent to the local cemetery, which doubled as Mary Osborne's outhouse.

While she was away, an old codger tipped forward on his seat and warbled, "I weep for Donal dead," or something close.

"Will you give us a song?" Mary Osborne demanded before Jamie was barely settled back into her stool.

"I'm not much of a singer," the new wife tried.

Mary would not have it. "Every human being has a song."

"I can't remember the words to any," Jamie protested.

"Look at you now, all beautiful and young and newly married. You must sing, for your husband and all of us gathered now."

"Go on lass, give us a song," the fella nearest added.

My bride looked at me helplessly, perhaps gazing into our strange future.

"You must," I chuckled.

So it was that Jamie, whose love of silliness I have always adored, bequeathed upon Ireland, land of haunting ballads, the immortal words of a ridiculous advertising ditty that started: "I went looking for a noodle, a different kind of noodle, that is golden light, tastes just right. And I found what I was after . . . a golden noodle."

She'd found her noodle all right. It was me.

The next day we drove up to Howth. Bun's gate lodge, the arch of vines, and undoubtedly my robin had all vanished, replaced by four concrete bungalows that looked as if they belonged on the moon. Flash money was already contaminating the land.

More recently, the producers of *Riverdance*, that spectacular of modern stage-Irishness, purchased a "tear-down" bungalow by the now unmanned Baily Lighthouse for £1 million and replaced it with an 8,500 square-foot house with indoor swimming pool and subterranean parking for five cars. Then they grabbed up a neighboring Georgian house for £3.9 million, followed by another dwelling on the other side – such is life in the new Irish Beverly Hills.

If only Ireland's new rapaciousness was confined to a single address. In 1984 it was impossible to know that the carefree days of even those back-of-beyond pubs like Mary Osborne's were numbered, like so many other pages from Ireland's past. Developers now pay hundreds of thousands of euros for any pub license that can be transferred to city establishments worth ten times that; these reincarnated city pubs are then dressed out in Paris-Los Angeles-Prague chrome 'n' leather fittings meant to evoke swank foreign dreams. Meanwhile, Dublin syndicates have filled warehouses with sufficient bric-a-brac to create endless reproductions of these supposed icons of Irish authenticity all over the world – six hundred export kitsch pubs were thrown up in the year 2000 alone, in places like Beijing, Paris, Houston, and Milan (there are ninety others in Italy). I once met a Cork musician who had been dispatched to belt out ballads in the six Irish pubs a syndicate had recently created in Dubai. He loved it.

Irishness – "Oirishness," as the natives ironically pronounce it – cannot be trapped in a jar. Often, only a wild blunder can lead to the country's elusive heart. Heading back to Ireland on our first anniversary in June 1985, Jamie and I ploughed west from Dublin in a rental car until exhaustion set in. We randomly located a former "glebe" or vicar's house on a side road that now took in travelers. Bordered by lush pastures, it looked perfect. We strolled, ate, and retired for the night.

While preparing to pay the next morning, I examined a map of

Ireland on the entrance wall. Something odd at once caught my eye. "Sorry," I said when the owner appeared, "but I couldn't help noticing the pins stuck into your map. Inishbofin, Brittas, and Borris, Terryglass, Mulhuddart, and Howth – I've been to every one of these places."

"How extraordinary," the tall, auburn-haired woman said.

"There's a family named Wilkinson that has houses in every place where you've stuck a pin. I had a dear friend named Bun Wilkinson who took me to every one of those spots."

"What? *I am a Wilkinson!*" she exclaimed. "Bun was my uncle!"

My, my. "This is amazing. We're about to head over to Carlow to see Paddy, Bun's son. He won't believe this."

"Well, he better! Paddy and Anne will be here in two hours! Wilkinsons are coming from all over the country for a family reunion. Put your bags down. You're staying."

Ireland the inscrutable, the nursery of serendipity, was at it again. So we stayed up until three o'clock in the morning – the traditional hour for the first guests to depart Irish parties – while Paddy fiddled, everyone sang, and tales were traded with characters who threw out words like DJs screeching vinyls in nightclubs. Eventually, we awoke with gasps for water and an enriched appreciation of how exquisitely such uproar had been perfected through centuries of Irish party empiricism. A little bedside reader told of glory eighteenth-century party days in grand homes like Mount Panther, Mount Venus, Mount Misery, Ballyseedy, Ballyruin, Ballydrain, and Bastardstown.

Jonah Barrington, the owner of a "pile" in the midlands, held one particularly rousing bash, featuring a hogshead of claret, mixed with a repast of slaughtered cow and chickens, bacon and bread. At 10 o'clock the next morning, the guests were discovered still crashed with insensibility around the dining-room table, with the evening's comatose piper sprawled on the floor with a tablecloth drawn to his chin. In the stables lay four more guests who had careered toward their horses before collapsing into the straw. Two of the parched guests in the dining room had passed out against a newly plastered wall. The heat from the fire had set the goo like marble against their hair, leaving the gone-native Anglo-Irish stuck to the wall. But the resourceful Jonah Barrington took his clicker out of his pocket and clicked it, whistling in the local wig maker to extricate the unfortunates, ultimately by ripping their muddied hair off with an oyster knife.

Our much more virtuous selves washed, dressed, and joined Paddy and Anne that afternoon for a leisurely cruise down the Grand Canal.

Nearly a decade later, we sallied around the west of Ireland and were startled by the pace of change: bicycles all but vanished, cars roaring down once tranquil lanes, garish new concrete bungalows replacing whitewashed thatched cottages everywhere.

Tick and tock went the clock to a sun-drenched August family holiday in a Georgian cottage outside Castletownshend in West Cork in 1998. Before us lay spectacular ocean vistas, with ruined castles and round towers on offshore islands and distant headlands. In the local pub, farmers filed in at the end of the long summer evenings to chat and sing; it seemed impossible to think that dozens of mass-produced dreary holiday bungalows were soon due to double the size of this picturesque village, with its cobbled main street sluicing toward a sublimely sheltered harbor.

Scrambling through gorse-ridden pastures, we discovered an ancient stone ring fort at the crest of a hill with views of endless bays, cliffs, and mountains – one of more than 40,000 megalithic formations casually scattered about the Irish landscape, invariably with no fanfare or visible sign indicating their existence. Runic whorls had been inscribed in a standing stone, and a murky underground passageway burrowed into an infinitely mysterious past.

"What's this, Dad?" asked Harris, forever fascinated by secret worlds.

"Who knows? Maybe an escape route from the Vikings who would lop off the heads of anyone they caught, or a chamber for killing wicked people. Go take a look."

Jamie, not understanding the beauty of bloodcurdling visions, protested that dispatching an eight-year-old into an underground chamber indicated a deplorable lack of judgment.

Not by Harris's lights, because he quickly squirmed out of sight. "Cool! There's some kind of strange ancient paintings on the walls," his muffled voice quickly called back to us. So transpired another impromptu initiation rite into our family's ancestral past.

On the next rise stood a haunting formation of prehistoric standing stones – ten-foot-high, free-standing monoliths once known as the Five Fingers, although one has toppled over and another was dragged off long ago to become a folly in the gardens behind the mock castle of the ruling Townshend family, so imperious were the Anglo-Irish landlords of an earlier era. One could also gaze down into the estate where Edith Somerville-Ross, with her cousin Violet Martin, wrote *The Irish R.M.*, *The Real Charlotte*, and other celebrated novels describing the privileged ways of their class and an Ireland now gone. Some homicidal fools from the local IRA knocked on that door one evening in 1937, and pumped her nephew full of lead, fifteen years after the Crown's presence had been driven out of Ireland. Senseless.

What did it matter now? The bitter religious divides and hierarchies of foreign domination have long since withered in the south of Ireland, where Vikings, Normans, and transplanted Brits – and innumerable modern wanderers like ourselves – have all been swallowed up and transformed by the island's wily potency, and the seductive spirit that keeps hypnotizing anyone who long strays upon its soil. So I hiked the fields with the boys and took our young Laura to fling out our fishing lines in the next cove, and click, click, click. Even when we landed nothing, we hooked visions. Little did we realize that we were reeling in Ireland, and that two years later the catch would be complete.

Chapter 6

Cork City is infested with odd characters and many speak in parables. On fine afternoons one of the street artists tapes an eight-square-foot canvas on a sidewalk to labor on a masterwork that will never be completed. His boombox swells out maudlin refrains from the movie *Titanic* as he begins each afternoon in art hell. Droves of tourists gawk at the near-photographic likenesses of Leonardo DiCaprio and Kate Winslet reaching toward each other across a starry night while their doomed vessel sinks into the blackness beneath their ethereal forms. Leo and Kate are permanent fixtures, never to be changed by a single brush stroke. But the street artist takes pains to blacken yesterday's details from the margins before renewing his caricature for a few appreciative dropped coins. His creativity is limited to doodling a fresh iceberg or crowded lifeboat in one of the tableau's corners.

Watching this charade after leaving the Hi-B on a late August afternoon, I thought about how difficult it is for visitors to Ireland to resist feeding upon similarly complacent constructs. A mental canvas is unrolled upon arrival, already dolled up with visions of a timeless green land that the tourist wants to be far different from home. First-hand viewing may produce a few fresh details in the margins of the visitor's preconceptions, but the stereotypes are painted back in at every chance.

Of course, nobody surpasses the Irish at making merry with this tendency. A few years back, there existed a kind of Cork drinking club called the Clancys, which had a loose affiliation with a similar collection of eccentrics in London. Hearing that the Brits were coming over for a tour of the southwest, the Clancys decided to show them the Real Ireland. So they recruited three local midgets, each smaller than Small Denis, and outfitted them with elfin jackets, tricornered hats, leggings, and pointy shoes. The wee fellows were then secreted to a Ring of Kerry field that the visitors' tour bus, with several stewarding Clancys on board, was sure to pass at dusk.

"Stop here," one of the Clancys shouted as the coach approached the spot. "There's a famous fairy circle just below and at this hour we might just see them."

"Sure, mate. We'll go see the little people," scoffed the Brits.

But the visitors halted nonetheless – and shortly dropped their jaws at what waited in the hollow. There, sitting on a stool, was a leprechaun nailing shoes, another beside him whistling on a miniature flute, and a third stirring a little magic pot. Lost in reverie, they didn't cast a glance at the white-faced Englishmen – until the embedded Clancys roared with laughter.

A wicked joke, but scratch the Irish hard enough and you may still hear a thing or two about fairies. A country-born but city-smart friend named Lourdes, a teacher with a fashionable spiked hairdo that would fit in perfectly in London or New York, told an anecdote a few months after our arrival.

"When I was about ten or eleven, I met a neighbor in the lane one day, an old lady named Mrs. Crowley. She looked so distraught that I asked what was the matter. 'Have ye any news?' I asked, because that is what everyone said when meeting back then. She said, 'Someone has disturbed the fairy circle and the livestock are gone out of their senses.'

"This might sound crazy to you now, but the truth was that a farmer had in fact that very morning plowed close to the village's ancient fairy circle, and the horses had taken a terrible fright, broken through fences, and scattered for miles in a way that no one had ever seen before. You may be skeptical, but something strange happened to set them off like that, and I am telling you that even today, no Irishman with any sense would ever build a thing on an ancient fairy circle."

"No question about it," nodded her partner, Hans. "There are realities still that nobody quite understands. When my mother was young, she heard a strange wailing outside at midnight and went into the fields to investigate. The sound was most horrible and got louder and louder as she approached a nearby row of trees. And what did she find there but a banshee keening and plaiting her white hair, then suddenly vanishing before her eyes. Two days later, my grandmother died. You can call that coincidence if you wish, because she was already ill admittedly, but it's enough to scare you, truth be told."

The tricky path between truth and stereotype must be tiptoed gingerly when a family of five has to forge a changed life in a new land. Favorite clichés get shattered in the midst of the simplest transactions.

A world-favorite stereotype is that the Irish are a supremely open people. Right. And Eskimos are just waiting to rub visitors' noses too. Well, the Irish can be extraordinarily friendly, and will certainly talk your ear off when in the mood. They can also be suspicious and clannish and vacillate between every extreme of the emotional spectrum with an elusiveness that can leave a visitor dangling in confusion. In Cork, a simple inquiry about someone's work status, even if you have been asked a dozen questions about your own, can engender long scrutinizing glances, as if the interlocutor might be wearing a secret tape-recording device. "Keep yes and no unsplit. And give your say this meaning: give it the shade," advised the Romanian poet Paul Celan. In the southwestern counties of Ireland, collectively comprising the province of Munster, ambiguity has been perfected to a level that would do the Sphinx proud. In fact, the native Irish language doesn't have a solid word for "no." Road signs, when they exist, never say "stop." That would be too straightforward. It's "yield," even when anything short of a dead halt will lead to a screeching smashup. "I will, yeah," Corkonians say when they mean "never."

During a later journey to the beautiful island of Valentia off the Kerry coast, the director of Ireland's westernmost marine emergency radio command center – an institution predicated upon the need for instant direct communication – waved out over the nearby mountains as if seeing inscrutable gnomes. A native of not-so-distant West Cork, Gene O'Sullivan said, "I've been here for thirty years and do not begin to understand these people. Sit down to have a pint with them and they'll ask the most personal and embarrassing things without blinking. But ask them anything about themselves and they reveal nothing. Ask them if they think the black clouds overhead will bring rain, and Kerry people won't answer. They'll just say, 'Sure, there could be a change in the air.'"

In Ireland, the Kerryman is considered the "cutest" – meaning most shrewdly cunning rather than handsome – of individuals. He's often called "a cute Kerry *hoor*" (a phrase applied exclusively to men) on account of his infinite capacity for duplicity, but the Kerryman is actually a cultural archetype. Pithy anecdotes about Kerry cuteness provide insights into the mysteriousness of the entire race, and, we soon found out, apply with considerable aptness to the clannish and clever ways of Corkonians.

Things in this part of the world are simply not as they seem, until at least one comes to understand the meaning of cuteness, and the omnipresence of gates. People in Ireland's southwest work invisible ones constantly. Look at almost every house, be it ever so humble, and the first thing you will notice is a closed gate.

Our house in Cork came with a solid iron gate with a latch that clanked like a prison cell's. At first, we seldom bothered with the thing. We still imagined Ireland as being a safe and freely mixing place, and had no interest in perpetuating some archaic class divide, just because our side yard, called a "garden," was more generously proportioned and hedge-sheltered than the small squares of lawn that serve as most children's play areas in Ireland's cities. So the kids piled in, sometimes a dozen of them creating a three-ring circus out there, with two or three in the apple tree, another dangling from a rope swing, a bunch playing soccer on the lawn, and a couple more playing hide-and-seek in the hedges.

After years of chauffeuring twenty-mile round trips for two-hour play dates, Jamie especially relished the easy comings and goings of neighborhood pals for the children, even though the growing hordes seemed to be proliferating unnaturally and were laying waste to our kitchen stores. "Do you think someone's put up signs urging every kid in Cork to play here during the school holidays? They eat crisps as if the second Famine is returning, and I think they're going to crawl into our beds if we don't look out," she fretted one late summer afternoon.

"At least none of them mean any harm," I rejoined, not realizing you should never ever tempt fate in Ireland in this way.

Sharing too readily on this island, it soon became apparent, can be taken as a provocative act, exciting suspicions of boasting and preening. Unbeknownst to us, certain neighbors began to talk about our gate behavior. To them, it was as fate-tempting as disturbing a fairy circle.

Meanwhile, a couple of less-than-friendly teenage boys from a bit further afield began examining the fantastical sight of our always-open gate. The boss had a squat body and dark eyes that seemed fraught with the confusion of adolescence. Often they'd hulk near the beginning of our walkway while a seemingly more innocent younger girl with them would venture forward a few steps to the edge of our lawn and wistfully eye the to-and-fro. Our landlords, who had lived in this house until we arrived, had manipulated the garden gate like prison wardens, and never allowed more than two kids in at a time. Suspicious and mean, that seemed to us. We still imagined that every kid within earshot would welcome our democratic new ways, which was as naive as thinking that all Irish people are delighted when an acquaintance gets a new job or car. Hah! To understand Ireland, one must learn to hear whispers.

One day, Laura came home in a hysterical state after the younger sister of the Chief Scowler spat upon her for no apparent reason. We had no idea what motivated this – Laura's foreign accent? Our strange gate behavior? Our newness? The size of our garden? Furious, I marched forward and gave the young culprit a good dressing-down. But this was far too direct, and not at all the way things are handled in Ireland.

Undoubtedly the young lass had gotten the idea she wasn't fully welcome in our garden, whether this was or was not true. So she got even. Little did I know that it was not our place as newcomers to remonstrate. Her heavy-set older brother made that clear by driving his bicycle straight at my much smaller boys whenever they ventured onto the common pavement of Bellevue Park. Appeals to his better nature fell flat, so then I warned him that I would not tolerate further bullying. That evening we returned from a pleasant stroll and discovered that our kids' garden play furniture had been smashed to bits.

Suddenly, our new lives seemed less carefree.

Another neighbor came by for a hello, and a "No, I couldn't possibly, well okay, just a sip of wine." We did the how-do-you-do, then moved to the Big Issue. "My mother thinks you're crazy not to close the gate. She's been talking about it every day, but she's like that."

He'd given us a direct warning, then disguised it, as Irish people always do to cloud their meanings. In Cork, the lexicon of the unsaid runs deep, and conflicts are discussed in parables.

In the nearby John Henchy's & Sons public house, I met a raconteur with shoulders as broad as Bun's and a surname in common as well – a distant cousin named Seamus Wilkinson. He told riveting stories about his native Galtee Mountains in Tipperary, about his father's exploits in the Irish Republican Army during the War of Independence, about various foreign adventures, about, it seemed, everything near and dear. Wonderfully gregarious, Seamus soon brought us a gift the next morning of fish he'd just caught. Yet it took ten months before Seamus revealed that he spent many weekends looking after the dying and infirm in the local hospice and chaperoned a yearly contingent seeking miraculous redemption in Lourdes.

"Why do people in this country hold onto their secrets so fervently; why the half-closed gate?" I asked my new friend.

"If you tell people too much, they'll start talking about you," Seamus said.

Out. In. A newcomer to Ireland had better learn those nuances. They speak of gatekeeping, of ancient suspicion and deep guardedness in this land where the legions of informers to the occupying British and the Normans and Danes before them were the most reviled of toads. The burgeoning economy has created countless entrepreneurs like Seamus, who is a very successful builder. But nearly every one still watches their back and works their invisible conversational gates deftly, like dealers in a sleight-of-hand game of shells. Too much openness will merely get you dismissed as naive.

"You don't hear me talking about the mortar and the damp-proofing on my building sites, do ye now? When you go in a pub, you just talk about things that are light and easy and see what drifts up to the surface," said one of the more self-assured persons I'd met yet.

Another acquaintance from Dublin, which now holds nearly half the country's population, put it more strongly. "Just be cautious, because you never know who's listening and what will happen with the information they get about you around here. Tell people as little as they need to know, especially here in Cork. In Dublin, they can be as 'in your face' as any American, but they are not that way here at all. There is a certain Cork type who says one thing when he means another, and if you respond too directly, he'll just look at you and smile. But this kind of fellow actually despises being challenged or suffering the slightest offence, especially by a foreigner. It's like the Japanese when it comes to saving face. Hit this type of guy between the eyes with any criticism or misgiving and you make yourself a bull's eye in his sights."

Our first weeks seemed blessed with the benevolence of my old friend Bun's guiding star. In one of the most memorable episodes, a nephew of his named Tim Jackson took my family out for a weekend sail from Crosshaven, a village half an hour south of Cork. His boat was moored at the Royal Irish Yacht Club, which, true to the county's penchant for hyperbole in boasting the tallest and longest buildings, straightest road, and the like, is known as "the oldest yacht club in the world." An accomplished sailor, Tim expertly tacked us around Cork's magnificent harbor ("the vastest in Ireland," naturally), before returning to the most venerable yacht club in the world.

Unfortunately, our approach was intercepted by a demonic wasp, the species in these isles being avid dive-bombers of all things fragrant in late August – cans of cola, glasses of wine, a section of peach, you name it. Just as the mooring hove into sight, this kamikaze zeroed in on my redolent nostrils. I swiped in self-defense, knocking my absurdly expensive brand-new, glare-resistant, graduated bifocal glasses into ten feet of some of the fastest-flowing and most impenetrable alluvium in the world, a fluid so black it could be poured by the pint from a Guinness tap and no one would glean the difference.

The afternoon seemed ruined, and my wallet hit hard. Desperate, I sought help in a pub across the way, extracting from quiet drinkers the names of a half-dozen scuba divers, all of whom turned out to be on holiday somewhere else – endlessly forbearing no longer, the modern Irish travel with world-class abandon these days (Tenerife, Capetown, Crete, Thailand, and Australia being standard fare). My phone calls were pathetic, because the punters, which seasoned drinkers in Ireland are sometimes called, ended up having to dial the various numbers themselves, seeing as I could no longer see.

Just when I was about to give up, someone suggested the name of one Vincent Fahr, a Cork City fireman who doubled as a volunteer harbor search-and-rescue man. Vincent, in the middle of his dinner when I rang, heard my plight and my foreign accent, and was on the scene within ten minutes, to the undoubted relief of the punters.

Rugged and friendly, Vincent hurriedly donned his wetsuit, oxygen tank, and mask and prepared to descend into the water that was growing blacker with every thickening cloud.

"Aren't you going to take a flashlight?" I asked, forgetting that the Irish called them "torches."

No. Vincent explained that he would feel his way through the foul bottom muck inch-by-inch with his bare fingers, because his movements would unleash blizzards of muddy sediment that would render a light useless.

Having recovered all manner of lost treasures and even drowned bodies previously, Vincent seemed confident when he disappeared into what can only be described as the watery equivalent of the La Brea Tar Pits. At first, our hopes rose as frequently as the erratic trails of bubbles signifying his eel-like explorations of the ooze now at least fourteen feet below. But there was no joy. A lavish yacht drifted past with its crew tinkling wine goblets, while the water grew depressingly more opaque. Our children, originally fascinated, lost interest as Vincent's bubbles crisscrossed the gloaming water. Having never discussed his fee, I busied myself with counting his exhalations, figuring a thousand bubbles might easily cost me a (pre-euro) punt, and there seemed to be millions of them. For nearly an hour, Vincent groped his way through oblivion, and by my calculations our bank account was nearly exhausted.

"The man's determined to find your glasses," said my wife.

"Who knows where the tide has moved them?" countered Laura.

Suddenly, after fingering the muck so interminably, Vincent Fahr blasted up through the dark surface like Neptune with a trident, his fist holding a pair of eyeglasses instead. "Are these them?" he asked.

Our roars of "eureka!" were so raucous, we could have been banned then and there from the decorous confines of every yacht club on earth. But we had found a hero in Vincent; Vincent had refused to let us down. Vincent was living proof that a spirit of selfless dedication still runs down the Irish backbone. Vincent had crawled through an ooze from Styx, just to help us.

"How much is it going to cost?" a niggling inner voice began to ask as I slapped him on the back. "You're incredible," Vincent was told as he loaded his gear back into his car. A long pause ensued while the happy smiling continued.

"What do we owe you, Vincent?" I coughed.

"Why, that's up to yourself."

Could there be any worse response, I thought, while beginning to fork over a sheaf of twenties.

"Stop right there," Vincent interrupted after seeing the first note.

"Wait a minute. We interrupted your dinner; had you crawling in the mud for an hour; you used a full tank of oxygen and all to fetch a pair of eyeglasses – that's not reasonable. Take at least two."

Vincent Fahr offered a slow Sphinx-like smile, and sheepishly reached for a single bill, protesting that even that was too much.

"Welcome to Crosshaven," he said and turned away to arrange the gear in his "boot."

And this was Cork. This was the Ireland we had been seeking, full of kindness and welcomes yet for a family from afar sailing forth on its hopes. Veiled warnings some had offered had no bearing, not for us.

Chapter 7

August eased toward autumn, and things seemed to keep falling sweetly into place. True, the Chief Scowler and his trusty sidekick kept parking their awful adolescence behind our now closed gate for a quick afternoon snigger and rock toss at the younger children, followed by a dumping of their astonishing number of junk-food packets in our lane. But these episodes usually were more brainless than bothersome, and we figured they'd just peter out in due time.

In reality, the only thing that shattered our peace was the now constant decibel-blasting cannonades our doorbell released as streams of neighborhood kids called for the boys, and sometimes Laura as well. Jamie, for her part, claimed the infernal noisemaker was a harbinger of happiness.

Meanwhile, I began teaching the Irish kids a thing or two about our North American sports, organizing street versions of ice hockey, or the fluttering plastic Wiffle-ball version of baseball. Our children, in turn, mastered the local game of "tip the can," which is a variant of hide-and-seek developed to suit an urban Irish childhood in the frequent company of parked cars.

The kids' busy confraternity had the added benefit of allowing their father to sneak off for his own explorations. On a couple of further late-afternoon visits to the Hi-B (a place Jamie so far avoided), I got to know a marvelous character named Owen McIntyre, newly recruited to start an environmental law program at the redundantly named University College Cork, where the autumn term had not yet begun. A glorious talker with a hyper intellect and irrepressible self-confidence, Owen hailed from distant Donegal, perhaps the least spoilt county in Ireland. He nonetheless epitomized the country's new vigor, free of Famine-legacy poor-mouthing, begrudgery, secrecy, and distrust.

You want to talk about the bazaars in Turkmenistan? Owen's been there and will tell you about that. Vodka swilling in Moscow? Getting stuck on a mountainside with Serbian toughs? Just turn the switch, and his stories fly forth. So here he was now with his raven-haired partner, Maria ("partner" referring to the unmarried, protracted state of mortal sin that about a third of all Irish Catholics now opt for as a thumb-nosing to the once almighty Church). As new to Cork as ourselves, they were inquisitive, enthusiastic, and vital. That Owen was fifteen years younger mattered nothing, just as my age divide with Bun only seasoned that relationship.

"Aye, it's an extraordinary thing that your family is doing. I admire it greatly and I can well surmise that your wife must be a remarkable spirit. I know I can speak for Maria as well in saying that we would be honored to meet her," said the loquacious Owen.

"Absolutely," agreed Maria, a Connemara native brought up in London and thus possessing a uniquely mellifluous accent, in this country where subtle shifts in intonation can typically be pegged with one sentence. "We should meet as a foursome."

"Why not right now?" I demanded. "Come to our house. I'll phone Jamie to make sure it's okay."

"That's fine with me," the wife, being a game one, said.

In about twenty-seven minutes we were all lounging in the sun wok of our stone-walled patio, while Jamie soon set to ferrying out plates of steaming pasta tossed with black olives and sautéed chicken. The conversation so easily ranged the world, while the children blessedly played elsewhere, that the pop of corks assumed a certain rhythm as dusk settled.

"Perhaps we should take a nightcap to the roof? You can see all of Cork from up there," I suggested. A go-for-it look did I get from Owen, and Maria and Jamie were by now giggling so fervidly that resistance from those two was not on the cards.

Out the top window we all noisily clambered to our rooftop viewing pad. Across the road, shades lifted and curtains parted. In silence, we beheld the astonishing panoramic views. Window panes from houses on every hill fired into prisms of liquid silver and bronze. Whorls of clouds whispered across the darkening sky.

The vista evidently inspired Owen. "Jamie, David," he blurted in a rush that halved the first vowel in each of our names, "I hope you will accept a few words of an attempt at an Irish welcome, in gratitude for your gracious hospitality and that exquisite dinner."

My wife's rapt gaze said work away. For Owen is not only charming, but tall, handsome, and exceedingly flirtatious when he hits overdrive.

"Jamie, with your beauty and grace, you shouldn't seek employment – it should seek you, unless this town is comatose beyond hope. I know that I can speak for Maria as well as myself in saying" – here a huge jet rumbled across the heavens – "we have enjoyed your company as much as that of anyone we have met in years."

Translate the above to an American male leaving a dinner party: "Thanks, pal."

Female version: "That was neat."

Hang on, though. Owen McIntyre, under the merest sliver of rising moon, was still waxing. "Would it be too much for me to touch my glass to yours, Jamie, to wish you and your family every joy?"

How in the name of Bono could one say no to this verbiage? So I had no problem with the extra second, or was it ten or twenty, it took for the traditional quick clink to proceed my way. In fact, I refilled everyone's glasses, just to keep hands busy.

"Aye," Owen pressed forward. "We have had some wine tonight, of course. But what I want to say is that on evenings like this, the drinks are almost an afterthought. They merely help like-minded souls come to understand one another a touch quicker. What I am saying to ye now, and I sincerely hope that I am not being too forward, is that it has been a great pleasure to share your company, David. It has been a privilege, and I feel that we are on the way to becoming friends for a long time."

Clink. By all means, clink. A casual observer could be forgiven for thinking that our pressed-together glasses were holding the two of us up. But I was actually deeply pondering all the while the ties that unite a certain gene pool all over this earth: about shoeless forebears eking sustenance out of godforsaken plots in the west of Ireland's hardscrabble; slaving through the penal colonies in

Australia; digging the canals and railway beds of North America; or changing English sheets through eternal spinsterhood, or something like that. Well, come to this roof high above Cork City on such a starry night, you forlorn Gaels of yore, and you will rejoice in what has become of the land of your blood, I think I thought.

"Look out, Owen!" Maria suddenly cried as her beloved abruptly leaned over the edge of our roof's hip-high wall with one hand lunging for a passing luna moth – at least that's what he said it was, though it looked like a bat to me.

"It's time to go. This has been lovely," Maria said with simple grace, as she shoved my dear new friend headfirst toward the open window, nearly four feet above our deck.

After ushering our visitors down the stairs, Jamie and I returned to our eyrie. "Look at how blissfully unhurried our new lives have become," I said, then continued into a speech about how conversations here, especially with Owen, amounted to a verbal equivalent to Cubism, with small utterances splintering into tangents that kept redefining whatever it was that was struggling to be said. "Even the way they pour pints is unhurried," I summed up, as Jamie hoisted herself through the window, having heard enough.

In the morning my beautiful, loving wife gave me a jab in the ribs. "Hey, wake up. We promised the kids a field trip to Clonakilty. Remember the music festival and all that?"

"I'm still feeling unhurried," I groaned, reaching for a pillow.

"Ditch the Oirish act," Jamie commanded. In minutes, she had herded the children and my reluctant self into the car.

In about three miles we learned that "unhurried" no longer describes Irish driving. In years past, we'd shared "bockety" lanes with phalanxes of sheep and meandered on rural byways whose grassy verges were called the "long acre," thanks to cows nonchalantly helping themselves to the pickings there. But that was before the Celtic Tiger quintupled Ireland's yearly car acquisition rate and made the once-sleepy island the per-capita king of automobile purchasing in Europe. Our guests of the last evening had pointed out that the Republic's citizens now pony up about £10,000 in tax alone for the privilege of driving their fancy new wheels – a sum that not long ago would have garnered a fine house. Consequently, they work many extra hours to pay for their gilded coupes and thus have to drive very fast to get where they are going so that they can relax.

But we were scarcely prepared for the new ferocity on wheels. The newspapers often described hour-long jams in Dublin and half-hour ones clogging up smaller cities like Limerick, Galway, and Waterford, but rarely mentioned the time-stopping black holes where all forward motion ceases at random points across the island; these are called roundabouts. England, France, and Boston have them too, but Ireland's are different, a kind of vehicular Pamplona.

Until now, driving on the left hadn't been too difficult, partly because we mostly walked. But then, we hadn't yet met up with a particular ring of Cork madness known as the Kinsale round-about. This engineering marvel splices the four busiest roads in the county – one diverting tens of thousands of cars through the new Cork harbor tunnel, another serving as the main south artery out of the city, a third as the northbound connection from the airport that attracts 1.9 million passengers a year, a fourth sucking traffic in from the west – into a lanyard of perpetual bedlam. Handsome plantings are rumored to sprout from the grassy center of the Kinsale roundabout, but we certainly weren't about to gaze upon them, what with hundreds of vehicles simultaneously converging from all angles.

"Stay on the left? The left of what?" I cried to Jamie as two lanes of traffic screamed past on that side and two more jockeyed on our right, before one of each of these abruptly vanished, forcing its cars to veer into the dead center of the revolving mess.

We went around twice, struggling to read the typically cryp-tic Irish road signs while steering for dear life. Finally I careered onto the open road. Relief was short-lived. The N71, like many of Ireland's new highways, was surprisingly good (thanks to vast, never-to-be-requited European Union investments) – for a stretch. But motorists at our rear zoomed perilously close, assuming the demeanor of Luftwaffe pilots with a fresh kill in their gun sights. And why not? At that point there were almost no traffic police or radar speed traps in Ireland, and no one ever issued tickets for strafing within three feet of the next car. Not surprisingly, Ireland has the second-highest rate of road fatalities in Europe, more than double those of jam-packed Britain, triple icy Norway's, and just behind those found on the sheep-clotted hairpin mountain turns of Portugal. Statistics say that Ireland is the seventh most dangerous place to drive on earth, with the top five entrants coming from the far ends of the Third World. Of course, Owen McIntyre had pointed out that a quarter of all Irish motorists have never been trained or even tested – the ubiquitous L sticker on many of the nation's cars means Learning Permit and most are bleached by years of exposure to rarely seen sunlight due to loopholes and delays without end in the country's motor vehicle system. The cardinal rule is: when in doubt, accelerate.

Centuries ago, the ancient Celts were famous for cattle raids in which bands of largely naked individuals on horseback would swoop down upon unsuspecting neighbors or best friends. Screaming deliriously, they would issue a thump on the head and make off with a cow, then celebrate the feat with a night of mead drinking and bardic poetry while the heifer wandered back to its owner, who would enjoy the same pastime the next evening.

On this particular Saturday, barristers in Jaguars, eighteen-year-olds in *Mad Max* motorcycle gear, and old farmers in smoke-belching bangers were gleefully pursuing the same adrenalin-pumping ritual. When discovering our attempt at enjoying a pleasant drive, they all suddenly materialized in waves, flashing their headlights, leaning on their horns, and accelerating within side-mirror inches of the dawdling sixty-mile-an-hour motorist from afar before finally "overtaking" into the face of oncoming traffic.

A bit worse for wear, we made it the thirty-some miles to Clonakilty, a pretty town with trim houses painted in the lovely pastels the Irish use to defeat the winter murk – vermilion and aquamarine, lavender, plum, and peach are just a few of the improbable hues that one discovers upon entering "Clon." One stretch is so self-consciously florid that local wags call those dwellings "the Smartie houses," seeing that they resemble the colors of an English candy called Smarties.

Life in these parts was once anything but bright. The brutal legacy of the Famine in the west of Ireland was in fact the anvil of future revenge. In an 1846 letter to the Duke of Wellington, a Cork merchant named Nicholas Cummins captured a few choice vignettes from the nearby hamlet of Myross, today as sweet-looking as could be. Cummins could have been talking about any parish in this region, whose ruthless landlords kept exporting grain to England in the midst of the Famine's unspeakable want:

> In the first [hovel], six famished and ghastly skeletons, to all appearance dead, were huddled in a corner on some filthy straw, their sole covering what seemed to be a ragged horse-cloth and their wretched legs hanging about, naked above the knees. I approached with horror and found by a low moaning that they were alive; they were in fever – four children, a woman, and what had once been a man . . . Suffice it to say that in a few minutes I was surrounded by at least 200 of such phantoms, such frightful spectres as no words can describe. By far the greater number were delirious, either from famine or from fever. Their demonic yells are still ringing in my ears, and their horrible images are fixed upon my brain . . . My clothes were nearly torn off in my endeavours to escape from the throng of pestilence around when my neckcloth was seized from behind by a grip which compelled me to turn. I found myself grasped by a woman with an infant, *just born*, in her arms and the remains of a filthy sack across her loins – the sole covering of herself and the babe. The same morning the police opened a house on the adjoining lands, which was observed shut for many days, and two frozen corpses were found lying upon the mud floor, *half devoured by the rats.* A mother, herself in fever, was seen the same day to drag out the corpse of a child . . .

Perhaps inevitably, Clonakilty produced Michael Collins, the War of Independence commander who cracked the British intelligence system and orchestrated the insurrection's relentless campaign of ambush, sabotage, and arson, including burnings of many of the great nearby houses of the Anglo-Irish. As ruthless as he was charismatic, Michael Collins was also responsible for the fatal ambushes of numerous agents of the Crown as they slept in their beds. To his generation, the Famine was *yesterday* and they therefore felt no qualms in treating the British to a helping of the same quagmires the Americans would later discover in Vietnam and, ultimately, Iraq. But Michael Collins was also forced to negotiate the thankless compromises that led to the formation of the Irish Free State, the bitterly rued pill ever since being that the British retain control of the heavily "planted" (in other words, deliberately stocked with chiefly Scottish colonialist farmers) six Protestant counties of Northern Ireland. For his troubles, Collins was promptly murdered just down the road from Clonakilty in the 1922 Civil War, during the brief carnage in which dissident IRA guerrillas rebelled against their Free State brethren for having acquiesced to the notorious "treaty."

Modern Clonakilty, we could quickly see, had shaken off its brooding on its Famine past and now embodies the brightest aspects of the Republic's burgeoning progress. It is an amazingly thriving place, with geranium-bedecked restaurants, tasteful shops, and stone-fronted guesthouses arising in such an outburst of civic pride that the community was recently named the winner of Ireland's national "Tidy Towns" competition. At the center of the main street sits O'Donovan's Hotel, one of Ireland's numerous comfortable, independent hostelries which are so much more engaging than the mass cut-rate hotel franchises that provide accommodation in too many countries. O'Donovan's also boasts an Asian café in the back alleyway where Irish peasant women used to spend their days skinning and salting fish for daily wages that wouldn't buy a fork of fried rice now. We decided to order a restorative drink in the hotel's pub, motioning the children to mill about in the rumpled lobby.

The call was for two pints of Murphy's, the softer, mellower Cork version of the better-known Guinness, which is no longer owned by that august Anglo-Irish family but rather a Spanish conglomerate called Diageo that also controls other important international cultural icons such as Burger King and the Pillsbury doughboy. Murphy's – long managed by a powerful Cork family of that name – has become the property of the Dutch brewer Heineken, which has predictably re-baptized its stout operations as "Heineken Ireland." This is equivalent to the Japanese taking over the American national landmark the Rockefeller Center, which they in fact did some time ago. In both cases, nobody complained. Such is progress.

We moved into the cafeteria with the kids and assembled trays of fried fish and sandpaper-surfaced chicken nuggets, called "gougons" in Ireland, complemented by the usual mountains of chips. A young woman impassively waited at the till.

"Are you okay?" the teenager asked, which did not help my road-frayed nerves. Did we look terminally ill? The phrase was dumbfounding, and in this country, where language is so often wielded with a fine brush, such mindless utterances fall with a deafening thud. For the last few weeks we had heard, ad nauseam, the same words greeting shoppers who approached Irish cash registers with their arms wrapped around masses of expensive clothing or toys. In most countries, people thrusting wads of cash over check-out counters are not asked, "Are you okay?" but rather, "May I help you?" We couldn't help wondering if the phrase "Are you okay?" really was a nod to the old indolence of the land, meaning, "Why the hell are you bothering me?"

"I'm grand. How are you?" I responded, waiting for the inevitable three-beat response. Ever-observant Laura, knowing my hobby-horses inside out, caught the sarcasm and scowled. Variants of such amiable how-are-yous are asked all over the world, and in many places are even answered brightly. In Ireland, no positive reply can be offered – that's bragging. Better to feign unhappiness.

"Not too bad," the clerk said right on cue. Irish people always say that to inquiries regarding how they are faring. The words convey that the people mumbling them are not yet dead, nor have they had their entrails recently cut out by invading Norsemen, nor their entire family stricken with typhoid only to depart in the night on a pestilential Famine ship. The response expresses the

Irish infatuation with poor-mouthing, meaning a stoic sharing of life's miseries with the rest of the unfortunate inhabitants of their godforsaken wet bog of an island. "Not too bad," I knew by now, is never, ever to be rendered with a smile. The point is to convey that one's as miserable as everyone else, even though public opinion polls consistently show that the Irish today are actually among the most cheerful and optimistic people in Europe. The phrase is undoubtedly a remnant of the post-Famine psychology that has never caught up with the "Smartie" age.

Eating helped my mood, and we ventured outside, by now forgetting the frenzy on the roads. The music festival was materializing, with traffic diverted and the town's main thoroughfare flooding with pedestrians. A great cluster of them gathered in front of a bevel-windowed old pub called De Barra's, which, Ireland being what it is, has hosted as its most celebrated regular and provider of Friday night entertainment the former wah-wah amplified bass guitarist for the Jimi Hendrix Experience, Noel Redding. Today, three trad musicians sat on stools on the sidewalk, all as clean-cut as bankers, tuning wah-wah-deprived fiddles. As it turned out, their first song was based on a series of letters a heartbroken father had written to a son who had emigrated to Boston in 1860 – never, like millions of participants in the Irish diaspora, to be seen again by his family. The words could have as easily been penned to one Owen Monaghan, namesake of the little son I'd just hoisted onto my shoulders, who departed forever from County Monaghan in 1844 to a miserable factory job twenty miles deeper into Massachusetts. They could have been directed as well to millions of others who would never return from Australia and South Africa, Argentina and Ontario, anywhere at all that would have them.

The ballad was so poignant, its mournful fiddles and tin whistles and aching words so expressive of the terrible exodus from places just like Clonakilty, that I began brushing away tears. Jamie, I saw, was doing the same thing. Laura looked from one parent to another and caught our emotion; even Harris stared off wistfully. Here lies then, ye transplanted children, another sad initiation rite to your past, I thought. Yet the level of literacy and devotion to history that resonated through the singers' rich baritones, and through the crowd's rapt appreciation, seemed immensely reassuring to me, a sign that even the young Irish remained steeped in the tragic poetry of their past.

On this gentle afternoon, the band, called Natural Gas, had no intention of dwelling on a mordant note. Their next offering concerned the universal pub musicians' impatience with donkey-eared listeners, and it started with a refrain epitomizing the disrespectful "foostering," or fool's play, of loudmouthed drinkers.

"Hey you with the head! Put down your bloody *bohdran*! Pick up your pint instead!" the number begins, referring to the tambourine-like skin drum (pronounced BOW-ron) used by Irish traditional bands. "Say two acts of contrition for the poor pub musician. If I had a son, that's not what he'd be, for they have to put up with hooflers and tricksters and chancers dropping ten quid in their fee."

This flourish coaxed forth a peculiar dark-eyed man with a loud red-and-white-striped shirt, enormous yellow tie, and brace suspenders holding up a pair of floppy vaudevillian trousers. Transported by some private reverie, he butterflied his arms forward as if swimming through waves of incoming visions. Fishmouthing all the while, he laboriously worked his legs in various directions as if his pants contained stilts. For reasons known only to Clonakilty, this impromptu entertainer, whose face was as rigidly unchanging as a Noh actor's, is called Chicken George. When not performing, he's said to be a great conversationalist. But head-scrambling contradictions are the rule in modern Ireland, for De Barra's has also served as a favored venue for David Bowie and Paul McCartney. How could one not love the place?

Joining the crowd outside was a coven of barefoot individuals in brown sackcloth topped by mangy rats' nests of hair. The women, with blackened teeth and blue whorls and lines smeared across their faces, looked like hundred-year-old hags and cackled accordingly. The even wilder-haired and possibly uglier men sported ten-foot pikes.

"These festivals get over the top," I whispered to my wife, for in Ireland festivals break out in dizzying variety. Every town with enough children to fill a school can muster a pair of August festivals without a second thought, and the bigger localities keep it up for nine months – folk, food, fiddle, and farm festivals, dance, jazz, film, choral, art, literary, heritage, matchmaking, midsummer, spring, and autumn festivals keep coming at you and one sometimes imagines hordes of festival merrymakers changing their costumes behind the next ridge and descending like a thousand Comanches on every unsuspecting crossroads that has not fenced them out.

"They're a bunch of crusties," Jamie said, using the Irish term for a certain wave of recent New Age immigrants who are alleged to be soap shy. "Festival crusties."

There was no doubt about it. Not long ago, the west of Ireland was full of native Gaelic speakers who lived in a timeless world into which the Creator seemed to breathe an inordinate share of the world's dreams. The waves moaned on briny rocks and old women heard the terrible cry of the banshees; a mouse moved in a hayrick and the fairies were heard to be back at their mischief; a woman died young and her suitor saw her image in the moonlight for the rest of his forlorn years. In modern Ireland, loads of New Age people still see, or try to see, such visions, often sitting cross-legged before the few remaining stone hovels buried in the depths of some hollow or bramble-ridden boreen – which means a little lane, though a Cork City avenue is called Boreenmanna Road, which translates into "Little Big Lane Road."

These pike-wielding cacklers were indeed crusties, or in other words hippies yearning for a return to the land. The crusties moved in droves to the secret spaces of Ireland's west in the 1970s and 1980s to forge more spiritually rooted lives than they believed possible in the mass population centers of Britain, the Netherlands, and Germany. Many have acclimated nicely and are tipping away now at producing superb cheeses and organic vegetables, along with the usual baskets, clay pots, and water-divining trades. But some of the newest Rastafarian-styled recruits sit on Cork corners banging bongo drums with an irritating monotony. An aging troupe called Skibbamba will dance in place for hours in tie-dyed pajamas, with some of the mothers sporting babies in papooses who jolt their heads backward and forward in perfect, if helpless, time to the beat. Anyone so inclined can rent the entire bunch for a party, which just last week I'd promised Laura I would do for her wedding celebration in, oh, another decade or two.

"That's not funny, Dad," she stammered in disgust. Natives in West Cork, however, retain a tolerant balance in dealing with such exotics. Clonakilty recently suffered an interminable visit by a Californian who screeched rock anthems at otherwise harmonious street corners that the Lord expressly created for Irish people to complain about the weather and their aches and pains. Worse still, he began posting announcements of his forthcoming lecture on The True Meaning of the Age of Aquarius. When the hour of illumination arrived, not a single person showed up. Such is Cork cuteness, and the man vanished.

But modern Ireland is actually hugely enriched by the presence of myriad foreigners – from the actor Jeremy Irons, who recently painted his Cork castle pink, to Keith Richards of the Rolling Stones playing Buddha in the Wicklow Mountains, and the Swiss wheelers and dealers who in the 1980s bought an estate outside Skibberreen as a refuge for their government to weather nuclear war. In fact, a four-room schoolhouse not far from Clonakilty now educates nine different nationalities among its seventy pupils, including kids from a family who had just fled their ranch in troubled Zimbabwe. Through a mutual connection, we stopped at their rented farmhouse on our way back to Cork City and found a party in full tear. Inside, young Dutchmen with shaved heads were making horrible noises on their electric guitars, but on the lawn we were charmed by an aristocratic English writer, whose debut book had to do with the bank robbery he committed when fresh out of Oxford.

Next, a dark-tressed, dimple-cheeked young woman slunk our way, her bare midriff sporting a gold naval ring. She was Una, and it transpired that she had been raised on a crusty houseboat captained by a tin-whistle playing American mother.

"How interesting," I said. "Where does she live now?"

"Well, she's a divinity student these days and lives in a tiny little town called Cornwall, Connecticut."

"Una," I guffawed. "Your mother's eaten dinner at our house there several times."

Ah serendipity – Ireland is thy name.

Chapter 8

September dawned. "Hey, you with the heads, it's show time!" I called to the sleeping boys in their bunks, it being the first day of school.

This fateful morning is of course uneasy anywhere, but now our beloved boys, God save them, were about to be served up as not only the new kids in their classes, every child's worst fear to begin with, but – and here comes another initiation rite, kiddoes – also shoved forward for public inspection in strange uniforms amidst a gabble of accents, backgrounds, and expectations entirely foreign to their own. Even in the intimacy of his tiny American school, Harris the Procrastinator had always dreaded this turning point, so resolutely in fact that he had utterly refused to relinquish his grip on my leg when I tried to usher him into the first grade in the U.S. On that traumatic day, I had to bring him back twice. So there was no mystery regarding his motivation in fussing "for just another minute" over a Lego creation beside his pillow.

Owen is different: he adores any challenge that appeals to his particularly opinionated, and sometimes self-set nature. Fascinated since he was two by the inner workings of all things, he had recently unfolded a paper clip and driven both ends into a power point so he could be sure about the live power of circulating electrical currents. Never mind that his fingers were serrated like barbecued meat, he'd found out what he needed to know, and didn't cry. So he was raring for a crack at a new Irish school, was in fact eager to study his ancient ancestral tongue.

Porridge – what else? – was served and then the boys struggled into their new Catholic school regalia of gray trousers, white polyester shirts, and black clodhoppers. They were then tourniqueted with striped ties and black blazers ennobled with priceless braided rings of gold and school crests embossed on their breast pockets. A door-stoop photograph was quickly choreographed, with Laura, whose first day at school would be tomorrow, reluctantly appearing in the soon-to-be requisite black tights, gray skirt, red blouse, and striped tie of her more distant school, with her long strawberry hair falling over the shoulders of her official blazer. For years we had endured pitched morning battles about who would deign to wear what to school. So the simplicity of consigning the ingrates to unchanging uniforms was a relief. But the big question was whether Ireland's academic strictness, religiosity, and fierce attention to basics – the latter long since softened over in self-esteem-obsessed American schools – was about to consign them to a thousand emotional deaths, or expand their horizons.

We scarcely had a clue. Sure, I'd completed a frenzied sampling of nine different Cork schools a few months before, wrapped a blindfold around my head, spun around three times, and stuck a pin on an institution that said Christian Brothers College. Everyone said that the primary level of that private school, a ten-minute walk from our house, was A1. The crème de la crème of Cork went there, starting way back with the offspring of the "Merchant Prince" class who weren't much bothered by the Famine at all. Adult graduates of Christians' various institutions around Ireland were still complaining bitterly at the moment about the arbitrary humiliation and harsh corporal punishment they'd experienced long ago. "But sure, it did us no harm," lots would say in the next breath. "I'd never have learned a thing had I not been sufficiently scared of my teachers," a friend, who was a graduate of this system, once told us.

In fact, the principal of Cork's Christian Brothers primary school, once exclusively the domain of celibate priests, was now not only a female but a middle-aged mother of captivating warmth who had recently lost a young son. Deeply compassionate, Síle (pronounced Sheila) Hayes had even called at our door to extend warm greetings the day after our arrival in Cork. She was a breath of reassurance, especially because the Christian Brothers order, racked by scandals of pedophilia in the eighties, had not attracted a single new novitiate in the last five years. Cork's Christian Brothers

College – the primary school a feeder institution to an adjacent nine-hundred-boy secondary school that places many of its students into Ireland's best universities – has no Brothers at all on its teaching staff, not a one.

As we headed down the Wellington Road, it wasn't hard to keep the boys' minds diverted, the first day of school in Ireland being a bizarre testament to the creativity of the Celtic spirit. Mothers and fathers were all hand-delivering their kids to this rite of passage, shared by four schools within a thousand-yard nexus, and many were so overcome during their last-minute embraces that they parked in the middle of the road, on sidewalks and crucial intersections, and lost sight of the half-mile-long string of cars stalled behind them. Nothing moved and pandemonium ruled. Our fellow Corkonians handled this predicament with aplomb, however, by not honking or shouting but hitting the mobile phones for a thousand lamentations to other drivers stuck like themselves, half of them perhaps only a couple of hundred feet away. A *garda* or police officer (versus *gardaí*, the name for a rare gathering of two or more of them in one place) ambled from mist into reality, but it was instantly apparent that he had no rule-enforcing intentions beyond chatting with a friend recognized through a rolled-down car window just ahead of ours. Ireland has not tossed aside its implacable patience and forbearance, not yet. Everything will eventually be "sorted," if one just sits and waits, as our fidgeting boys were consigned to do, even if their hair was nearly standing on end.

Getting into the swing of things, we double-parked and ushered our anxious progeny into a holding-tank-like front room, where a grim painting of the Last Supper had absolutely no calming effect on the squirming masses of nearly 200 five- to twelve-year-old boys. Jamie and I folded our arms serenely and waited for the welcoming first-day-of-school speeches we'd by now heard for a good number of years.

But the pedagogues had a neat Cork trick for us this time: they said nothing. I looked at my shoes for a while, then Jamie's. I always thought her feet were nice, but still – there wasn't a lot new to see there. Meanwhile, the teachers and students watched each other with mutual dread, and one could envision spitballs being worked into readiness. Suddenly, a whistle blasted through the stillness, as deafening and shrill as a call to order at Alcatraz or Sing Sing. I looked at Harris – he looked at me. Don't leave me in this place, his eyes seemed to plead. But there was an unmistakable message to the parents in that whistle – go away.

"I liked what they said about nurturing the whole child," I muttered to Jamie as we walked away, baffled to the core.

My wife looked set to kick me where it hurts. "This isn't the time for sarcasm. I just hope you knew what you were doing with this place," she moaned, with a small tear streaming down her cheek.

The next day, it was Laura's turn. We set off to her venerable, 361-year-old Bandon Grammar School, which is a coed secondary school teaching kids aged from twelve to eighteen. In Ireland, children begin high school in the seventh grade in a belief that they are already equipped to master a greatly expanded range of subjects, including foreign languages, and more in-depth mathematics, geography, and world history than is sanctioned in the more hand-holding middle schools of North America.

Naomi Jackson, a vivacious niece of Bun, had ardently recommended her alma mater, without dwelling on the logistical challenges of getting Laura twenty-three miles down the road every dawn to the always congested small town of Bandon. This was the moral equivalent of telling new arrivals in Vienna to try an academy in Bratislava, or doting parents in Baltimore to make arrangements in Washington, D.C.

On tourist maps and brochures, Bandon appears to be about twenty minutes from Cork, but the reality is something else. After driving a half-hour with Laura fretting in the backseat, we slowed before one of Ireland's more puzzling roundabouts at a place named, apparently appropriately, Half Way. No new traffic was arriving or departing from the lonesome feeder roads stuck into this ring of motorized jabberwocky, but here was a very handsomely laid-out roundabout indeed. Had young roundabout trainees been given the chance to test their skills in this forlorn spot? No other explanation was apparent. But then we hadn't grasped that speculators had stealthily acquired a patchwork of nearby farms as part of an

£800 million scheme to create an overnight town of ten thousand inhabitants squashed into four hundred acres.

A few miles farther, the highway abruptly narrowed through the village of Inishannon, once the scene of repeated failed IRA attempts to blow up the local barracks of the British police constabularies in 1921. Every go fizzled like a vision from a *Road Runner* cartoon, but 315 of these outposts of the Crown were bombed and burned elsewhere. Historians tend to pay more attention to the IRA's fatal ambush of sixteen British auxiliaries about three miles away on a boggy stretch by the village of Kilmichael, the work done by a handful of ill-equipped rebels under the command of General Tom Barry, age twenty-one. Surprisingly, this skirmish is celebrated as the most pivotal battle of the Irish War of Independence.

The fertile soil of this part of Cork has always been prized in comparison to the barren ground of Ireland's extreme west, and thus attracted determined cultivation by the carefully planted Anglo-Irish. In the seventeenth and eighteenth centuries, the ascendant gentry systematically annexed the best small holdings of the native Catholic peasantry in the vicinity, a great number of whose owners were bled dry by the harshest landlords' tithes during and after the Famine. The Georgian-styled plantations grew stately, and their protective walls formidable, owing to the willingness of destitute masons to work for a penny a day, while the thatched hovels of the natives were reconstructed ever deeper in the barely tillable hollows. The rank-and-file citizens of Bandon, the once walled garrison town four miles past Inishannon, didn't fret. Their attitude was so virulently anti-Catholic that the place became known as "Bandon, where even the pigs are Protestant." The peasants' livestock, having some value in local eyes, were allowed to spend the night upon common grazing land within the town's domain, while their owners were banished to the hinterlands at dusk.

Bandon Grammar School's promotional brochures didn't mention that the town used to boast a sign by its entrance gates saying: "No Catholic, nor free thinker, nor dissenter may enter here – only Protestant gentlemen." One night someone with a different perspective scrawled, "Whoever wrote it, wrote it well, for the same is written on the gates of hell."

Until about a generation ago, no Catholic in the Republic of Ireland would have dreamed of sending his child to a school with a Protestant pedigree like Bandon Grammar's, nor would such a child have been admitted. Indeed, it wouldn't be long before one of Laura's new friends would take her aside and advise that she should never tell her classmates that she had been raised as a Catholic – "Papist" is the way it used to be put in the Republic and still is in the North. The truth, nonetheless, is that the bitter religious divides have largely evaporated in southern Ireland, where elite Protestant schools tend to call themselves "non-sectarian," and now draw 30 percent or more of their students from the once reviled Catholic masses. A very different situation still prevails in the troubled North, with Protestant mothers stoning and spitting at their Catholic counterparts seeking to infiltrate a supposedly "mixed" school in the Belfast neighborhood of Ardoyne.

But in the Republic, little enmity or even notice is paid these days to sectarian distinctions, although the punctilious Protestants do have some distinctive qualities. For one thing, being naturally more organized and respectful of authority, they are much better than Papists at managing traffic. Numerous speed bumps slowed our progress up the tree-lined drive into Bandon Grammar's seventy-acre campus, and not one parent stopped to gab in the middle of the road.

Laura looked edgy, nonetheless, which was disconcerting. This was a girl who had played ice hockey the past winter on a team of nineteen boys with but one other girl, who had ridden horses five times larger than herself when she was six, and relished lead roles in school plays that thrust her before packed auditoriums. An expert-grade ski slope coated with ice was a piffle as well, even though she wasn't particularly athletic. Laura, the dear heart, prided herself on trying anything. But where were we bringing her now? A few weeks earlier she had a brief tour of her new school under the wing of the personable young headmaster. But the place was empty then, and now the seventy-five "first-years" were spilling this way and that out of cars, all decked out in their immaculate uniforms, but carefully looking over their shoulders.

We parked near one of the modest concrete outbuildings

that fan out beside the somewhat dilapidated former manor house and patronage once belonging, like all of Bandon, to the Duke of Devonshire. His former pile was long since converted to classrooms, a meal hall, and library, with cramped *Madeline*-style dormitory rooms for the boarding girls on the upper floor. The school has quite decent facilities, with a floodlit, all-weather playing field; a soccer "grit pitch;" tennis courts; and an enormous gymnasium complex. Although sitting prettily on a cow-dotted hill, it bears little resemblance, however, to the grandiose visions of mock-Gothic campuses that the top American or British preparatory schools passionately pursue. But to our relief, Bandon charged a fraction of its foreign counterparts, and seemed, at least superficially, to sacrifice little in the transaction.

Many of the incoming students spoke with the reedy trill of the first- or second-generation English, called "West Brits" in Ireland, who still find their way into the grandest remaining country houses in these parts; and very few betrayed the lilting singsong of the euphonious Cork accent we had come to love. But filing into the convocation hall, they all seemed as vulnerable as kids anywhere struggling with their first day in a new school. After a few minutes, the headmaster issued a call for attention, and I readied my eardrums for another horrendous whistle blast. Mercifully, there was none. We ushered Laura forward to where another new girl with strawberry hair and freckles just like hers sat alone on an empty row of stools, looking like she would rather be anywhere else in the world. "She looks like you, Laura. Sit down there and make her comfortable," I urged. It turned out that this girl – despite sharing with our daughter the most classically Irish coloring of anyone in sight – was English. Quickly, they would become best friends. In fact, once Laura sat beside her new friend, she never looked back at the strange beings who had created her. Our daughter's adolescence, the go-away time, had begun. It didn't take a whistle for my wife and me to depart now.

All three seeds had been transplanted to new soil, and now our fates hung on how they would take.

Chapter 9

Inevitably, new rhythms took hold. Each morning Laura rose on her own at six, made tea, and dressed for school. A few minutes later, Jamie would start fixing breakfast and packing lunches. Around 7:15 I'd take Laura down to Cork's hideously Stalinesque bus station for her hour-long journey to Bandon, with a transfer at the far end, the same taxing trip to be repeated at the end of her school day, which sometimes lasted until 6 p.m. After dinner, the homework was stacked higher than she had ever seen before. Until now, she'd bicycled or been protectively driven the three short miles to her Connecticut school without the slightest worry, her every care looked after. Suddenly, every commonplace security was gone. Remarkably, this girl, who'd only just turned twelve, was too excited to complain. Laura's self-confidence amazed us. Hers was a vision of a child maturing before our eyes.

Returning from the bus station each morning, I would hear a revelry bugle wafting from the nearby military barracks to rouse the more tender souls of the Irish army. Peculiarly, it would often sound four more times over the next hour, sometimes with bagpipes mixed in, the local soldiery evidently being a more sleepy bunch than our young daughter.

By now, the boys would be waking for their sweet cereal, packed, like so many other confections in Ireland, with at least twice the sugar punch of its counterparts in America – which may have something to do with why the Irish talk so much. Just before nine, we'd escort Harris and Owen through a sentry gate to the walled officers' compound of the army barracks, then down past leafy, bird-song-rich lanes and playing fields where the dew sparkled in the sun. By the time we reached their school's back gate, the world was fresh.

Owen loved his first-grade teacher, and Harris was relieved to discover that his classroom was not the house of horrors he had feared – not yet. No sooner would one of us ferry them home around 3 p.m. than the super-charged doorbell commenced splitting eardrums as their eager new friends called to play in the garden.

About an hour later, I'd often watch from my top-floor office window high above as the duo of crisp-strewing malcontents, now often joined by an immense friend, began their afternoon's slink down our lane, sometimes crawling as if seeking invisibility, for a new afternoon's installment of sniggering and menace toward the youngsters playing on the other side of the hedge. With newspaper stories constantly circulating about the sometimes ugly treatment of dark-skinned asylum seekers in this island of the welcomes, we should have grasped by now that there were elements of Irish society that abhor outsiders of every kind, and in fact savor the challenge of trying to scare them back to wherever they come from. But we didn't.

For a while, we merely tried to ignore the creeping and crawling things outside. Our boys, for their part, were scarcely troubled, so long as they played on the right side of the protective gate.

In the evenings they were kept busy anyhow memorizing the principal towns of the twenty-six counties and all the exotic river and mountain names of the Republic, or in Owen's case, learning to say "dog" in Irish. Sometimes they grew snappish, one or the other joining with a new friend in an abusive "slag fest" – a prime Irish sport – insulting their sister or brother to curry favor with the ever-shifting allegiances outside our door.

"Don't you understand how important it is that we stand together as a family over here?" Jamie or I would scold. Nice words, but they fell on deaf ears. In truth, there were bitter fights about first goes at jams, juice, butter, bread, biscuits, toothpaste, television, and maddeningly short shower times before the heater conked out – the typical fodder of parent hell.

But mostly our problems seemed minor, even if I was worried about not yet having harnessed the same volume of work assignments that always seemed to materialize back home. True, I had my occasional website feature column as the guru of new developments in the medical device industry, but arrangements for the next big ticket newsletter were falling on deaf ears – and, alas, the magazine and newspaper work I had counted on rekindling was, shall we say, materializing "slowly." Too often, I found myself sitting at my desk and staring at the far hills in hopes of inspiration or at least a ringing phone. The process became something of a pantomime. The light changed so constantly that one had to circle the room again and again, like a caged cat, to open and close shades and switch lamps off and on to cope with the baffling transitions from filmy gray to strange shimmer, followed by floods of heavenly brilliance, and then back through the kaleidoscope once more.

But Ireland remains rightly famous for its infinite avenues of procrastination. So Jamie and I solved early anxieties by enjoying some leisurely lunches, pretending we were on an idyll in, oh, say Provence. A couple of the nicest were savored at the nearby Arbutus Lodge, a stately nineteenth-century inn with a veranda over a tranquil garden descending toward the grain elevators that rise up like tin porkpie hats over the River Lee. The food was excellent: roasted chicken and shallots and what appeared to be leeks landslided beneath creamy garlic potatoes, washed down with a tasty New Zealand chardonnay. Another afternoon saw us picking at wholesome salads in the balcony restaurant above the downtown English Market, which is a gloriously colorful, vaulted-roof arcade wherein earthy butchers and fish-beheaders man stalls beside petite sellers of Brie. Ghoulish monkfish and sole; blood-red slabs of beef and fowl hanging limply from scrawny necks; stacks of sweetly scented bread; vegetables and fruits just in from Kenya and Spain; local cheeses from West Cork; fresh Italian pastas; Lebanese olives; Israeli artichokes; and Skippy peanut butter – you can buy a mouthwatering array of foodstuffs from the booths in that emporium. Indeed, one can eat infinitely better in Ireland than was possible even ten years ago. One can feast, and until we got the hang of how much we were actually spending, we did.

It was hard not to celebrate. So one evening of that first week of school, I brought Harris with me to a lake in an abandoned limestone quarry in North Cork for a little fishing. Mostly he was captivated by the task of rowing a rented boat, as if he was the one steering our family ship of state forward. In the rosy light, one fat trout after another surfaced to take my flies, and I let Harris reel them in. In Ireland, big fish have always cast a mystical wake; ancient Irish poets used to lie for hours in remote river pools seeking wisdom from the bubbles released by passing salmon. Their breath exuded knowledge of the godhead.

"Are you happy here?" I asked as we climbed back into the car.

"You mean sitting in a car?" he responded, always wry.

"You know what I mean."

"Ah sure, it's grand," Harris said, proud of the new expressions he was picking up.

I probed. "Not everything is going to be grand, you understand that?"

"Well, I miss Robert. Most of all I miss catching snakes with him and exploring the woods, and I don't like it that there's no snakes or woods outside our door."

"I can understand that. But you've got so much else, so many new friends, and for the rest of your life you are going to be a larger person for having experienced what is happening now. It's going to be difficult sometimes, but when things bother you, just tell me, and we can try to fix them together."

"It's okay, Dad," he said and abruptly offered a hug.

A sweet silence fell over our trip back to Cork City – there was love in it.

Things were going so swimmingly, I received sanction for another Friday afternoon visit to the Hi-B as September waned. Voilà, I instantly gained a stool at the front ranks of the Cork senate, and there my education continued. Apparent, it soon became, that the cantankerous Brian O'Donnell was far from the only star attraction in this place, because the pints de jour this afternoon were being poured by a woman with an opposite, boundlessly warm nature – Esther.

Never had I seen a more engaging bartender. Discreet enquiries quickly revealed that every afternoon two-dozen men or more wander into the Hi-B simply to be cheered for a pick-me-up or two by Esther's rollicking charisma. Some stay longer, and one could easily understand why. Here, the regulars whispered, was a woman who always appreciates and never scolds or asks one to take out the garbage – the male dream.

There must have been some kick in that first pint, because I became instantly enraptured. A painter, I thought, could exhaust his palette in portraying Esther's long brown streaks of hair falling nonchalantly from either side of a jolly moon face, and her glowing blue eyes, never tainted by a ripple of hostility. No supermodel, I would learn, captures as much attention as Esther does every day.

Fresh customers inquired, one after another, "May I have a pint of Guinness?"

"Of course you can, love," was her invariable response, regardless of whether they had been seen before.

Time drifted, and I heard three different men ask her to run away with them for the weekend.

"I don't believe running is something you should undertake without a medic," Esther chortled, which was gracious considering the appearance of some of her suitors. She said that her boyfriend, Toss, of these last eighteen years wouldn't bother being jealous – "not with the customers I serve here," Esther roared.

Suddenly, a certain velvet-voiced gent made his presence felt in the bar. By now, I'd learned that half the adult population of Ireland shared an obsession with this crooner, whose insouciant, seductive tones emanate from every third pub, shoe shop, and bank. "Nel Blu Di Pinto Di Blu – Volare, oh, oh, oh!" Those were the immortal words echoing now through the Hi-B, where Dean Martin, R.I.P., rather than the viper-vanquishing Patrick, seemed to be regarded as Hibernia's true patron saint. The Las Vegas Brat Pack boy may be enjoying a brief posthumous surge of attention in various countries, but his boozy aura clearly reigned supreme over Ireland. John Fitzgerald Kennedy was all but forgotten, although his portrait had once reigned in every Irish foyer, along with companion ones of the pope and Jesus, the latter with an exposed, and often electronically illuminated, giant red heart. Now it's Dino Crocetti who croons eternally in the let-the-good-times-roll soul of the modern Emerald Isle, with a fag in his lips, a drink in his hand, and a girl on his arm – the way every other Irishman would like to carry on to the day he dies.

I'd tasted the Hi-B's seductive fruits before, but nobody had warned me about what was coming next. Here now was Esther, who never touched the booze or nicotine herself, crooning giddily "Little Ole Wine Drinker, Me" and "Memories are Made of This." Suddenly a half-dozen customers began belting out in unison, "When the moon hits your eye like a big pizza pie – that's *amore!*"

Merriment washed through the place in waves. An irresistible smile spread across the small face of Jimmy Cosgrave, a former butcher close on eighty and a classic of the ever-amiable, retired gentleman-laborer type still ubiquitous in Ireland. Jimmy, dressed to the nines in a white shirt, tie, and suspenders under a neatly pressed jacket, proved good for a few pints – until his wife gently steered him toward the door. Geezers in Florida beach-chairs do not have it so good.

Sitting close to the pay phone into which he incessantly dumped coins for brief, cackling calls to mysterious contacts, presided the Hi-B's resident sculptor, John Burke. "Burkie" had an inimitably gruff voice so rasped with drink and cigarettes that it sounded like it emanated from a clanging boiler stationed hundreds of feet down in his torso. The son of a Tipperary IRA hitman known as "Two Gun Thady," Burkie soon showed himself to be a softie at heart.

In his younger years, he was acclaimed for massive abstract sculptures in the Calder mold. Fellows at the bar now sniggered that as soon as one of these was installed at the grassy center of one particular Cork roundabout near the airport, numerous drivers dialed "999" to report the wreckage of a fresh plane crash. Nowadays, Burkie tended to work on intricate tabletop constructions, as the money for the kind of big projects that he favored had grown tight.

"You come from a strange nation," offered Burkie, with dark sunglasses obscuring his mischievous eyes.

When Burkie said something was bizarre, I quickly learned, it was stone guaranteed. "I mean where else would you get pornographic ice cubes?"

No argument there.

"I used to love a bar in Manhattan called Maggies. It was just off Fifth Avenue somewhere. There was this Jewish fellow in there named Bob Goldman who once asked me what time it was. I looked at my watch and said 'Half five.' He says, 'Half five is two thirty.' Christ, didn't he have a point?"

"Nice one," I said.

"That was how we hit off, like. He took me up to the top of the Pan Am building and the next thing you know he's packing me into a helicopter and we're flying all around the fecking Big Apple half-cocked. After a while we came down again and had some more drink. Then he says he's taking me to New Jersey, where he lives. So I said, fine. We drove his car onto the Staten Island ferry."

"The what?" I asked, remembering the geography differently.

"The Staten Island ferry. I just told you. Anyway, Bob has this flash car with a driver and we head off down these huge highways. Then we stop in front of some factory and he says, 'I have this bunch of assholes working for me and I have to check that they're still awake.' There were all these Vietnamese or some goddam thing hunched over conveyor belts and an enormous machine in the back throbbing and belching exhaust and shooting out endless pink ice cubes shaped like tits with little ice nipples on them. I said, 'Holy Mother of Mercy, what's this, Bob?'"

Burkie was cackling, sipping, and furiously sucking on a cigarette. "'Everybody loves porno ice cubes in the clubs these days,' says Bob. Then he throws a switch and out come pink ice cubes shaped like girls' asses, thousands and thousands of them. I said, 'Bob, do you have anything for the homos?' and he throws another switch and out come thousands of iced pricks."

"Tell me you're making this up," I said.

"How could you? How can you not love America when it's capable of things like this? Then he tells me we're going to a Halloween party in some club and gets me to dress up like Richard Nixon. And guess what kind of ice cubes were in every glass?"

"What town did this happen in?"

"I told you, New Jersey," Burkie responded.

A silver-haired man exuberantly joined our conversation. He

had an extraordinarily lilting voice, the kind that Cork people use to singsong their way giddily through everyday speech, as if swinging happily through some diphthong-ridden forest of their imagination. The one declaiming so exuberantly now was a jazz pianist who presided over rollicking, impromptu sessions in the pub every Wednesday night. He was but a month old the first time his mother ushered him into the Hi-B so she could chat to friends who were taking a break from their shopping.

"I liked the place so much, I've come back for seventy years," the musician laughed.

"And we're wondering when the hell you'll ever leave!" Esther chortled. Then she leaned closer, saying, "Dave, this is Dick O'Sullivan. He's a *dote*."

This was high praise, because being called a "dote" in Ireland is an epiphany, a verbal halo. The word is untranslatable, not only into foreign tongues but also into English. It has to do, obviously, with being doted upon. But in Ireland, women – it is always women – take the verb and suffuse it with so much loving emotion that the word becomes burnished into a noun of all-encompassing affection. The replenishing of reality with wellsprings of warmth is of course what Irish women do all day long, thereby preventing the country from turning into a madhouse of nonstop homicidal bickering. After all, the most celebrated of ancient Celts in the eighth-century *Tain* manuscript, the boy-warrior Cuchulainn, a.k.a. "The Hound of Ulster," merrily lopped off the heads of about two thousand rivals, often for a single comment that displeased him.

"Oh, your daughter's nearly a teenager, is she? Well, good luck," offered Dick. "Maybe you've heard about the American, the Englishman, and the Kerryman who had the same problem," he said, proceeding to offer a rollicking off-color joke about the blindness of fathers toward developmental changes in their daughters.

By now, my head was spinning, yet my thoughts were already fixed on the idea that I could never leave Cork. At that moment, a narrow-eyed old geezer sat down on a stool and started rummaging at his side. "Esthaher!" he wheezed with his head drooping in dismay. "I'm sorry but I seem to have no money."

"Ah, not to worry John, I'll pour your pint and you can pay me another time," the patron saint of Cork smiled.

A moment later, John wheezed again, "Esthaher, I have no pockets. They're all gone."

Esther's devilish eyes now flashed the length of the suddenly gone-speechless bar. The geezer took a long quaff and, with lips rimmed in stout cream, stood up to head for the gent's. Only then did it become apparent that he had put his pants on backward. Laughter unto tears rained.

The time now was about 4:30, although it had begun slipping, slipping. A friend of Dick O'Sullivan's arrived, sipped, and commenced belting out an aria from Puccini, his eyes closing soulfully and his right hand lifting as if he were on the stage at Covent Garden and not standing unaccompanied in the middle of a bar where neither sanity nor sobriety is held in high regard. And why not sing? It was Friday after all, the flagship of the seven most appealing days of the Irish week, and the September sun, whose future appearances were likely to be scarce, was yet shining.

Brian O'Donnell slipped in, his fussy prosecutorial eyes darting about for miscreants as he helped himself to a prodigious brandy. He happened to train his glare upon me.

"I see you are further acquainting yourself with the asylum," Brian winked. "Ah, I think you'd better watch that fella beside you. He may claim to be a Richard, but he's been a Dick all his life."

A change of music, and the bar began to levitate to the strains of a brass section muscling into a bout of Wagner, with Brian waving his imaginary baton at the crescendo.

What a place. "I'm at the Hi-B and it's mad fun with a cast of characters you wouldn't believe, but I'll be home soon," I told Jamie over the phone, possibly without registering the desired effect.

But then I hadn't figured out that the clock on the Hi-B's wall was dangerously defective, as indeed are baffling numbers of Irish timepieces – every street corner clock in Cork tells a different time, just like the Liar's Tower. At that point, the Hi-B's hour hand hadn't yet climbed to six, and the world still resembled the one I had left at the bottom of the stairs. I met a roguish carpenter named Kieran to whom I warmed instantly; a statuesque Mary Louise;

and several Denises who began to blend into a single composite grinning Denis.

Lo now, there was Owen McIntyre suddenly bursting in with marvelous stories broadcast in his Donegal birdsong, in fact a raving monologue that seemed, as usual, to be launched rather than spoken from his lips. This saga had something to do with a fellow with a "savage" appetite for a "fierce" woman with "deadly" looks and a "mighty" wit, which energized the suitor's "massive" thirst along with thoughts about something "shocking." But the punch line was lost in his inevitable digressions. I told him I had a "wicked" need to go home for dinner.

"Come here to me," Owen said, which, even in my waning condition, obviously signaled an invitation to shut up. "You have plenty of time to make it back for dinner now – it will be at least twenty hours until the next one – so you might as well have another pint."

There are reasons why Irish people are not always punctual. The ritual of shared pint-buying is sometimes part of it. This rite never, ever comes in ones, but always in units of two. If you accept the first offer, as any polite soul must, but do not return the favor in an equal and opposite amount soon, you will be blackguarded for the rest of your days in whatever pub your ass has been parked. So we had a deuce times two.

"What we are doing here is not about drinking per se," Owen suddenly explained.

I stared in consternation at the various twenty-ounce glasses arrayed before us – drained, working, and due up next. It didn't seem like we were nibbling hors d'oeuvres.

"Drink is nothing more than opening a door," he started again.

To a flight of stairs I am about to fall down, I thought.

The talk, which flowered and digressed in all directions, was not easy to walk away from, until my wandering gaze discovered the clock's hour hand just completing its fifth revolution since the last spot-check. Where was Father Theobold Mathew when one needed him?

The taxi driver I found on Patrick Street did a good impersonation of that celebrated scold. "Do you know about the three stages of the Irish drunk?" he asked as I amiably swayed beside him in the front seat – in Cork, it is disrespectful for passengers to retreat to the back of a taxi and impede the flow of nonstop wisdom from the lips of the driver.

"I don't actually."

"The peacock, the monkey, and the pig."

"Sorry?"

"They all start as peacocks and turn into monkeys and the pig comes rooting around after."

"But I thought monkeys were a barrel of fun?"

"For a while, but they have to be watched closely because they will turn into pigs in a flash."

"How does one spot the change?"

"When they begin pissing in alleyways, and fighting for no reason, and vomiting on their shoes, they are pigs. Take a close look at the behavior of the young people of Ireland now and you will see the impact of two hundred years of a nation being continually jarred."

Charming. "I gather you're not fond of the drink yourself," I said as the bright lights of MacCurtain Street finally dimmed behind us, and I began to weigh the euphoric sense of discovery that informed my last sips in the Hi-B with the sour truths that were yanking down the drooping lobes of my formerly contented ears.

"Oh, I am," said the taxi man. "But I drink alone, at the farthest possible end of my local bar whose name I won't tell you and where you will never find me anyway."

Who would want to, I thought, fumbling for change as he came to a stop.

For some reason, my key and the front door lock exchanged greetings clumsily. But I pasted on a happy face and tacked with high hopes down the hallway into the ominously clean and silent kitchen, at the far end of which I discovered my wife scowling from a chair. Talk about adapting to our new land. She might as well have been rocking impatiently before an open hearth with a rosary bitterly twisting in her hands.

"I met the greatest people, especially Owen," I started, smiling perhaps as slackly as some other customers had done while evacuating the Hi-B hours earlier. This was no time for moral equivocation, so I steadied my feet. "I really feel we made the right choice in coming here. Our lives are going to work out great."

"That's good, because I was just reading a short story," Jamie said, "and it reminded me of your behavior tonight."

"Really?"

"Yes, it was about a man whose wife had just given birth to a baby boy. The midwife sent him out to get fresh towels. But he was so excited that on the way he stopped in at the local pub to tell all his friends the news. Everyone was so happy for him that they bought him drinks and he bought some back. At some point, he remembered that he was supposed to be on an errand, but he was too far gone to remember the thread. So he left with some coins in his hands and stopped in at the shop next door. When he got home he called up the stairs to announce his purchase. 'Honey, I'm back! I got the fish!'"

"At least he returned with something," I said, wondering if I had left a haddock at the Hi-B.

Chapter 10

The perfect antidote for bedtime sourness is to aim for higher altitudes in the morning, so the family, on some expedition or other every weekend, was wrested to search for an ascent into Waterford's Comeragh Mountains, irresistibly called the "Magic Road." Contacts from the night before had vowed that we would see things there that would turn our heads as they never had been before. Of course, in Ireland, people will promise whatever falls onto their lips.

The blurry assurances had something to do with sheer waterfalls, celestial mountainscapes, and gravity running in reverse. Well, wasn't that the point of our moving to Ireland? The family was dubious as we left the garish seaside stucco palaces of Waterford's tony Gold Coast, hard by the evidently drossly inferior Copper Coast, and struggled through various twists and turns in the hinterlands. At last we came to a shop at a remote crossroads whose astonishingly wrinkled proprietor offered nearly indecipherable praises of the day's light. "There's a rare might to it, that's for sure," said he.

The shop had a surreal quality, perhaps owing to the clouds of steam billowing out of a side door to the man's living quarters. Thence emerged the pungent odor of boiling cabbage and one could imagine the grinning cat face of a Mary Osborne look-alike stirring a cauldron on an ancient hearth somewhere in the next rooms.

More curious, however, was the place's merchandise, so threadbare and ancient that it looked as if it had been stocked via bicycle basket by a distributor from Flann O'Brien Grocers. The front shelves offered balls of string, tins of custard, and small vials of castor oil and glycerine, the latter old enough to have had their labels soaked through with untold years of exudations from under their caps. These goodies gave way to small clusters of canned peas and kippers, each ingredient separated from its fellows by generous foot-long empty spaces coated in historic accretions of dust. At the back stood a bin of dirt-encrusted carrots, every specimen so miserably stunted, leathery, and aged as to be perfect for making Bun's carrot whiskey.

But the most intriguing item was the proprietor's face, gap-toothed and spectacularly weathered from what must have been decades spent in the surrounding mountains chasing sheep. The *1892 Annals of the Cork Historical Society* describe a character named Tom Green with a very similar mien:

> His face must have been unusually plump in his youth, because in his old age, it was, without exception, the most remarkable make-up of folds and wrinkles, grooves and hollows, and miniature valleys and glens and mountains, that nature in an eccentric freak supplied to one of her sons . . . His head dress was a blue cloth cap, and in the expansive top of this he kept his pipe, match-box, and pocket-handkerchief, and stored his allowance of tobacco . . .
>
> Tom had one failing – whiskey. In these old times, a glass of whiskey, familiarly known as "a small darby," could be purchased for a penny; and he could always tell you whether the publican gave good or bad measure, because, as his teeth were all gone, his mouth exactly held a glass . . . He would then select a potato of moderate size, and, putting it into his toothless mouth, would subject it to a process of rolling until it had disappeared and made room for another. His expression was so intensely comical that an eminent firm of brass founders in the city had offered him five shillings for a cast of his face, as they wanted something fresh in hall door knockers.

Our present Tom Green was asked if there truly were any unusual gravity doings in the mountains above his shop. This fired a gleam of excitement into his deeply socketed eyes. "There most certainly is a strange power up there. It is enough to make a car run backward up the hill. And just think about the mighty weight in a car! How this can be, no one can explain, but it happens every time and you could set a watch to it, although of course time then would be going backward too, which might not be a bad thing, if you think about that. You just go up this road out here where the sign says Mahon Falls. Climb on past the cottages until you reach the high ground. Then you come to a cattle grid and, beyond that a small push, a white thorn tree with all kinds of trinkets in it. Stop beside it and go in neutral, and you'll see."

The narrow track wound into ever wilder country, framed by astonishing canyon-like expanses that resembled the Dakota Badlands. But there lay the grid in the road, and a moment later the scraggly thorn tree, festooned with colored strings and odd patches of cloth, waited at the bottom of a slight but definite incline. Silence reigned on this Magic Road of wind, stone, and gorse. "Will we be going airborne now, Dad?" smirked Laura as I halted the car, shifted to neutral, and prepared to roll onward. Nothing happened – for a second – but at least we did not go forward. But then, this one-ton station wagon, with its more than five hundred pounds of occupants, silently began to roll, inch by inch, meter by weird meter, backward – and up, up, up. We all stared goggle-eyed as the car slowly flubbered its way at least fifty feet in reverse from the queer tree.

"Your foot's on the gas!" Jamie shrieked.

"It is not, the damn thing's in neutral!'

In a few seconds, the car halted. But whatever had happened was beyond strange. Not believing my own eyes, and being well educated in the epistemological pathways of human knowledge, I proceeded forward in order to turn and test things from the opposite direction. Back to neutral, we returned after coming to a dead stop beside the trinket tree, and lo! the car, without benefit of combustion engine power, accelerated this time uphill at perhaps twice the speed as before. In fact, the thing refused to stop at the crest and kept gaining demented power until I jammed on the breaks. "Give me Spielberg!" I cried, and of course the children scoffed.

Were the sheep dotted high on the ridges laughing? Did their own feet adhere to the ground? Was Ireland dangerous to one's every bearing?

"You would have to find this spot, wouldn't you?" said Jamie, knowing that I had once written about a gravity-obsessed Roger Babson, whose college named after him in Boston boasts Isaac Newton's rebuilt library, a transplant from the original apple tree, and the core works of the Anti-Gravity Research Foundation, along with a twenty-foot-high globe marking dozens of spots around the world where bizarre gravity-defying phenomena have been voluminously recorded. But the Comeraghs' Magic Road was not indicated on that globe, so in the pursuit of science, we crisscrossed this enigmatic stretch over and over again to test which way the car's wheels would roll – uphill or down? – on their own. And soon we were joined by another car, and then a second, doing the exact same thing. Here we were at the top of the world in a conga line of gravity-defying Irish. Beautiful.

In search of more commonplace reality, we hiked to the glorious cascade of Mahon Falls, making a game all the while of competing with the kids to see who could count the most sheep hundreds of feet above us on the crests of the surrounding ridges. Everyone knows there are no reptiles or amphibians in Ireland, but the boys of course found fresh frog's eggs in a nearby ditch and squeezed their slimy spawn into an empty Coke bottle for later enrichment in their bedroom. Strange, strange is the Emerald Isle.

The journey home inspired us further. In the lovely coastal village of Ardmore we came upon a soaring eight-hundred-year-old round tower that protected the monks there from Vikings and local heathens. Beside it, nestled in the hill, lay the tiny, thirteen-hundred-year-old oratory of St. Declan, who some scholars believe brought Christianity to Ireland before St. Patrick. The whole hillside breathed with the sanctitude of holy ground, with the remains of a monastery surrounded by the graves of peasants and postmen, barons, sailors, and deans, and the dead from more wars than today's students can remember. At the sea's edge stood a quiet sculpture of the revered St. Declan embossed with the icons of his legacy – a bell, a sail, and a steeple-high round tower – inscribed with these words:

> When Declan was old he retired to his Hermitage, a place of solitude and prayer, to get away from his city where his monastery is located.
>
> In Art, he is often shown with his little Bell, which, according to legend, was wafted across the sea from Wales (where he had been visiting) on top of a large stone, after his servant had forgotten to pack it.
>
> "Follow that Stone," said Declan, and where it comes to land will be the place of Resurrection. It is in Ardmore.

This afternoon, there was no reason to doubt a word – about bells floating on stones, cars rolling uphill, fairy circles, the whole web of Irish wonder. In fact, we ached to share our experiences with the treasured friends of my parents and now ourselves, Dr. Michael Buckley and his wife, Hylda, who happened to be visiting Cork at the moment. One of their closest friends had organized a party to celebrate our arrival in the promised land that very night. How could you beat it? We'd been in Ireland for seven weeks, and still our arrival was being toasted. So we dropped off the kids and found our way to the elegant 225-year-old home of a kind of shadow mayor of our adopted city.

"Defying gravity, Neptune thrusting your glasses from the sea, and finding Brian O'Donnell and the Hi-B? Do you have any idea of the luck you are riding over here?" laughed Mick. "I mean, I can only rejoice in the things that have happened since moving to America. Hylda, the kids, the house, the practice, and all the rest. But I can never stop feeling that the most carefree years of my life were the ones I spent in Cork. I miss this place always. They laugh louder and longer here than any other place on earth, and they do it every day. I envy you."

We were sipping wine in the very formal sitting room of his dear friend Michael Bradley, proprietor of a prosperous grocery shop and "off-licence" or liquor store on Cork's North Main Street. Forty or more guests were assembled around us, our host being a friend of about every third person in Cork and a master at organizing parties at a whim. His gracious consort, the recently widowed Hilary O'Sullivan, served smoked salmon on slivers of brown bread from a silver tray, proffered with a warm solicitation after each taker.

Mick Buckley, nearly seventy, left Ireland in 1958, along with 40,000 other members of his impoverished generation. He and his Cork-born wife, Hylda, had as always their youngest daughter, Mary, who was born with Down's Syndrome, lovingly at their sides. Mick, who has about the gentlest eyes ever issued, looked over the merry crowd and nodded, "You'd better treasure this."

How could we not? Our host, Michael Bradley, impeccably attired in a pinstriped suit and blue and gold tie, was introducing us with a diplomat's fanfare to similarly stylish barristers, restaurateurs, colonels – dozens of distinguished members of Cork's upper classes, a number of whom belong to the select local families still called the Merchant Princes. None of this crowd would ever be caught dead in the Hi-B, and yet they had a spirit that was every bit as mirthful and quirky as was found in that place.

Palates were constantly refreshed, and the conversation pranced in its inimitable Cork way. Suddenly our host tapped his glass with a spoon.

"Let's have a toast to the new Corkonians," he announced, his lips puckering with the trickster look that half of Ireland wears so well. "I know you will all join me in wishing Jamie and David a splendid time in Cork, even if Americans do sometimes arrive in peculiar ways. Why, I believe there is a song about this."

With that, the urbane Michael Bradley promptly burst into "Yankee Doodle came to town, riding on a pony!" Nearly every remaining guest joined in with, "Stuck his finger in his hat and called it macaroni!" and suddenly placed their generally far from young hands on each other's shoulders to form a train of pretend ponies as they cantered singing from room to room. Ireland of the welcomes, begod.

A few days later we met up again with the Buckleys in Kinsale, an exceedingly pretty, if promoted-to-death, harbor town famous for fine restaurants, quaintly winding lanes, and lavish parties in seaview houses that cost over a million pounds. The property-selling agents like to call the place Ireland's Riviera, and the briefest excursion on a sailboat, which ply the surrounding sheltered inlets in great number, yields views of shimmering, cliff-ringed bays that live up to the bill.

Our first stop was the nearby star-shaped Charles Fort, upon whose ramparts a hundred feet above the harbor the boys scurried about with their toy guns, to the great distaste of their rapidly maturing sister. One look at the surrounding greenswards rolling forever onward to blue ocean, the whole panoply shimmering under a dance of exquisitely delicate light, and I felt yet another jolt of love for Ireland. The happy yelping of our children boosted the heart higher.

"Isn't it wonderful," said Hylda, "the way the kids can run free here with no whistle-blowing park rangers roping people into official tours? Thank goodness the Irish still just leave you alone to do whatever you want at your own pace." She herself had an arm lovingly encircling their daughter Mary, and that, too, was touching. One of Ireland's untold secrets is the communal love that is poured out to the disabled. Perhaps this stems from the fact the country has never legalized abortion as a means, used so widely elsewhere, to eliminate looming birth defects, or perhaps it's because the Irish still retain some heightened sense of compassion for the unfortunates once confronted everywhere in their impoverished land. Or maybe it even owes to the country's extra wattage of surviving Christian faith. But a newcomer is struck by how much more visible and also cheerfully woven into daily life are the infirm in Ireland, where the warehousing of those with a handicap is still regarded as a moral failing. At this moment, gazing meditatively on the far ocean, I certainly wasn't dwelling on such weighty matters. But all these truths hung like a whisper around us.

I looked around at the atmospheric site, and Mick Buckley, his voice soft as an Irish April, began to unravel its history: Charles Fort, along with another redoubt across the channel named after King James, was built in the 1600s to protect the great fleets of barks and frigates that once used Kinsale as their last port of call before heading off for refills of West Indian rum, Chinese silk, and other supplies vital to the day-to-day life of the British Empire. These fortresses were also intended to dissuade the Spanish from repeating a certain local visit in 1601. That was the year when the powers-that-be in Madrid dispatched an invasion fleet to join with a native uprising intended to crush the might of Elizabeth I, and return the Irish to rule over their island. The Spanish expeditionary forces succeeded in seizing Kinsale's castles, but landed far south of where they had been expected, and were soon besieged by an English counterassault that forced them to hunker down where they were.

As a result, rebel chieftains named Hugh O'Neill and Red Hugh O'Donnell were forced to lead their six thousand soldiers from the still unvanquished northern kingdom of Ulster on a brutal sixteen-day winter march south. They would have been wise to bide their time to test the strength of the British army upon arriving, but instead quickly launched a mass frontal attack. For fighters accustomed to hit-and-run raids, this was a bad mistake, and the results were tragic. If only the Spanish had joined the action from the rear, the Crown's forces might have been pincered and the course of history changed. But Don Juan de Águila's three thousand soldiers blithely stayed put as a powerful British cavalry attack crushed the Irish rebels. The Spanish packed off and, after a few more flare-ups elsewhere, organized resistance to British rule essentially collapsed for two hundred years.

The Irish remnants retreated to the lunar landscape of West Cork's Beara Peninsula. The British, aided by traitorous locals, caught up with them there and hung eighty captives in the square of today's quiet fishing village of Castletownbere. One by one, the remaining defiant Irish chieftains abandoned their motherland in an exodus to the Continent known as the Flight of the Earls. Quickly, the British consolidated their rule, and carried on with destroying the country's great abbeys and ancestral castles, seizing prime acreage for their distant nobility, and generally driving the local peasantry off to land fit for goats. They referred to the native Irish as "foreigners" and forbade such types from selling so much as a potato on Kinsale's pretty streets. The sadness of Ireland's history, ancient and recent, is evident throughout the southwest for anyone who cares to pause.

Nearby lay the village of Ballinspittle, which is a sleepy crossroads with perhaps a hundred houses and three pubs. Mick and Hylda took us there next to view a famous grotto with a life-sized, blue and white cement statue of the Blessed Virgin set into a steep hill. In the mid-1980s, this spot teemed with supplicants praying for miracles. The word had spread throughout a still backward and mystical Ireland that the statue perceptibly swayed as if imbued with a numinous inner life. God's hand was to be seen touching Ballinspittle.

We all stood before the shrine with a kind of rapt consternation. It did not move a centimeter, perhaps thanks to a hammer attack (since repaired) by a crazed Californian a few years earlier.

Every few minutes, passing drivers would slow, roll down their car windows, bless themselves, and hurry on.

"Drive-by blessings," I said to Dr. Buckley.

"This county has changed fifty years in a decade," he replied wearily, "and religion has gone to hell." But he made the sign of the cross himself, and his faith had clearly never wavered.

We came down to a headland that spilled into the Atlantic with cliffs pushing out from either side like arched wings. The entrance to this promontory was guarded by a stone wall topped with barbed wire, and a man at the gate moved forward suspiciously.

"What's this?" I asked Mick.

"It's one of the most exclusive golf courses in the world, called the Old Head of Kinsale. They say this place was one of the first ever settled in Ireland, and people used to come fishing and walking here from all over, but the owners have stopped that. The course is said to be fabulous, but very expensive."

"And very hostile," I said, filing this item for further investigation.

The next weekend we ventured to Paddy and Anne Wilkinson's distant Carlow refuge. Hidden by the rioting growth of pine trees they had planted nearly two decades before, their mountainside home had always seemed to be curtained off from the intrusions of modernity.

But a new car sat in the steep drive; and the ever-thoughtful Anne, who had recently been promoted at her work for the department of the environment, looked different, more modern and self-assured than I remembered. She and Gwen opened a bottle of Sauvignon Blanc and swirled it in their glasses, sniffing to decipher hidden aromas. Broiled salmon in a soy-ginger sauce, wild rice dotted with local mushrooms, and a nicely sautéed medley of fresh garden-grown vegetables were heading our way. It was delicious, and why not? Ireland had had it up to here with the donkey-cart images of old. Gwen had traversed the world's oceans with a South African boyfriend who had become a star on the global sailing race circuit. She had enjoyed local wine in places I couldn't even find on the map, being a citizen of a culture unimaginable at her birth.

"The changes have been good for us, you know, and I would never want to go back to the way things were before," Paddy said, sprawling his long, loose limbs in various directions from his kitchen chair, just as his father might have done. "Sure, it's troubling, too. This entire country is only one or two generations away from the soil. We never had any time to prepare for the modern ways that have come in almost overnight."

Paddy gazed out to a field upon which neighboring farmers used to fleece bawling sheep with lightning-quick hand shears, a practice now thoroughly electrified. "We're all much better off, there is no denying that. Just back in the eighties, it was hopeless here, with unemployment over 20 percent, maybe even five times worse than today. Those desperate days did nobody any good at all."

"What would Bun feel about all these changes?" I asked.

Paddy, who still draws his water from a hose stuck into a spring farther up the mountain, didn't hesitate. "He'd be glad to see the hardship and the emigration ending, that is for sure. But I don't know that he'd love Ireland quite the same as he did. He'd know too well what we have lost."

"But where on earth is life as much fun?" I questioned, and Paddy grabbed my arm.

"Well, I wouldn't live anywhere else myself," he smiled.

Chapter 11

The idea of shape shifting between one identity and another runs deep through Celtic legends, but we soon discovered that "going Irish" is nonetheless an exceedingly tricky quest, even when blessed by the continuity of my Wilkinson connections. Challenges to our every sense of self materialized constantly. Our perplexed small-town American bank, for example, addressed a major fund transfer to "Cork, Thailand," leading to a four-week detour of vital moneys through the Far East. Meanwhile, the cash cow – the corporate newsletter meant to support our curious adventure – suddenly got snuffed. One thought of Roger Miller: no home, no food, no pets – ain't got no cigarettes. So some local publications were touched for assignments and possible employment for Jamie, who had lately been writing for the august *New York Times*; but business leaders and feature editors alike, evidently all graduates of the gnomic Office of Motor Taxation, flatly refused to return phone calls or letters, or otherwise confirm that we existed. You might think that the booming Irish economy would welcome arriving hopefuls with open arms, but, when money is involved, that is not always the clannish Irish, and particularly Cork, way.

We were, as the Germans call it, *fremd*, which means both foreign and circumspect – at least professionally. Making our status as "outsiders" even more acute, the adolescents messing about on our lane outside our gate seemed to share the feeling on a much more personal level. They set with an autumnal vengeance to the challenge of driving us out of Ireland, often devising techniques of inspired virtuosity. Pissing on our gate in broad daylight; hurling water balloons at our door; and tossing pebbles at our car, the ammo finely selected so that it was just small enough to scratch the windows and paint without smashing glass and committing an obvious crime – these boyos were accomplished.

Their malevolence seemed so unpredictable that we worried over the safety of our kids, especially Harris who, though considerably smaller, was still closest to their size. In the face of their taunting harassment, he soon took to retreating behind our protective hedges at the first shambling sight of this bunch who, despite our fervent wishes otherwise, had now stepped up their sport.

A number of times we tried talking to them, but they would not even meet our eyes. Their looks toward us were ever blank and utterly fearless, as if there were no common rules of humanity – or law – linking us together. We felt like targets and nothing more.

"I can't stand it anymore!" Jamie, who had repeatedly tried to reason and even plead with the adolescent smirkers, finally erupted one day.

"That's it for me, too!" I said, and finally called the ringleader's father.

"Look, we are obviously not from Cork, but we just want to fit in. Everybody knows that adolescents the world over like to act up, but what is happening to us feels like an assault. How this started is irrelevant. Can you please help see that it ends?"

The man, sounding as worn down as any father of adolescent boys, said he would look into it.

A few nights later, a stranger approached me in a pub. "I understand you have been making accusations about certain individuals. If I were you, I'd cease this intimidation and insinuation instantly, or there could be difficulties."

What in the name of halitosis had happened to the spirit of Ireland, I wondered. What toll was all the new affluence and indulgence taking on the next generation? Perhaps I'd totally failed to grasp the sinister aspects of the country's intractable defiance of order, the rancor of willful anarchy noted by writers from Joyce and Flann O'Brien to Patrick McCabe.

The more important question for the moment was how to protect ourselves. Calls to the police proved fruitless – because where was the evidence? Wheels turned, and click: we decided to build an irrefutable record of the puerile pursuits at our door. So whenever the group appeared, a barrage of snapshots greeted them. What a marvelous sight it was to see these little blighters run.

But the combination of adolescent mayhem along with the chilly indifference of potential employers sometimes depressed us, suggesting that delusions lurked in our dreams of building fresh Irish identities out of thin air. The early welcomes by our neighbors and new friends like Owen McIntyre had been heartwarming, but it now felt like this land of our forebears, from which we somehow expected to be accepted as if returning kin, might take its sweet time in letting us fully through the door.

I had an old habit of seeking solace in solitary fishing expeditions. On certain early October afternoons, I therefore wound my way to nearby streams. One of these toppled out of a charming waterfall and purled through a green glade, unspoiled enough to make one think of a mercurial ancient Ireland where a cornered soul could lie in the water and turn into a salmon and then swallow a hazel berry full of divine wisdom and soar off as an eagle. The place was gorgeous, but, alas, fish bereft and a little short on supernatural intervention.

So I worked my way downstream, coming to larger pools, and more promising riffles and runs, and over these I unfurled my long lasso casts. Here, the desired transmogrification finally succeeded. Behind me, I discovered a pack of Aran sweater-bedecked Americans oohing and aahing and busily photographing my every move, as if I now was the embodiment of Ireland's timeless bucolic ways – the original postcard Celt. Such was the barminess that had taken over my identity.

Further shape-shifting awaited at Cork's annual traditional music festival, as Laura and I discovered upon entering a pub called the Corner House one drizzly afternoon. Inside, eight grizzled musicians plucked away at banjos, guitars, mandolins, an upright bass, an auto-harp, and a gleaming Dobro resonator guitar – just about every instrument upon which man has tacked on a string – in a foot-stomping Irish interpretation of old-time Appalachian bluegrass. Laura hunched beside me at the back of the place, where younger crisp-swallowing kids sprawled on the floor, the homier

Irish pubs being locales where three generations can mix without a bother.

The unique Celtic cultural experience on tap consisted of feverish renditions of the "Yellow Rose of Texas" and "Are You From Dixie?" This was clearly your basic mad-hatter mix of Irish incongruity all over again, making one feel for a moment most peculiarly at home, especially when the group launched into a lonesome-voiced, twangy number called "Give Me Back the Five Dollars I Paid for My Wife." Every thirty seconds, a Cork dude in cowboy boots and a ten-gallon hat screamed "Yeehaw!" None of these Willy Nelson look-alikes were remotely from Dixie, unless you look at life through Cork's unique lens. The province being called the Rebel County for reasons of both temperament and history, a good many of its citizens internalize some imaginary Mason Dixon line so deeply that they show up at local hurling, Irish football, and soccer matches waving Confederate flags. In fact, a truck driver at the top of Military Hill has an enormous rig with Rebel flags painted on the doors and his road tag of "Big Jim" emblazoned between the headlights.

Jamie came by to collect Laura at the end. Curious, I ensconced myself into the post-session company of the Lee Valley String Band, whose core members have been playing together for thirty-three years. Here was a leather-capped butcher named Mick who sings ballads as he chops carcasses, a banjo player named Mick but more often called "Black Dog," and another Mick who pens drawings and writes original songs when not driving a forklift. Perhaps because their older brothers were "Micked" first, others were dubbed lesser names like Hal and Kevin, and in one wizened, white-bearded case, Christy. That one had a magical ability to strum a steel guitar, chain smoke, serial drink, and sing with the piercing heartache of a bereaved mountain man – at the same time. My kind of lads, and they had just come back from a rousing session before seven thousand folk festival fans in Denmark.

"They're so good, they could draw crowds like that any time they want in the States," I said to the Corner House's owner, the redheaded and impish Fergal MacGabhann, which is the Irish spelling of McGowan.

"Just getting the eight of them out to Denmark was one of the biggest organizational challenges Ireland has ever faced. It was Cork's Dunkirk," Fergal laughed as he artfully dribbled a perfect G clef into the creamy head of my dark pint of Murphy's. He entices the band to play for free every Monday night – they've missed only two sessions in the last decade – by offering as much free drink as they can down while performing. From what I saw, Fergal might want to check this arrangement with his accountant.

Black Dog laughed, "It's a bad habit for a bad group." He shook his salt-and-pepper beard dismissively at the idea of Lee Valley exporting, as so many others have done, the Irish song and dance routine for fame and fortune abroad.

"We just don't give a fuck!" roared Christy, fingering his double-fretted contraption called an auto-harp. Christy's preferred nutrients had left him so thin, he looked as if he was drawing sustenance from the aftereffects of calories ingested in his school days. A purist, he told me he had always revered the great American bluegrass singer and songwriter Bill Monroe.

On a visit across the pond a few years back, the famous folk man asked to be brought to Christy's house for a late "Sunday morning" introduction (in Ireland, two o'clock on that particular afternoon is referred to as "Sunday morning"). Christy, who had been imbibing the night before, heard the knocking and the halloing at his doorstep all right, but refused to vacate the therapeutic folds of his bed.

"But it's Bill Monroe," one of the musical Micks shouted.

"And I'm Adolf Churchill," Christy bawled and pulled a pillow over his head.

No matter.

"We're getting older, and we still don't give a fuck – and you can quote me on that," Christy chuckled.

Alright now. If these fellows could drive forklifts and chop mutton with an adopted song in their hearts, then why couldn't we?

Autumn was passing – the season is never called "fall" in Ireland, where deciduous trees remain sparse, having done most of their falling to build British masts a long time ago. One November afternoon, a horrible rumbling commenced outside our door. It sounded like a Zeus job. The sky grew frightfully dark and we saw trees in our tranquil garden suddenly bending sideward as though intending to shimmy in the windows and doors. Then our house high on Military Hill seemed to tremble, which was impressive considering that its walls were nearly two feet thick. Amazed at how winds surely topping seventy miles an hour almost instantaneously blasted into foment, I hurried upstairs for a better view. The black maelstrom overhead held whirling branches and, for all I could tell, the limbs of stray cats. Then volleys of thousands, no millions, of pellets of water began to tattoo our windows, and the sound was like something out of the Charlton Heston sections of the Old Testament.

"I guess this is what they mean by 'lashing,'" said Jamie.

"It's scary," Owen whimpered.

Instead of huddling with the family, I was seized by an urge to venture out into the storm, like the fools who race to the beach to witness an incoming hurricane. After arriving in America, the Norwegian novelist Knut Hamsun set off for Minnesota on the roof of a late-nineteenth-century railroad carriage in order to experience the full wildness of the continent. Joseph Turner had himself strapped to the top masts of British frigates to refine the veracity of his paintings of howling seas.

Myself, I walked down the hill toward town. The experience was like a Gene Kelly stroll in the rain as reinterpreted by the producer of a Hollywood horror movie. It instantly brought back the true flavor of working on Bun's cottage in Kerry, those halcyon days spent sinking calf deep in mud while rain without end ran down our noses and ears.

This was worse. The torrents were not only pelting the top of my head but coming in sideways, endless sheets of water blasting laterally just above pavement level and into my calves, thighs, and groin. Exhilarating, I told myself, that was the word. But as I stumbled onward through the gusts, the wind kept yanking the tails of my raincoat up toward my shoulders and exploring what lay south of there. After a short while, my trousers were soaked to belt-level and water dripped from a region normally considered private.

Like a shipwrecked mariner, I at last lunged soaked and shivering into the Hi-B, where a blazing coal fire beckoned from the corner.

"I wouldn't linger there too long, if I were you," warned Kieran, the carpenter extraordinaire.

"Why not? I'm drenched."

"Because Brian will think you're blocking the heat from everyone else, or more importantly, from him. He has ideas about how much heat everyone is entitled to," said my friend with the fierce chin, glittering eyes, mad wit, and long, graying, swept-back hair of an Irish chieftain.

"That's absurd."

"That's what you say. But c'mere. Brian once caught a man shivering on that very chair who had the nerve to throw a couple of extra bits of coal into the hearth. The prick instantly pulled the pint out of the man's hand – a nice brimming fresh pint, like. 'That's my pint, Brian, and I paid for it,' your man said. 'Well that's my coal, and I paid for it, and you're barred for life.'"

Still dripping, I moved toward a stool.

"This is it. It won't stop lashing now for months," groaned Kieran. Lashing, hammering, pelting, showering, misting – the Irish have nearly as many words for rain as the Eskimos do for snow. And why wouldn't they, with studies showing that the cloud cover in this eternally sodden country has increased by 20 percent in the last century, and the number of cloud-free days has dropped from sixty a year around 1910 – more than once a week – to an average of nine in the last decade. In this year of 2000, a County Mayo village called Crossmolina would have rain every day for three and a half months.

"So much for fecking Irish summers," moaned one of the Denises. "I'm shipping out of here next year, forever. Australia's my next stop."

"It kind of clears the system," I tried.

"You've got to be joking, boy. This is awful, it is misery – there's a place at the bottom of the ocean reserved just for us," forecast a man named Noel Brasil, who turned out to be an accomplished songwriter, and a favorite of the great singer Mary Black.

The next morning I struggled back down the Wellington Road into possibly more appalling conditions, holding a school-bound boy in either hand, in hopes they would not be blown off to Cardiff or Liverpool. It was amazing how much a transformation of the weather paints a changed sheen on things. A smear of dog shite seemed to loom up every ten feet, and these were invariably splattered not in the gutters or street but the dead middle of the sidewalk. Cork – the Venice of the North – I now knew not only had the straightest road, tallest and longest buildings, and oldest yacht club in Ireland, but the heaviest saturations of wilfully uncurbed dog shit of any place on this dog-fouled earth.

The fouling by humankind seemed worse. We'd noticed the truth weeks before, in a visit to the soaring St. Colman's Cathedral above Cobh (pronounced cove), that lovely former seat of the British Admiralty that the occupiers decked out with stately Georgian and Victorian terrace houses, cordoned with marines, and called Queenstown. That outermost way station for transatlantic crossings once hosted up to six hundred merchant ships every day. Later, it became the disembarkation point for three million half-starved native Irish escaping the Famine and its aftermath. The emigrants there would disappear into the filthy, disease-ridden holds of "coffin ships" that presented the same conditions, minus only chains, as African slaves endured en route to the new world. Typhoid ran so rampant that up to 30 percent of the passengers never made it across the Atlantic alive, and curious modern explorers could walk from one end of Grosse Isle in the St. Lawrence River, upstream from Quebec City, to the other without taking their feet off of buried Irish bones.

A wrenching sadness still permeates Cobh's main pier, the last port of call of the *Titanic*, where a fine heritage museum ably evokes the full heartbreak of the town's history and Ireland's once impoverished southwest. "Never again," say the Jews, meaning that they will never forget nor stop honoring their Holocaust dead.

It is not the same with the Irish, despite a similar experience of near genocide. Cobh should be a sacrosanct place, enshrined as Jerusalem, yet even the hallowed museum there is ringed by shops selling cheap keepsakes to tourists. From the water's edge, the ascent up the steep stone steps to the carillon-belled cathedral should be rendered as a Stations of the Cross-like passage commemorating every terrible vicissitude against which the Irish once struggled. But instead, this walkway is a testament to soulless neglect, despoiled by uncountable heaps of beer cans and plastic rubbish. Remember not our tragic past, but our present indulgence, reads its message.

Wellington Road's sidewalk was equally depressing as I steered my sons down the slope toward Christian Brothers. Crisp bags, cigarette packets, "Scrumpy Jack" cider cans, even soiled nappies, lined the pavement. The most repulsive droppings came from the local "chippers." Half-finished sprawls of discarded french fries and flattened hamburgers were coiled into cornucopia-like paper wrappings oozing grease in the rain. A Fermoy car dealer named Tom Monaghan had recently become so disgusted by the ugliness on Ireland's streets that he was trying to turn the feel-good national "Tidy Towns" competition on its head by launching a "Filthy Towns" award. On this godforsaken morning, Cork deserved first place.

We picked our way onward. As usual, Laura had been dropped off at 7:20 at Cork's unspeakably grim bus station for her hour-long trip to Bandon. The maturity with which she was handling this challenge was extraordinary. I prayed the boys would be so resilient, as I hugged Owen goodbye and ushered Harris toward his classroom. Suddenly, a bloodcurdling scream of "SILENCE!" erupted from the other side of the closed door. My feet recoiled and my body froze. The shriek sounded like the work of a mad Celtic chieftess prior to a ritual beheading, yet the source was a sweet-looking woman of no more than thirty. Wow.

"Go on Harris, it's okay. She's just clearing her lungs," I nudged the ten-year-old forward into the waiting circle of tribal sacrifice, trying not to connect with the dread in his eyes. One scream at children like that and a teacher most anywhere else would be blacklisted for life. But our bearings were by no means solid yet, and I wasn't sure how I was supposed to respond to this sort of challenge in Ireland, what with all the warnings about keeping meanings carefully clouded. So I straightened Harris's tie, wished him luck, and tripped over myself to get the hell out of there.

"Silence!" the shrew bellowed again. And people say there are no banshees left in Ireland.

That night, Harris began to sob as I tucked him into bed. "Why do we have to be in Ireland? I hate it here. I hate my school and I hate my teacher, and I want to go back home now."

Our presence on this isle felt utterly delusional. What good had we accomplished by yanking our children from the security of their contented former lives? Much wiser and braver than us seemed the dinner-party talkers from Sidney to Richmond-Surrey and South Hampton and god knows where else who shrugged off their wine-happy promises to set off for exotic shores soon, knotted their ties, and put their responsibilities back in place every morning, whether they liked it or not.

"I'm worried that we've made a terrible mistake. I feel sick with guilt," I said to Jamie, before reluctantly dialing the home number of Síle Hayes, the principal of the boys' primary school.

"I heard the screaming again today and I was appalled," Mrs. Hayes said, interrupting my hesitant complaints. "It will be sorted."

A week later, a shaken Harris announced that his teacher had been fired and then stormed from his classroom in tears. Seventeen other parents had complained, which was remarkable, in that the Irish until recently simply acquiesced to whatever harsh treatment their children received at the hands of school authorities, since these usually were meted out by an all-dominating clergy. Nonetheless, people were beginning to "stand up for their rights," as Americans call it. But the process is still conducted very quietly. In fact, in Ireland most complaints are made with a whisper.

Chapter 12

Writers love nothing more than to picture themselves slaving at work, especially in some romantic garret in a faraway land. What they hate most is doing it. So it was that I would wander the shady lane outside our house, pretending I was thinking, while looking up with a mixture of fondness and revulsion at my office window with the panoramic views that were supposed to imbue me with inspiration. But Cork is not a place that allows lonely cogitators to take themselves too seriously, not, at least, when the annual jazz festival blows in at the end of October.

Cork's four-day celebration of jazz is the mother of all Irish parties. The city turns into a carnival as 50,000 revelers arrive on trains, planes, and cars to hear the offerings of a thousand musicians, a good few from distant lands.

The Hi-B was not listed as a venue. Yet one afternoon I discovered a cigarette-thin, elegantly smooth pianist called "Professor" Peter O'Brien playing an electric keyboard that had materialized out of nowhere, with his girlfriend bowing a fiddle madly at his side. Bebop, big band, and the blues began breaking out in hotels and pubs all over town, much of it first-rate. Cork people use the word "ballhop" to describe a particularly riotous extravaganza. The jazz festival was a ballhop alright, despite ceaseless torrents banging on every venue's window. One of the best sessions involved a swinging homage to Jelly Roll Morton, masterfully executed by a blue-eyed, graying Kerryman called "Stride" O'Brien (no relation to the professor), with a few numbers added by his Dublin friend Brendan Lynch. A chat afterward resulted in the mention of Professor O'Brien's performance in the Hi-B the day previous.

"Pete actually played there?" the Kerry musician questioned.

"Yeah, it was superb."

Pause. "Do you think I might give it a go tonight?"

"I don't see why not," I offered grandly.

A phone call had the music-loving Brian O'Donnell at our side in minutes, the arrangements sealed. A slender young Audrey Hepburn look-alike who did Ella Fitzgerald like nobody's business wandered by, so I invited her too.

"I'm just saying, now, isn't it remarkable that you've been here such a short time and can arrange these things as if you lived in Cork for years," Brian said.

In short order, there commenced in his den one of the most inspired and intimate concerts of the entire festival. By the end of the evening, Stride O'Brien and Brendan Lynch were playing side-by-side duets as a delighted Brian thanked me profusely.

The next afternoon, I returned for my bouquets of praise. Jamie had been informed that I would be celebrated for all time in the Hi-B. But something felt off as soon as I walked in the door. The Mahler at that moment was loud enough to make a man beg for Brahms.

"Too bad you weren't around last night," Brian said, his memory of the session evidently gone sketchy. "There was the most beautiful piano playing in here and you would have loved it."

Ouch. Suddenly the Hi-B did not seem the carefree clubhouse that I'd imagined the night before. I left abruptly, reminding myself that Ireland, except for the dance of certain young tormentors and the Noh masks of certain potential employers, was treating us kindly. True, Harris's second teacher had just quit without warning, although Christian Brothers quickly found another replacement. The boys were nonetheless settling in well, playing rugby on weekends and endless games of "tip the can" in our park. Laura was glued to her new mobile telephone, nurturing burgeoning friendships; and Jamie, having by now successfully shrunk every shirt in the house, had developed some possible contacts for obtaining work, and was primed for new challenges.

Now three months into our adventure, we decided to celebrate our various blessings with a trip to a place in County Kerry called Sneem. And why Sneem? Because we liked the silly sound of it, suggesting as it did a peaceful holding ground for phantasms like sneetches. The name is thought to derive from the Irish *Snaidhm na Cailli* – the knot of the old woman or hag – though nobody knows why. The true meaning could in fact be obscene. Leering from Ireland's buried pagan past are numerous stone reliefs, some embedded in medieval church walls, called *sheela-na-gigs*, which show enough knotted female circularity to boil the blood of a prurient priest.

Anyway, Jamie and I had some Sneem history ourselves, having happened upon the village during our honeymoon after getting hopelessly lost in the badlands of the surrounding mountains, which are called MacGillicuddy's Reeks. After escaping this fastness, Sneem had seemed like a tranquil haven, with its rows of brightly painted limestone terrace houses sweetly stacked before a pair of broad central greens that are called squares, even though they are triangles. Between the two, the Sneem River surges under a narrow-arched stone bridge, then spills down into a harbor and the great Kenmare bay beyond, which is also called a river though it is not.

As we wound for the second time down through Kerry toward Sneem on an early November evening, the village seemed little changed, although a strange welcome materialized in the form of a wild goat sailing off a ledge and nearly landing on the roof of our car.

After making arrangements at the Bank House B&B ("Welcome to my home," said the kindly proprietor), we went out to savor the vista of spectacular russet brown mountains, feather dusted by drifting wisps of white clouds with an artfully applied crescent moon glowing in the inky dusk behind them. We had our walk, our meal, and a deep sleep in a dimension of pure silence. The next morning broke in glory, the sun raining light upon the river, the sky a filmy blue above the ring of surrounding peaks with their curious names likely harkening to the ancient Celtic mother goddess, Brigid: Coomcallee, the hollow of the hag; Maulcallee, the knoll of the hag; and Clouncally, the meadow of the hag.

Suddenly, a rainbow materialized between two distant pyramid-shaped peaks, then intensified as it plaited all the primary colors and some afterthoughts into a vast arc that misted onto a nearby field. Moments later, a second, even more gorgeous rainbow magically came to life a few parallel feet away, or so it looked in rainbow reckoning, beside the first. Laura, hanging close like the younger child she had been only yesterday, began hurrying with me toward their side-by-side landing points so tantalizingly close to our path. To our amazement, the beginnings of yet a third rainbow began to shimmer into place alongside the fellas overhead, and Laura was shouting wonder when the entire display abruptly disintegrated into the ether. Nope, the Kerry morning said, you imagined the whole thing.

Jamie and the boys joined us as we passed a sixteen-foot, stainless-steel tree sculpture, "planted" for some reason by the president of Israel in 1985, and drew up to an intriguing sign at the other side of the village. It read: "The Way the Fairies Went." Hmmh. The sign pointed down a narrow lane with a small, drab nineteenth-century church decamped at its end, under the altar of which is said to lay the remains of one of the laziest and most outlandish priests in the history of Kerry, Father Michael Walsh, R.I.P. 1866, who eschewed sermons and spent his days hunting the hills in Wild West buffalo skins. In front of it sits a white marble sculpture of a giant panda, with an inscription explaining that this was a gift from the Chinese People's Association for Friendship with Foreign Countries in gratitude for a visit by Cearbhall Ó Dalaigh, prime minister of Ireland from 1974 to 1976, and a proud Sneem man. Odd forces were definitely at play.

Beside the church lay a park where the grass wove thick and the birdsong sweet, but no fairy chatter could be heard. Instead, there waited a black, voluptuous sculpture of the Egyptian god Isiris, she the incarnation of fertility renewing without end. Beyond lay a mysterious series of fifteen-foot-tall pyramids of blue-gray Kerry slate, rising improbably beside the river and before the open water of Sneem's harbor.

With an uncanny sense of Bun's presence, I craned through an opening into the first pyramid. Inside, it was cramped, dark, and mesmerizing. Here and there, the walls were interrupted by narrow window slits of gorgeously colored stained glass, smooth as shards washed onto lonely strands, and these ascended like stepping stones of light toward the soaring pinnacle. The sun streamed its whimsy onto these exquisite prisms and the dripping-wet, cell-like inner walls. The effect was disorienting, as profound as Monet's chapel in St. Paul De Vence or Mark Rothko's mysterious shrine in Houston. The maker of these stone poems had conjured together all the world's most soulful prayers and blended them into a universal harkening to the divine – the inside of an Egyptian pyramid, of a Kerry hermit's beehive cell speaking of a devotion beyond modern comprehension, of a Gothic cathedral reduced to its bare oratory essence, of a prehistoric cave ridden with ogham swirls and animal paintings crying out to the supernatural. Of every one of these dimensions, these creations by an artist named James Scanlon breathed.

I wandered into the next three pyramids, as transfixed as a supplicant at Ballinspittle. The last was deliberately unfinished, partially open-sided, as if to invite viewers to fill in what was missing with their own imagination and faith. The place felt holy, drawing power from the church beside it and making the Mass proceeding there all the more profound. I walked by the river, which now seemed to be coursing with light instead of water, turbines of light churning under the stone arches of the venerable stone bridge, before fanning into a broad sluice in search of the sea. There were salmon in there, running back to the stream of their birth after a journey of thousands of miles. Wherever my old friend Bun had wandered in the dusk since his death, I felt that he too had revived, that he was sharing in this vision of James Scanlon, a seeker who had somehow eradicated the divisions between stone, glass, light, and psalm.

As I stood there, the Kerry mountains began to release a further curl of rainbow. The remote west of Ireland has been celebrated through centuries of legend and poem – for a unique power to renew the magic of apprehension, for shattering noise into the fundaments of silence. The ancient Irish poets used to seek inspiration by lying for hours with stones on their bellies in the chilling pools breathed up by springs. Here in Kerry, that would have been unnecessary. All one has to do is wake up and gaze upon visions that lie close enough to touch. Doing nothing more than that, I began to experience an inner jubilation, for the gift Bun had given me, for the gift of being alive, for the gift that is Ireland in its glory and that I hoped my children were absorbing well. Without thinking, without intending, I found my arms beginning to lift in exaltation.

The kids examined me strangely. I came back to terra firma and enlisted them to help collect some of the mindlessly dropped garbage that infested even this hallowed place. Then we went into the church to catch the end of the Mass.

Owen must have been affected by all this, because he asked to visit one of the local keepsake shops catering to the coach tours that choke Kerry in summer. Therein, he disappeared. After a minute or two he resurfaced with a tweed tam-o'-shanter on the top of his blond head.

Never mind that half of this Irish woollen tourist-market stuff is now made in Indonesia or China, or that few natives under the age of sixty wear it. Owen's intentions and his own visions were pure. He emerged grinning broadly, with his freckle-nosed, blue-eyed, mop head crowned by his budding Irishness, whispering, "It's my Paddy hat."

The purchase was made instantly.

Chapter 13

Where oh where had my own protective Paddy hat gone? A ride on a golf cart is supposed to be a tame affair, but the one I found myself enjoying a couple of weeks later should have been kitted out with some form of helmet and perhaps a parachute and crampons. A sheer cliff dropped 250 feet into the ocean from about four feet to my right and the treacherous gravel path was suddenly veering in that godforsaken direction as well. Why was I here? An American magazine had commissioned an article regarding the ultimate Irish Xanadu, the spectacularly situated and steeply priced golf course on the Old Head of Kinsale.

Jim O'Brien, the unflappable manager of the place, was at the wheel, proudly pointing out the sights as I held on for dear life. The surf roared below us, and a squall fluffed and vanished a few miles off, close to where a German torpedo rent the *Lusitania* on May 7, 1915, sending 1195 drowned passengers floating toward the Old Head, and the U.S. careening into World War I.

"Look there," Jim said, jamming on the breaks and pointing to an opening in the cliffs that was surrounded by countless bickering gulls. "It goes from one side of the head clear through to the other. There are fifteen caves out here that do the same thing."

Among other things, the Old Head is a national bird sanctuary, home to untold thousands of Arctic skuas, stormy petrels, great and sooty shearwaters, pomarines and hoopoes. It is also an isthmus of stunning beauty upon which generations of Cork people used to freely walk and picnic, a natural treasure that spreads into some of the most stunning and storied vistas that can be created by water, stone, and sun. In 1989, Jim's boss, a tough and controversial Kerryman called John O'Connor, bought the whole shebang from a local farmer for about £225,000 and, despite agreeing otherwise with the local planning authorities, began to seal off public access to what rightfully should be an Irish national park.

Jim led me to the dilapidated remains of a seventeenth-century "brazier" lighthouse – only three others exist in Ireland – which once featured open fires on its roof. "It was later said to do service as a whorehouse," he laughed devilishly. "Some of our guests have asked if we could restore it to its former glory." And the wallets and attitudes that come with those visitors make it possible that they were not joking.

Back by the Old Head's narrow neck, one could see the crumbling remains of a twelfth-century stone tower that once reigned over a castle belonging to the Norman de Courcy family who called this place home for centuries. Somewhere close by supposedly lay the ruins of an Iron Age fortress called Dun Cearmna, which the course's brochures link to the mythological origins of Ireland. The claim is that it was the home base of the second-century B.C., pre-golfing Erainn tribe who gave the country its name, although Ptolemy's map reference to that crowd was as vague as would be expected for a man who never set foot on Ireland's shores and couldn't handle a mashie or wedge.

Jim drove me along fairways that looked yummy if you happened to be a golfer or a cow, and chortled on about various visits by American celebrities, senators, and athletes, including Tiger Woods, Michael Jordan, and the billionaire emperor of a Florida garbage-hauling and video-shop kingdom, Wayne Huizenga. Here slept a purported fairy circle; here on the rocks below a certain putting green, the steamer the *City of Chicago* split in two in 1912. Scattered every which way around this fantasy land were newly propped up imitations of ancient Irish standing stones: Disney Ireland.

In the clubhouse, a low-slung, glassy, stone-faced affair that looked like it belonged in California's Malibu, the guest-book glowed with epiphanies. "If God were to come back as a golfer, this is where he would play," someone had scribbled. The Creator golfs? I wondered. Even the hoariest parts of the Old Testament had not revealed the universe to be this perverse. I looked out at the lighthouse's white tower shimmering from the end of the headland, doubting that the spiked and spangled shoe crowds had a clue about how bitterly their privileged play went down with the local Irish who have been banished from this hollowed peninsula, and branded anew as "foreigners," just as the British had labeled every Irish-speaker in these parts only two hundred years ago.

"We're pretty much targeting an American audience," Jim had confided over lunch, when I asked about the greens fees that run to US$250 a round, or about ten times the going rate in the rest of the country. It was clear that this enterprise had deliberately tried to price itself beyond the reach of almost anybody with a native Cork lilt.

"One of our plans is to foster enduring connections with the Old Head through lifetime international memberships, which will be priced at fifty thousand dollars," O'Brien offered, saying "dollars," not punts, nor pounds.

What about the helicopters we'd seen roaring over Kinsale to hurry time-pressed executives in for their mashie bashes around the Old Head? "Americans don't like to drive on our narrow roads," Jim explained. "They find them slow and dangerous."

The pursuit of leisure was definitely getting frenetic: forty choppers a day now crisscross Ireland to bring golfers to their expensive tee times at such places, what with the number of visiting linksters exploding from fifty-two thousand a year in 1988 to a quarter of a million today.

But things can get worse: Jim's boss hopes to begin ferrying golfers in by blazing-quick motor launches, once he completes a planned £15 million luxury hotel on a parking lot in the heart of Kinsale. Meanwhile, another group was floating plans for a local £40 million pleasure palace, including not only a lavish swimming pool but also an ice-skating rink, on a spectacular greensward outside of town. The famous Australian "White Shark," Greg Norman, backed by a group that includes a former U.S. Senator, was meanwhile finishing off his own spectacular $30 million course on the coast of County Clare. This one came with a luxury hotel and enough holiday homes to double the size of the local village of Doonbeg, from where one can kiss the Clare ambience goodbye. The same kind of theme-park reality is now scheduled for one of the finest estates in Kildare, the grand Carlton House, which belonged to Edward Fitzgerald, leader of the ill-fated 1798 United Irishmen rebellion, inspired by the recent American and French revolutions. If that hero could have envisioned the crowd about to traipse his lawns, he would have shipped himself off to Timbuktu.

But there was an uplifting aspect to my journalistic exploration of this new Celtic world, for being armed with a provocative story in Ireland, especially one potentially redolent of fresh dirt, is a ticket to introductions and inside-conversations without end.

"It's the greatest regret of my career that we did not manage to purchase the Old Head as a national park. We had the opportunity to do so, and failed," lamented a senior Cork planning official who refused to be named. From bureaucrats, naturalists, and lifelong begrudgers, I heard chapter and verse about how O'Connor's "Ashbourne Holdings" had systematically cut off the dawn-to-dusk free public access that had been specified in the planning agreement. The outfit had demanded insurance fees from would-be strollers, then insisted upon identification cards to prove that candidates for a walk were official ornithologists, whale watchers, and the like. Finally, the head man just told everyone without a pocket full of greenbacks to bugger off.

One day, I joined the magnate in a Cork restaurant that is struggling to ape the trappings of power-lunch hot spots in London, Manhattan, and modern Dublin. John O'Connor proved to be as big as John Wayne and just as blunt, with thinning gray hair covered by an American baseball cap. Outwardly unaffected for a man who owns a lavish hundred-acre seaside estate in Kerry, he was sporting a polyester windbreaker that wouldn't have cut mustard at Augusta or Pebble Beach. He ordered a glass of wine and then followed this with a bottle, as a table full of cronies waited like fawning courtiers a few feet away.

"Creating that course was the golfing equivalent of building the Channel Tunnel," O'Connor offered, his blue eyes studying me hard. "To start with, every tree hugger in Europe tried to shut us down," he added, and began reviewing the lawsuits he had to battle right up to the high courts of the European Union. O'Connor maintained that the public never had any legal right of access to the Old Head. "Golf courses were considered an agricultural use of the land when we started, and not subject to any planning council stipulations, so you can't rewrite the rules," he insisted.

O'Connor then related how his landscapers trucked in three-quarters of a million cubic meters of topsoil from up to thirty miles away, plus nearly 300,000 salt-resistant plants from California and New Zealand, along with giant stone-pulverizing contraptions from ski resorts in the French Alps, to improve drainage on the hardpan of the Old Head.

"It was a labor of pain," O'Connor said wearily. At that moment, his mobile phone rang with a call from his neglected imps at the next table. He cracked not a smile, saying that "98 percent" of the golfers who visited what he liked to call his "national monument" were foreigners, but saw no difficulty in the irony in what to him was simply a matter of running a successful business.

"We have discovered that the public and golfing don't mix for safety reasons," O'Connor said, alluding to several incidents in which casual walkers had supposedly been injured by careering golf balls. So, after eight hundred years of foreign domination, famine and pestilence, the Republic's gravest dangers were golf balls falling out of the sky?

No answer.

The story kept opening conversational gates, especially in Kinsale. "It's abysmal. I was walking on the Old Head all my life and now no local can get in," said the bespectacled Brian O'Neill, who presides with his mother, Mary, over one of the most unspoiled pubs in town, the Tap Tavern.

"It makes you think of Nazi Germany, with the barbed wire and the guards," complained a wizened customer by the tavern's glowing coal fire. A retired pharmacist complained that his letters to the county council demanding the restoration of public access to the headland were exercises in pissing in the wind. How a supposed "national monument" could become a no-go area for local citizens was a subject that evoked outspoken spontaneity in an otherwise often whispering populace. It felt as if everyone was focusing for the first time on the brutal toll being exacted by their nation's new infatuation with wealth at any cost.

"He's been in here, alright," Mary, the fiercely independent, white-haired co-owner of the Tap Tavern, said of the Old Head's impresario. "He had a bunch of his cronies with him one night and set his eye on that whiskey there," she pointed toward a bottle high on a back shelf, whose amber contents were glowing under a small blue-shaded lamp. The label said Academy Whiskey.

"It is a fine and rare whiskey that has not been distilled for eighty years," said Mary. "But himself had the cheek to say to me, 'Mary, we would like a drop of that Academy Whiskey now.'"

"'You certainly will not. It is not for sale,' I told him."

Her son Brian smirked.

"'I'll give you ten pounds for a taste of that whiskey,' says he, showing off," Mary, looking a tad malicious, related.

"'You won't,' I told him. But O'Connor is a big man, so he offered twenty and then forty. 'It's not for sale,' I repeated."

"It must be good stuff," I said, not revealing that I by now knew that the developer frequently sauntered into the Blue Haven Hotel around the corner, expecting to be handed a fat cigar and bottle of fine wine on a silver tray at every appearance.

Mary grew heated. "He had all his friends around him, and was playing the big shot, so he said, 'I will give you five hundred pounds for that bottle of Academy Whiskey.'"

The look in Mary's eyes would have made stray cats run for cover. Two centuries ago, Kinsale, like nearby Bandon, was so thoroughly English that they forbade the outlying Paddies from so much as lingering on the town's streets. To the casual visitor, the place may look like a theme park willing to assume any shape that will please outsiders. But it is not yet so. The locals nurse bitter feelings about anyone who tries to tell them where they can and cannot go, even if they hail from points as close as Kerry.

"I said to him, 'John O'Connor, for all your riches and your golf course and your grand Kerry castle, you do not possess enough money to buy that whiskey from me. It is not for sale to anyone, and especially and most of all not to you.'"

With that, Mary crossed her arms in a harrumph, and disappeared into a back room with a mop.

Chapter 14

We were heading into the Irish season that is best spent in bed. By December, the dreary light made its feckless appearance around nine o'clock in the morning, glowing with all the joy of wet ash, and then began stubbing itself out about six hours later. Meanwhile, the rain hammered down, now without cease. Somehow, Laura roused herself in the blackness two and a half hours before dawn, dressed, breakfasted, and woke one or the other groaning parent for a lift to the bus station that was often still peopled with walking detritus from the night's previous indulgences. At least somebody in the family was moving with purpose.

Even the car grew sullen. By now, its white roof had taken on the appearance of a petri dish coated with green slime. A turn of the key set the drowned carburetor wheezing like an emphysemiac grabbing at the rails on their bed. The moment the family settled themselves inside the car, every window became so steamily opaque with condensation it was impossible to see the road. Then again, our flagstoned garden walk and children's swing set had become coated with their own dank green films, while mushrooms sprouted beside the shower, and the slugs or snails or whatever they were at our door stoop – those will not be described.

Some visitors to Ireland become so demented by the wintry darkness and damp that they actually believe it promotes health, as the meticulous naturalist, historian, and nutter Charles Smith, M.D., testified in his account of his extended tour of southwest Ireland in 1774:

> Perspiration in winter, during the twenty-four hours, in
> a quiet posture, within the house, was equal to the urine

secreted in the same space of time, which was at least thirty-eight ounces. In summer, perspiration was double to the secretion by urine, or, at least, a third more; and when assisted by exercise, it was to what we eat and drink in proportion of five to eight nearly. In the autumn, the air being mild, perspiration was a third part more than the urine, otherwise not more than one-fifth part. In December, perspiration was a fifth part more than the urine; but in January it was as five to three. In winter, when the spirit in the thermometer stood at sixty-five, though the perspiration by day, promoted by exercise, did not exceed fifteen ounces, yet the perspiration, by being nine hours in bed, hath been forty ounces, and sometimes sixty; so that vigorous exercise by day is scarce a balance to the lying ten hours in a bed in a long winter's night.

More true to our perception was a Ray Bradbury story about a drenched planet upon which the sun comes out for a few hours once every seven years, and where a girl was locked in a closet for a few hours and sadly missed the only chance she would have in her entire childhood to see the splendor of full daylight. It must have been penned in Ireland. Jamie's visiting brother and his wife saw about fifteen minutes of sunshine during a ten-day stay. We dutifully drove them this way and that around the bucolic countryside, not one field of which could they discern through the deluge.

"Ireland's so green and lush, so why are there no cows here at all?" demanded the extroverted sister-in-law, Gayle, a North Dakota farm girl herself, at a neighborhood party given by Shaun and Breda Higgins. It is almost impossible to silence an Irish celebration, but this did it, exciting universal guffaws in a country that still remains among the most agriculturally oriented in Europe.

"If I were to stand on my roof, I could see them when the weather is fine," said Shaun. "The only reason you can't see them from the roads now is that you can't see thirty feet."

A malaise seemed to take over the island. Among the most disgruntled were the secondary-school teachers who shut down the nation's schools for seventeen days carefully selected around peak holiday and weekend points in order to inflict maximum inconvenience upon parents, the object being to force their demand for an immediate 40 percent pay rise. Railroad and airline employees joined in the fun by squelching those essential services, so the taxi drivers decided "why not us too?" Worse, the bartenders in Dublin threatened to stop working. At last some government ministers concerned with labor issues broke their silence and said enough is enough, that the me-first avarice of this era could spell Ireland's downfall if people did not curtail their ever-increasing demands. Two months later, the ministers quietly voted themselves a 28 percent pay rise.

Numbering ourselves among the church-shopping class of modern Catholics, we kept trying out different outposts of solace. A strange one on Cork's Washington Street laid out its possibilities on a printed entrance-hall sheet, in a language reflecting its proximity to every major solicitor's office in the town.

NORMS FOR INDULGENCE FOR THE COMMEMORATION OF ALL SOULS

1) From noon on November 1 until midnight on November 2, all who have confessed or received Holy Communion or prayed for the Pope's intention (one Our Father, one Hail Mary, or any other prayer of one's choice) can gain plenary indulgence by visiting a church or oratory and there reciting one Our Father and the Apostles Creed.

This indulgence is applicable only to the souls of the departed. Confession may be made any time during the week preceding or the week following November 1. Holy Communion may be received on any day from November 1–8. For every other visit to a church made during this time, a partial indulgence for the same intention may be made.

2) The faithful who visit a cemetery and pray for the dead may gain a plenary indulgence applicable only to the holy souls on the usual conditions once per day from November 1–8. The conditions above apply also.

Having not yet retained legal representation (which is a good idea the moment one sets foot on Irish soil), we could scarcely figure out the prescribed sequences of praying in that place. It seemed simpler to attend services at a nearby church, but that didn't prove very uplifting either, seeing as the priest, who had recently been brutally mugged, drifted his eyes during services to some spot on the altar's wall where he seemed to be struggling to make sense out of what had become of Ireland. In this chapel, one prayed for the tender of the flock.

The season's grimness evidently had some agitating effect on our secret admirers. One dismal morning we walked out to discover that our car's rear window had been smashed to bits during the night. New chipper filth was strewn across our lane, and the Opel's lichen-ridden fenders looked suspiciously cleansed as if the nuisances had been working again at their Olympian talents in the pissing department. This was more than enough, and, nearly thrashing the phone against the wall as I dialed, I demanded that the *gardaí* please show their faces at last.

The nearest comedians should have been rung up instead. After a leisurely interval, a couple of somewhat distracted individuals in uniform showed up at our door, foot scuffling and weather analyzing, then taking statements, and with a little flourish of connectedness, proffering apologies for the disorder in their precinct, while promising they would look after us now. Gazing out the window perhaps an hour later, I was elated to see one of the miscreants being beckoned to a slowing cop car. For a second, his eyes narrowed with concern.

"Jamie, watch this! They've got him!" I cried, nearly whooping.

"What do you mean? 'Got him?' They're laughing like old friends," she growled. Sure enough, our young friend had an arm casually resting on the police car's door; chastened he did not look.

That night, I set out for surveillance on our dark lane. Suddenly, I found myself surrounded by a teenage pack swollen with new recruits. Testosterone hung in the damp air. This was discomforting, because the Irish art of vigilante score-settling runs deep, and because the night's group was also bulked up tonight by someone who was a good six inches taller than myself, who proved to be: The Brother.

Oh my, but did The Brother talk, speechifying about what a blissful youth he had spent on this same cul-de-sac where there was never any trouble nor foreigners like us, and about what a harmless fellow was yon sibling, just look at him in his inno-cence – there in the black of night where he may or may not be smirking.

Dangerous the scene appeared; six chipper-stoked diges-tions does not make for good odds, without the potential for a Cuchulainn triple salmon flip out of trouble – and yet, I quickly discerned something decent about The Brother. He in fact listened thoughtfully, and hearing truth in my complaints, even promised that my family's troubles would cease. We shook hands, and after a long moment of consideration, I put out my hand to each of the boys, telling them in their turns that, having been a teenager once myself, I would gladly forget everything if we could just move on. And so, and verily, was peace made . . . for a time.

Nonetheless, the chop in our lives was not altogether smoothed. It soon became apparent that Jamie's quest for employment was moving no faster than the strike-ridden public transportation whose plenary indulgences seemed to have long since expired. Her searches of the help-wanted ads uncovered S & M-sounding openings for "guillotine operators," "Arctic drivers," "rigid driv-ers," "panel beaters," and "abattoir" (slaughterhouse) workers, along with an insatiable demand for "I.T. specialists." It seemed that the most interesting and creative jobs all lay in Dublin, which was three hours away by train, when those were running. This did not help. There were evenings when she was downcast, and she let me know it well.

It was challenging, having so many aspects of our identities in flux. Anxiety and conflict increased. Not for nothing did Jamie's favorite song become Stephen Foster's hauntingly beautiful Appalachian/Irish crossover tune, "Hard Times Come Again No More."

I told a fellow customer in a downtown pub about my wife's frustrations and formidable, if ignored, abilities. The man, who ran a successful local business, listened closely. A passionate socialist, he often proclaimed his desire to help the entire human race. Sip. He hated suffering of every kind. Puff. He hated capitalism. Clink. Religion, too. Sure, and let's sip. He believed in the fundamental goodness of mankind and would dedicate his life to assisting same. Glug.

"Have your wife call in the morning, and we'll talk," he said, outlining a position he would soon need to fill. Natch, he didn't answer the next eight phone calls. But this of course merely under-lined the first rule of adjusting to life in Ireland – never, ever, believe any promise that is made in a pub.

This business of communicating in Cork was clearly very tricky. We were speaking the same language as everyone around us, but missing a certain inaudible nuance. Some friends finally explained that ours was a "who do you know" problem, that a secret grapevine ripples through every section of the island and that we had not yet established a personal identification code for gaining access to it. Quite simply, we were unknowns. The Irish like to deal with knowns, gossiped-from-head-to-foot knowns. If you want a plumber or a mechanic or a visitation by just about any human being who can stand upright in Ireland, you better have a name to mention – an influential solicitor, a distant cousin, or a friend of a friend of a friend – or you will officially be regarded as nonexistent. We hadn't comprehended that we did not yet fully exist, which is a peculiar problem to confront after nearly five decades on earth.

"How can we possibly know that you are who you say you are until six months have passed?" the bank employee had asked, obviously in earnest. Owen McIntyre confirmed our suspicions. He railed that the entire nation should be prosecuted for collu-sion in restraint of free trade, that supremely qualified native-born individuals with impeccable credentials garnered overseas were routinely frozen out of good jobs for the same "who-do-you-know" problem. An eccentric local poet scoffed, "Don't you know that *perestroika* has never made it to Ireland? Think of how the Russians do business, with cash envelopes and veiled threats used to move every transaction forward. They're ten times more open than us. Try Russia, you'll find more opportunities there."

One day, we had an American-born neighbor in for tea, despite his protestations that he was only free for fifteen minutes. He stayed for ten times that, so much did he have to say about the exasperating, impenetrable, inscrutable, obstinate, obdurate, duplicitous, fawning, feigning, deceiving, and plain curious nature of Irish communication he had been puzzling over for the last five or six years since marrying his Cork wife. It had taken him ages to land a low-paying job in a nursery school, despite having lengthy experience in the same line in the States. Rough going, he warned, lay in our path still – but he swore it was somehow worth it.

Another time, we met an English tourist who did not hedge words. "I've been here for three weeks," he said, "and been mind-fucked every night. But I've never been laid once."

Somehow, the kids for their part were adapting more smoothly. Laura was off to weekend sleepovers in grand country houses, while the boys worked on their continuing transformation into Cork street urchins. Owen fell into the requisite lilt. "I will, yeah," he'd say when asked to take out the garbage, pronouncing "will" as if it had three Es while insisting that we call the stuff "rubbish" and its destination a "wheelie bin." Alas, as much as he loved studying Irish in school, he became too self-conscious to don the Paddy hat anymore.

In Connecticut, the kids would by now be sledding, skiing, and gliding across frozen ponds. In Ireland, their element was mud. Harris, called "dirt boy" for similar proclivities as a toddler, took to the stuff passionately, wrestling down anybody within arm's reach in our garden to ensure that they were both filthy within seconds. One night, however, the children at last got to taste an Irish version of their former wintry element. A traveling theater troupe flung magic over an otherwise dreary evening in the old market square called Cornmarket Street. Hoary characters on stilts and in dragon suits emerged from the blackness to the roar of eerie electronic music, while hundreds of children watched in rapture. Suddenly, a huge fan-like contraption blew torrents of white

Styrofoam flakes over the crowd. The children raised their hands in wonder as the stuff spilled onto their hair and down their necks. It was just as Ray Bradbury had described in his story of that other meteorological transformation when the sight of the never-before-seen sun shocked witnesses. Then the machine coughed up its last flurry, and the mist wrapped its forgetfulness back around the night.

We walked by the Lee and savored the fairy-tale-like upside-down reflections of the lit-up buildings on the dark water, the shimmering green light that is played on the bridges every night. Our new home, half built on dream.

Cork could not be fixed in time. The Christmas season crescendoed onward, not like a familiar reference point but an extravaganza choreographed by Cecil B. DeMille. The streets filled with new faces by the thousands, as if country people had suddenly been vacuumed from every hollow to join in a frenzy of common shopping, jaywalking, and tribal socializing. The restaurants and pubs were jammed; the shops became mauled the way they once were in Irish country towns on cattle-trading Saturdays. Toy stores were laid waste and clothing shops saw their goods strewn wildly about the floor in this 3.2 billion-punt cattle mart that is Christmas in Ireland. Only the limply hanging turkeys in the English Market remained calm.

In the newspaper, there was no notice of a Messiah concert or caroling festival, and few signs of the religious spirit of Christmas past, but the churches took in throngs of the devout. Cork has enough splendid churches to dazzle any visitor, the most famous being a French Gothic fantasia named St. Fin Barre's with elegant 240-foot spires that enchant every view of the town. That flower of Protestantism is named after the founder of the eighth-century monastic settlement that planted the seeds of modern Cork, before the Danes thundered in with their broadswords and created the first real town in this part of the tribal island.

On the streets, there were buskers everywhere, including the minstrel with the saw, now making magic with "Come All Ye Faithful" and "Holy Night." The corners teemed with volunteers shaking collection buckets in search of donations for the old, the poor, orphans, sick children, a new hospital ward, the lifeboat service – you name it. So there lay Christmas.

Me, I kept far from the maddening shopping crowds until the last possible minute. But the appropriate presents were finally hoarded, and with relief I entered the Hi-B on the afternoon of Christmas Eve, having tucked in my pocket a small gift for Esther, a token of appreciation for all the kindness she had bestowed. Despite the bedlam inside, a moment arose to discreetly make the transfer.

Esther, topped with a red Santa hat and sporting flashing Rudolph bulbs on either ear, launched into a raucous chorus of "You better not shout, I'm telling you why," that was joined by a hundred voices raised in mad unison. The mood at the North Pole could not have been more euphoric. But then Brian O'Donnell surfaced, waving his arms disparagingly.

"You're all being far too loud, like a rabble with no place to go," the owner snapped, his tongue darting about his lips. The frigging scrooge. But then his business card did warn: "With a talent to abuse."

I noticed a journalist named Denis – wasn't everybody? – helping Esther transport her various trinkets out the door – seven bags full, when I stopped counting. A few days later, I asked how many presents she had received.

"One hundred and eighty four."

Our children did not make out that well, what with their treasured dog and the extended family that wreathed every previous Christmas with love having been left far, far behind on a day that featured endless rain and no snow. But the morning still brought them their small mountains of gifts. After Mass, and phone calls to our mothers, the kids' new friends and several of ours came by to exchange cheer, and Jamie cooked a sumptuous goose. Yet we saw shadows over our shoulders. Sad rugby socks hung from the hearth in place of the lovingly embroidered needlepoint stockings that had been forgotten in packing. No better way to arouse parental guilt than falling down on the job at Christmas.

The next morning we brought Laura to the airport for a present that required no apologies – a solo trip to visit a Parisian friend she had made back in Connecticut. Not even a teenager, she would venture by herself to Ariane Laporte-Bisquit's family near the Eiffel Tower, and then visit the grandparents' cognac-producing chateau in the south of France. And we were worried about her?

Chapter 15

New Year's Eve and tick went the clock of our changed lives. We were standing in the middle of Bellevue Park with our neighbors and gathered masses of kids preparing to watch the annual fireworks sail up from the city below. One of the scrawnier troublemakers was there too, but even he was smiling, and I began to look at his visage with thoughts about how my sons could well be progressing toward their own difficulties in adolescence. Hadn't I been insufferable at that confused stage myself? And how could one not smile tonight? All of Cork's exuberance was due to burst forth above the spotlighted spires of the town's fairy-tale churches. As midnight struck, laughter and song filled the air, and the kissing went on to extremes.

The only problem: it was now 12:15, and not so much as a star graced the drizzling sky. Up and down the sidewalks, from between parked cars, and from high windows, people stared at their watches. Time crawled ahead, mobile phones were frantically dialed, but the wizard in charge was not taking calls. No fireworks materialized, not so much as a single dud.

"For fuck's sake," our neighbor Diarmuid muttered, which is the all-purpose Irish refrain for expressing disgust.

Of course, the timing or even the promise of the fireworks had never been confirmed in the regional newspaper, perhaps because the organizers had not thought of phoning them or vice versa. So naturally no explanation of the missing fireworks would ever be printed either. This was the mysterious Cork way, where you either hear about some magical event on the grapevine or are left standing out in the cold, wondering and muttering "For fuck's sake" until your kids are shivering and your champagne has gone flat.

The next day broke cold and gray – "for fuck's sake" weather if ever it existed. But, lo, things changed as they always do in Ireland. Ever so slowly, the afternoon whispered wintry premonitions and finally released a display more wondrous than mere fireworks: snow. Regarded with all the awe of an eclipse, snow is a substance that is never taken for granted in Ireland. It is an epiphany, a mesmerizing force whose appearances Irish writers, like Joyce in his famous story "The Dead," use as a stock reference to forces beyond human comprehension. If the Brits had had any wits about them, they would have pumped fake snow over the land at the start of every uprising.

The boys went delirious as the first wet inch of the stuff landed, joining friends in slipping and sliding and tossing soggy grenades. A neighboring Zimbabwean college student and babysitter of our kids emerged squealing with delight, having never seen snow before. "It's unreal! It's magic!" she shouted. Darn right.

We were bound for Dublin the next morning, although the trip in a snowbound Ireland was not easily made. The temperature had a bite to it at dawn, and there was such a depth of snowfall – nearly four inches, the heaviest storm since 1983 – that scarcely a Cork car was moving, certainly not one on our prodigious slope, and we didn't intend to try driving either. So we trudged, slipped, and slid the downhill mile to the station and made it to the capital city fairly much on schedule, staring in amazement the entire way at an eternally green land that had turned ghostly white.

At the other end of the line, a couple with their own Irish saga collected us at Dublin's Heuston Station, across from the Parkgate Street army barracks where I'd once stolen carrots for Bun's elixir. We first met Dave and Rose Van Buren at a mandatory Catholic retreat outside New York City for betrotheds needing to scrub away their various states of sin. Rose was a mercurial, dark-haired, trilling farm girl from Limerick; Dave a droll, black-bearded, and gentle-eyed native New York son working for a legal firm, while writing poetry on the side. We struck up an instant friendship, and in the years to follow our children became friends and we stayed friends after the homesick Rose dragged her beau back to Ireland a decade before, while nudging us to follow.

Dave was now managing an Irish Internet chat site called

"Paddynet," an idea with the dangerous potential to clog up global communications should the populace ever set to electronic chatting as obsessively as it gabs via mobile phones. Rose toiled as a part-time nurse, when not tending to a brood recently expanded to five. With much to discuss, we set to a meal in a slick new emporium with foot-deep cushions and television screens flitting with the sparking hooves of Irish export step dancers. Then off we maneuvered down the road that bisects Dublin's vast Phoenix Park, where a motorcyclist commenced walking his machine like a recalcitrant cow through the drifts ahead.

The Van Burens own a classic semidetached Irish house, identical to its neighbors, in one of those endless recent developments that ring Ireland's cities. Their "park" in Castleknock, where the Norman conqueror Strongbow smashed through the 1171 siege of Dublin by Irish earls and allied Norsemen, is the kind of place a passerby can easily underestimate. But the Van Burens' children play with countless friends in the security of a cul-de-sac where every window hosts not only squinting but protective eyes, and the adults all know each other and socialize as regularly as fish in a common bend of a stream. To our kids, this family, cramped in their modest abode that was as tight as Mother Hubbard's shoe – and in fact had a mother-in-law in it somewhere – were wealthier than us, because three times more children played outside their door than our own. "The politics of the street," as Rose put it, was their life, with of course a little prying and one-upsmanship thrown in.

Supper for thirteen materialized in the form of frozen pizza and chips. Nobody minded because Ireland remains a place where the old saw of "the more the merrier" is the first rule of life, and pretensions to superior manners are generally reviled. Sisters and neighbors kept filing in and children vanished in an aunt's embrace.

"There are moments when you want to scream, and it's a challenge even finding the kids' shoes in the morning, but we have a good life here, you know," said our placid host, the son of a prosperous Westchester County, New York, family who had by now "gone Irish" hook, line, and sinker.

"Half of our friends live right next door," Dave smiled content-edly. "We never once could find a sense of community like this in America, and the coldness of our life there drove Rose nuts."

The Van Burens' doorbell resumed ringing. By 9 p.m. maybe forty people had jammed together in their small rooms, including a half-dozen of Dave's fellow participants in that rarity of rarities – an Irish barbershop chorus. The baritones hummed and ser-enaded as the children shimmied with joy at the sound of their father's deep, sonorous voice. By the end of that evening, Jamie and I set to euphoric warbling along with our fellow guests, while our three kids watched the scene with bedazzled amazement.

Alas, Dublin the next day did not seem quite so perfect. Glassy skyscrapers hulked like pillboxes of rising wealth over the carefree, vagabond city I had once known, while huge cranes stood ready to hoist faceless new Lego-bits of Ireland's stealthily traded afflu-ence into place. Ten-room brownstone office buildings at the most fashionable Stephen's Green addresses were being let for nearly US$200,000 per year. And the traffic was insufferable. A recent survey had noted that of all the world's cities, Dublin is second only to Calcutta in the length of time it takes to deliver a package three miles – forty-five minutes.

It was cold. The minstrel who enchanted Cork by bowing his bent saw appeared on bustling Grafton Street, looking like a lost beggar before the indifferent masses filing in and out of glamor-ous shops. The bearded, unkempt rogues of old were no longer wavering between fabled watering holes, their routes having been taken over by seekers of cosmetics and Italian shoes. My creamy-skinned old chanteuse of a girlfriend who had a dresser drawer as her crib, where was she? The passionate but kindly young com-munist with whom I had stolen carrots for Bun's whiskey, had he even existed? In the middle of my left palm, there remained a small hole from a long sliver that had jammed in while a friend and I painted County Meath stud-farm fences for the "nobs." This was my only keepsake now.

Ice gleamed on the street and just in front of us a middle-aged woman, unaccustomed to the dangerous stuff, slipped and cater-wauled, breaking her arm. Oddly, we, the foreigners, were the only ones to administer comfort until an ambulance arrived. Then we returned to the same corner, and an elderly gentleman lost his footing in the same spot. Was there some message in this pantomime? Had Dublin become a place where Ireland replaced its old ways with a new and dangerously slick sheen?

We strolled into dolled-up clothing shops and a couple of the still superb Dublin bookstores I had so much loved as a student. Pubs I once savored held people yakking everywhere alright, but many of the customers now looked insufferably earnest and flash as they blathered into mobile phones their dinner plans for everyone to hear, in this town where tea at Bewley's or a fry-up at the café (pronounced "calf") equated to putting on the dog just a few years back. Couldn't they see the Dublin I used to know, with its characters from the country who cinched their pants with rope, and shawl-cloaked vegetable-stall women who bawled into the morning, crude and carefree? Couldn't they see Bun there beside them, his head tilted in laughter, admiring the circus of Irish life?

So very much was gone. All I had was a hole in my hand and a peculiar Irish dream in my head. At some point in the previous evening, I had been asked about my, er, long-term plans. "I don't mean to get too deep or anything," the man said. Sure, he didn't.

But the question made me ponder the unfolding arc of our lives. I sidestepped it for a few minutes before suddenly blurting out an idea that I had only recently begun to take seriously. It involved giving voice to all the Cork vitality that I'd witnessed, the stories of ancient connection, harsh controversy, and fresh achievement that revealed themselves to us everyday. Bun had built his dolmen, his beehive and his magical Irish cottage. If that man had taught me anything, it was to keep fishing after dreams. Well, my old friend, I would build a magic Irish magazine.

Chapter 16

The snow quickly melted, the monsoons eddied into the precincts of memory, and the January sun strengthened with frosty nights followed by mercifully lengthening days. Naturally, the world's greatest weather martyrs cursed every twitch of the thermometer, but compared to the New England winters we'd known, the season was easy street.

There were many fresh articles to write while I plotted and schemed to launch my Irish magazine, and Jamie was beginning to turn the corner too. Ultimately she found her way through to yea-sayers to her talents that should have been obvious all along. Suddenly, she was tending burgeoning projects with the Cork Opera House, the main performing-arts theater in Ireland's southwest, and the Crawford Municipal Gallery of Art, and thereby meeting a dozen new people every day. Our purgatory of non-existence seemed to be ended, the six-month probation period complete. Jamie's enthusiasm fed my own, and the horizon spelled opportunity.

If Ireland no longer lived up to its nostalgic time-worn billings, there was at least a positive side to it. Cork, county of 430,000, urban center of 220,000, was bursting with new enterprises, unsung artistic pursuits, and heady schemes for the future. Promise scented the air. Spanish urban planners had been enlisted to make over the city center, with new pedestrian thoroughfares and public spaces, even as a massive drainage scheme began to alleviate the River Lee's nose-holding foulness. Developers rubbed their hands and whispered over tables at the projected doubling of the airport's size and the prospect of recasting derelict dockyards into a new world of waterfront cafés and boutiques.

Constantly, in that capital of our transplanted lives, too, I met beacons of a changing Irish world: an air-conditioning contractor (*air-conditioning in Ireland?*) who signed up £100,000 in new glass-sheathed corporate park assignments in one day; a thirty-three-year-old who had bought his third glamorously remodeled super-pub; a fellow with a garage fish-smoking operation now supplying delectable wild salmon and mackerel to New York; people who flew back and forth to London as if they were commuting down the road.

The Cork that captured my attention was a small and irrepressible city fueled by grandiose visions, a little engine that could. The entire county clearly danced to a resurgent tune, bent on erasing the ancestral defeatism of the Famine-obsessed poor-mouthers and begrudgers of the past – and the imagery of quaint backwardness milked forever by the Irish tourist board. A Clonakilty spa was busy enticing Irish matrons to toss off their inhibitions and lie naked for £300 seaweed baths and peculiar prone showers while an *Englishman* kneads them into contented pliancy. In the old days, such a Brit would have been shot for his naughty caprice. But flashy indoor tennis, squash, and swimming palaces were cropping up right and left, and California dreams of walloping squash balls and splashing into pools were imprinted on the population's freshly minted credit cards. A car wash used to be something God bequeathed upon Ireland with a downpour, but they too had become ubiquitous, typically part of gas station complexes selling throwaway nappies, gourmet coffees, and everything a family could need for a week.

"We're in danger of becoming the fifty-second state," warned a local character, without quite putting his finger on the fifty-first.

Whether the tourist approves or disapproves, ould Ireland is all but gone. Take any recent British or American innovation, repackage it for the island of heady notions, and one might make money. The country in fact seemed to offer one of the most entrepreneurial environments I'd ever seen.

Troubling issues, however, came with the territory. Were fattening wallets killing the nation's identity? Rising mountains of waste, choking traffic jams, and unchecked development were obviously taking their toll. In its zeal for progress at all costs, the government was pushing a $6 billion master plan for building thousands of miles of new motorways that would bisect six thousand farms, while, near to home, wreaking havoc on the beautiful valley of the River Lee.

Lawlessness had also become rampant with the nightly incidence of violent assaults, often upon innocent pedestrians, having risen exponentially, while rape and armed robbery, almost unheard of in Ireland's dirt-poor past, exploded in kind. The flood of dark-skinned "asylum seekers" from impoverished lands too often encountered ugly confrontations with the downtrodden rungs of the social scale. The threads of change lay in unraveled skeins on all sides.

As far as I could see, the local newspaper was but scraping the surface of these profound transformations. So here came one peculiar transplant's notion: launch a provocative, color monthly magazine celebrating Cork's renaissance, while probing the vast nether regions of all that Ireland conveniently ignored. Didn't nearly 450 regional magazines thrive in America, mother lode of new business ideas?

"Go for it," most said. "Munster, the entire southwest of Ireland, is crying for a new vision."

The only problem was raising, oh, about half a million quid.

The kids quickly noted the change in their parents' spirits. "If you start this magazine, Dad, won't we have to stay here for years and years?" the ever-penetrating Laura asked as she idly dipped a finger in a sugar bowl one night. There was mascara under her blue eyes, silver polish on her nails, and she looked half a head taller and disconcertingly more mature than when we boarded the plane back in August. "It's obvious that you are all geared up."

"I like Ireland, but America is way, way, double hundred times better," protested Owen. Only days before, this innocent tadpole had dispatched a postcard to his beloved friend Myles, his soul twin, saying, "I am far away, but you will always be the friend I love."

Harris sometimes looked dazed. His fellow urchins incessantly blasted the doorbell and seemed to swing out of the trees to join in with his life, but the boy had by now been subjected to his fourth change of teacher, the latest seeming to be far more decent than her predecessors. His beloved reptiles, his favorite sports, his formerly intimate world, his security, all had been taken away from him by the people he should have been able to trust. Rugby, the only competitive sport Christian Brothers offered, felt to him like an ass-backward knock into the mud. And so he retreated into a hermetic, fantastical world of enemy-zapping electronic games, with a boy's dreams filled in by grunting Esperanto-speaking shades.

"We really need to create more special experiences for the kids," Jamie said one night, and she was right. I worried that this Irish adventure had become top heavy with our own concerns.

The next evening we all went to the "panto" which is a slap-stick holiday season theater experience traditional across Ireland and the U.K., if largely unknown elsewhere. This particular pantomime was a *Cinderella* extravaganza involving a mugging/dancing/singing cast of two hundred, with a couple of dozen of these comprised by a chorus line of three- to six-year-old girls in sequined blue dresses. In true panto tradition, the ugly sisters offered many a bawdy double entendre for older listeners, and audience participation was mandatory. "OH, NO I WON'T!" an ugly sister loudly declaimed about some grubby chore she, rather than Cinderella, was meant to execute. "OH, YES YOU WILL!" five hundred children bellowed back on cue, in a hallowed panto interchange. Great stuff, as the Irish say.

"Things are going so well. Shouldn't we all stay in Ireland for a long time?" I probed while tucking the kids into bed.

"OH, NO WE WON'T!" they roared back.

Chapter 17

I discussed the Great Irish Magazine Idea with anyone who would listen. And behold, Ireland's tricky turnstiles began to unjam. Despite scant prior experience, Jamie set to successfully raising funds for a major Picasso exhibit for the erudite director of the Crawford Gallery, and he became interested in my quest as well. Quickly, the erudite Peter Murray pointed the way to a rich cast of local designers, photographers, and writers, along with the astonishing number of Cork-born multimillionaires abroad who might contribute to a publication about their home soil.

A hot Dublin investment firm referred influential local consultants, whom I hired to help beat venture capital out of the bushes. Suddenly, Ireland seemed like a place where movers and shakers could be more easily approached than anywhere I had ever been, once one was armed with a master thread.

So I called on an ambitious twenty-seven-year-old named Trevor White, who was at that moment launching a glossy monthly called the *Dubliner*. In cluttered upstairs digs there, I found the young publisher disconsolately staring at stacks of invoices on his desk. Ghostly pale, perhaps from reading his pile of bills, and boyishly handsome, he had the alabaster mien of Oscar Wilde's Dorian Gray at the precise point when the first cracks began to spread across his until then untroubled features.

"I'm not sure you want to be getting into this," he warned. "But go on and tell me what you're thinking."

The scheme was laid out in punishing detail. Trevor's head slumped over his desk as I spoke.

"I don't know if you realize how hard this will be," the young publisher offered, aging even as he spoke. "Ireland can be an unbelievably stingy and closed shop, especially when it comes to advertising. You better be fearless."

"Are you saying 'Don't do it?'"

"No, you're the man. Just learn something from what has happened to me. Cork is overdue for your idea and I think you're the person who's going to make it happen."

I chose to be heartened, and became more so upon discovering an omen above the departure platform at the cavernous railway depot of Heuston Station – a huge billboard promoting another new regional magazine called *Galway Now*.

Imagining that nuggets of information lay waiting everywhere, I called to the Hi-B the next rain-soaked night. Owen was holding court, talking about some "fierce" or "massive" thing. A charming property agent named Hugh McPhillips – a potential advertiser for my magazine? – appeared, fresh from rally racing his expensive sports car through death-defying terrain to the north. The water shedding off his clothing, and pooling at his feet, suggested he should have been nosing a hydrofoil up the River Lee.

"It's a full-moon tide and the river is windblown and coming up fast. I'd get out of here if I were you, boy – that is, if you want to make it home tonight, because the streets are already sloshing," said Hugh.

Ridiculous, I thought while descending to the hideous basement men's room, where I found my feet engulfed by a half-inch film of rapidly rising water.

The Lo-B.

I lingered a while longer, partly because a scrawny, fortyish man from the North had started talking passionately about the troubles there. I related a story about hitchhiking with my German girl-friend through Derry in July 1974. She and I confronted British armored vehicles and buses dripping broken glass, the occupants of the latter banging drums and bawling military ballads. It was a classic aftermath of the annual Orange Day parades, when hoards of jeering, jingoistic Protestants bluster through "Taig" strongholds to proclaim that they, the descendants of William of Orange, vanquisher of the 1690 Catholic uprising at the Battle of the Boyne, still rule the North.

In the seething border town of Strabane, I had ventured into a pub to buy cigarettes. The bartender grabbed his telephone, figuring me and the affected beret of my youth to bear all the hallmarks of a dodgy unknown. I hurriedly made my purchase and left. The next afternoon, a masked gunman raked the local mayor and chief of police with a murderous fusillade in the same loo where I had stopped for a piss.

In the Hi-B, the Tyrone man listened closely, his eyes squinting beady and hard. He leaned forward, his breath stinking. "What if I told you my cousin did that?"

"That would be shocking," I said, feeling unnerved.

"What if I told you he didn't, and I was just winding you up, for fuck's sake?" the visitor said with a coiled menace that suggested the first question might have been nearer to the truth.

I studied his sallow face closely and said nothing.

"I'm just playing with you now, so forget you ever heard this carry on, and go back to the States or wherever the feck you come from," he said, draining his whiskey and departing abruptly. A circle of coldness remained where he had just stood, as is often the case when a certain type of Northern man makes his presence felt in Cork. By now, I had met several locals who claimed to be active in the IRA, but they were, as far as I knew, pretenders. In all save the roughest social strata, such sympathies are often worn as nothing more than a rhetorical badge. Tough young males with a Northern accent are generally given a wide berth in Cork, so weary are citizens of the Republic of the hard carriage and explosive anger that is bred by a lifetime's exposure to daily menace up north, where Protestant pipe bombs are still thrown into Catholic kitchens with a sickening frequency, while the IRA keeps shooting out the knees of whoever crosses their thuggery.

The waters on Oliver Plunkett Street were assuredly rising. But there is no stopping Owen when he gets discoursing, especially after learning about the conversation I had weathered.

"Your man was talking shite. Aye, you simply never – *never*, do you understand? – pass on even the suggestion of some secret knowledge like that. Not a whisper – do you hear me? – if you're from the North and you value your family's safety," Owen, who was brought up in Donegal town, six miles from the Derry border, said with more than his usual vehemence.

"I've seen those parades. I know them frightfully well," he said of the 2800 sectarian marches that take place in Northern Ireland every summer, three-quarters of them loyalist tantrums meant to exercise the ever-growing Catholic minority into a fresh crossfire of primitive violence. "They make bad blood boil from one end to the other of the Six Counties. But c'mere, when I was growing up in Donegal, there were such fine, welcoming feelings between Protestants and Catholics, we'd even march in each other's parades to show respect for our neighbors' traditions. But if you drove for twenty minutes, the world became sheer ugliness. Every family knew someone who had been maimed or killed across the border."

"Jesus Christ," interrupted Hugh, glancing out at the floodwaters below, at least a foot deep now. "They'll be coming down the street in canoes before you know it."

"We might as well wait for the ebb tide," winked Owen. Brian O'Donnell soon offered his usual command for everyone to get lost, regardless of the prevailing meteorological conditions. "Drink up now. Last call!"

The regulars pretended to be hard of hearing. In Irish public houses, everyone knows that the first plea to depart is soon followed by a clock-stopping period officially designated as "drinking-up time." Stalwarts linger through this period to probe for possible openings into a more uncharted dimension known as "after-hours."

"He's looking like Oisín tonight," whispered Hugh. He was referring to the voyager through a magical Irish reality known as Tir na nÓg, where time altogether ceases. The legendary pre-Christian Oisín was led there on a white fairy horse and told, if he should wander, to never, ever, get off his supernatural steed. Oisín spent three centuries in Tir na nÓg, never aging one minute, while cavorting with the comely maiden who brought him there. But being Irish, Oisín eventually set out for a bit of roving. Naturally, upon reaching his home province, he climbed off his high horse, and thereupon set to aging hideously, his face instantly transformed into that of the 320-year-old man he in fact was.

On this mad night, Brian O'Donnell wore his Oisín look avidly, perhaps because his eyes were making merry upon a maiden fair. So it was that certain denizens hunkered low and rode off on our personal white steeds, which happened to have four legs made of wood. Oisín O'Donnell worked his imaginary baton over the Wagner crescendos that emanated from Tir na nÓg's trackless regions. Time was other people's problem, life eternal.

At some point, Oisín tired. He shut off his arias and the transformation that ensued was gruesome to behold. In seconds, the proprietor's face easily took on the weight of three centuries. Into streets still ankle deep were the assembled human wrecks banished, wetting their trouser cuffs as they proceeded. Pitiful was the departure to behold.

Was the wife happy upon confronting the hideously aged figure who returned to her side?

Guess.

The next morning, Jamie climbed into the saddle with me for a journey to County Kerry to visit Noelle Campbell-Sharp, erstwhile doyenne of the Irish print media, and another potential helper for my magazine scheme. Various gut-wrenching turns through the mountains finally brought us down a near cattle track to the coast and the tourist coach-pounded Ring of Kerry road with a turn soon looping toward Ballinskelligs. This continued to a magnificent headland north of Waterville, still so unblighted by holiday-home horrors that the area serves as a prime playground for some of the most influential people in Ireland, among them our hostess and her friends.

Noelle's art gallery was the rendezvous. A circular, thatched-roof stone affair, it looked like a deluxe bungalow in a game resort I once visited in South Africa. But its whitewashed interior walls displayed an array of finely executed landscape paintings and quirky sculptures, which piqued my curiosity.

Now in her late fifties, Noelle Campbell-Sharp had thrived as a shrewd marketing maven in Dublin, and then became a Bentley-driving publisher of a long list of magazines aimed at capitalizing on the Irish public's craving for glossy images befitting a modern "fifty-second state." In a radio interview she'd once summed up her editorial vision as "Let them eat strawberries." Her most successful publication was *Irish Tatler*, an offspring of the English flagship of gossip that had made her a handsome profit when she'd sold it off a decade or so before.

Hardly glamorous, she was in full Kerry mode upon arriving, a windbreaker yanked over her shoulders and her blond hair straggling around a broad face showing no trace of makeup. We sipped tea at the far end of her gallery beside an enormous hearth, smoldering with fragrant brown clumps of proper, hand-dug turf.

One could hardly imagine her being best friends with the Irish gossip columnist queen Terry Keane, who was rumoured to have spent twenty-seven years consorting with Charlie Haughey, the notorious former prime minister (*Taoiseach*). It is said that he used to whisk her off for weekends in Paris or the various country houses of his discreetly guffawing Hibernian friends. This was of course the same "Champagne Charlie" who is also alleged to have attempted to smuggle guns for the IRA and squelched every 1980s attempt at ending Ireland's proscriptions upon contraception and divorce, while lecturing the Republic about the sanctity of family values and churchly ways. At this moment, magisterial Charlie was now holed up on his Kerry island estate not twenty miles from where we sat, forever hounded by the press and the tribunals investigating the corruption that had so deeply infested the Irish politics of his era.

Our hostess, who has sipped from many a fluted glass with Ireland's ruling class, clearly had her own knack for working the strings of leverage. About ninety seconds were allotted for my description of the would-be Cork magazine. "Magazine publishing is a brutal business," she allowed. "I know what I'm talking about because I dragged eleven of them into success when everyone said no woman could do such a thing. What we are doing here in Ballinskelligs is not easy either, but if you have enough vision and energy and the goal is right, anything is possible. That is how we're proceeding because our projects here have the potential to revive this entire part of Kerry."

A young English woman offered us tea. I knew that Noelle had recently created an artists' retreat nearby called Cill Rialaig, along with some eccentric creation dubbed the Ballroom of Imagination and Desire. Alas, a squall of Kerry talk made it impossible to get a question in edgewise.

"More than a hundred artists and writers from around the world now come every year to live in our retreat and soak up inspiration from these mountains and seas. We ask for nothing in return, but some give us paintings because what they experience here is life-changing. We are also trying to create the most important public art museum outside Dublin, which could be a tourist magnet for this entire region. But does the Arts Council bother to even come and visit? Look, here's their latest letter. I regret, blah, blah. Funding limitations, blah, blah. Can you believe this? If they just came to Cill Rialaig they would understand the meaning of renaissance. Shouldn't anyone in the arts comprehend the meaning of renaissance? Once you stand by the cliffs there and soak it all up, you will see. Margaret Atwood will be here this summer."

Whoa, girl. Noelle barely left breathing space between her words, with not a one said about the launching of a certain Cork magazine, the well-advertised reason for our tortuous three-hour drive. One couldn't help thinking of the words famously uttered by New York City's garrulous former mayor, Ed Koch: "So enough about me already. Let's talk about you. What do you think of me?"

We climbed into her golden Mercedes and sliced through the village and onto the winding lane that led to her artists' retreat on the headland. "Look there," she blurted as we passed a driveway crowned by five ten-foot-high standing stones. "John O'Connor lives down that drive, the man who created the magnificent golf course on the Old Head of Kinsale. He's on our board of directors. Have you met him?"

Gulp. "Name rings a bell somehow."

"They say he put up one of those stones for each of his former mistresses and wives. I think for a while he was scouting me as the sixth, but I said, 'John, you are not going to turn me into another one of your megaliths!'"

Drive on, coachman, drive on. The road narrowed into a single lane, with the eroded left side hugging cliffs that sank in a free-fall two or three hundred feet down into the crashing Atlantic. I frantically clung to the door handle, then jammed my feet onto imaginary passenger-side brakes. All the while, Noelle blithely barreled into blind hairpin turns, talking nonstop, even though it would spell certain death if so much as a sheep materialized from the opposite direction.

Finally she stopped.

"You look a little green," said Jamie as we climbed onto the gravel lane, the wind whistling off the ocean and burnishing the sinewy pastures and rocks of the magnificently desolate headland named, peculiarly, Bolus.

"Never felt better," I gasped. This was partially true, because the incandescent afternoon sun threw a silver fire on the sprawling bay with its surrounding mountains, gleaming strands, and far headlands all exhaling vapors of mist. Whorls of the stuff breathed around the bony pair of islands called Scariff and Deenish; and miles out, the hulking Skellig rock, home to other-worldly monks for centuries, soared up like a hallucination. The most accomplished painter would despair of ever doing justice to such grandeur.

A single whitewashed cottage, possibly still beyond the reach of electricity, nosed up from a sheep-clotted hollow. It in itself was art, a portrait of life at its most elemental, listing in harmony with the landscape. A stringy old man appeared at its door and waved with the unhurriedness of someone tied to this place for untold generations and who likely had never wandered more than ten miles in his life. Ruined hovels lay a bit closer, the kind of dark, dirt-floored two-room dwellings where the fellow's ancestors would have shivered through the ages past. Noelle called hello to the farmer, with whom she was doing a Kerry dance about her flirting desire to purchase these last remnants to complete the resurrection of the nearby Famine-era village.

"A lovely man," she said. "But he's a cute one when it comes to selling the patch."

We walked back to her artists' retreat, a succession of five sensitively restored stone cottages at the edge of creation, all discreetly warmed by simple modern conveniences and bright skylights over airy studio spaces. They were stone heaps before Noelle shouldered into the place, one pile having been home to Séan Dhónail Mhuiris Ó Conail, an illiterate nineteenth-century fisherman, farmer, and famous *seanachi*, or traditional Gaelic-speaking storyteller, who spellbound listeners with his stories from a clockless world that effortlessly preserved tales passed through the centuries. One of this father-of-ten's gems was translated and written down thus:

> Three brothers they were who went to sea in a ship. They spent a long time at sea without meeting land, and they feared they would not meet any, but finally came to an island which was wooded to the shore. They tied their ship to a tree, and they went inland. They saw no one and met no one. They set to work then, and at the end of seven years one of them said:
>
> 'I hear the lowing of a cow!'
>
> No one answered that speech.
>
> Seven more years passed. The second man spoke then, and said:
>
> 'Where?'
>
> It went on like that for another seven years.
>
> 'If you don't keep quiet,' said the third man, 'we will be put out of this place.'

Improbably, another celebrated *seanachi* named Pats Ó Conaill inhabited the same settlement until the 1920s, his stories also magical. Undoubtedly not yet familiar with either fabulist, a freshly arrived, willowy German artist with mesmerizing green eyes invited us to her temporary new residence.

"It is out of dis vorld," she sighed. "But my easel posting is the screwed up. It has not been here."

"Just ease into things, everything in Ballinskelligs comes in its own time," Noelle said, breezing past. After noting the neatly modern appointments in the kitchen, she led us up to the loft bedroom with its stunning vistas. One could not dispute that this charismatic woman had indeed brought replenishing life to an ancient world, so very like the one I had sampled in Dingle with Bun, only just across the waves from where we now stood.

Noelle's ten-times larger stone house lay a couple of miles back toward the village. Commanding sweeping views of the same dreamscape, it boasted a fifteen-foot-tall, nineteenth-century anchor resting against its front wall. The sunken foundations of some ancient dwelling on the lawn provided the setting for summer garden parties. Inside, she'd kitted out her own homey pub at the eastern end of the house. Every room was fraught with quirks, including narrow winding stone stairs suggesting passages to castle keeps. Fine paintings and sculptures nested everywhere in the front reception rooms, with graceful statues fingering towards grand portraits. A cavernous rear banquet hall boasted an enormous oaken table designed to weather heaping platters and goblets for twenty revelers at a time. Bronze candelabra hung from the cathedral-like ceiling, one end of the mead hall featuring a galley kitchen reached by an iron spiral staircase. The walls, with sconces for more candles, were done up in terracotta embossed with runic whorls and ancient Celtic gods and goddesses in relief. The scene was fit for Irish chieftains, and Noelle naturally could not resist commissioning a mural featuring herself languishing on a throne, merry-faced in medieval robes and surrounded by similarly costumed friends, among them a beaming Terry Keane, stage left.

Noelle's house is the kind of place wherein one can imagine secret chambers behind bookcases, and intrigues playing out in the wee hours of the night. Our hostess made a point of showing us a distant guest bedroom whose door and walls were done in the kind of kaleidoscopic flourishes that ennoble classic gypsy caravans, and, sure enough, she had commissioned a nearby "traveler" to let his imagination run wild in this boudoir. Marvelous old circus artifacts and creepy masks sprung up in every corner.

We retreated to her home's pub, which altogether redefined the notion of a "local." While Noelle fetched a bottle of sherry from behind the mahogany bar, I eyed a collection of photographs that showed her in the full exuberance of youth, beside sleek sports cars and arm-in-arm with swell friends.

Meanwhile, she rattled on, mostly about her visions for the blossoming of the Kerry art scene. It became clear that the true purpose of our visit had been kept secret until now – it was to promote *her* quest and not mine.

"I don't mean to interrupt," I finally interrupted as the shadows began to darken in her quaint pub. "But we have to get back to our children soon because it's a long drive, and I was wondering what prospects you see in my magazine idea."

"Drive back to Cork? But that's crazy. You must spend the night here," she pronounced, looking slightly crestfallen as if the discussion of our project had been reserved as a highlight for the evening's dinner party.

"That's very kind," I said, wavering slightly. "But we have no babysitter lined up and really must go shortly. So I just thought I'd ask about the magazine."

"Oh yes, your magazine. Unfortunately, it's been several years since I've had anything to do with publishing. I've left that world behind," Noelle started hesitantly. Suddenly, an invisible gear turned. "I told you that Irish publishing is a murderous business. You wanted to deal with Cork, right? I have great time for Cork. You said something about having done up a proper business plan. Good. On the other hand, you might as well forget everything in your plan. Success isn't about plans. It's about one's force of will. But the local Cork market is teensy, maybe three thousand subscribers if you're lucky. The thing everybody starting a magazine forgets is that the editorial content is almost irrelevant. It's about advertising, advertising, advertising. You have to hire someone who can sell advertising in their sleep."

"That sounds good, but I was wondering . . ."

In full guru mode now, Noelle brooked no interruption. "You might have to give this person a stake in ownership, say 5 percent. No more than 10, certainly. Go for the national players, the ones with deep pockets and cachet – Guinness, Irish Distillers, Aer Lingus, maybe luxury car manufacturers, Waterford Crystal . . ."

High in the dusky sky outside, one could see a sliver of emerging moon. It would soon get interesting on those hairpin mountain turns, especially if we were subjected to nocturnal versions of Kerry's flying goats.

And the message was by now clear. Advertising – and more advertising. Fair enough, for this woman clearly spoke from experience, and her enormous vitality spoke for itself. "It's been splendid, but I'm afraid we really must . . ."

"That's mad," the lady of the House of Imagination and Desire insisted.

The sherry was refreshed. "John O'Connor will be joining me for dinner. I'm sure he would love to meet you both," Noelle pressed on. "He might even advertise in your magazine."

Feet shifted, eyes darted, embarrassed thoughts swam like fish seeking cover under rocks. There was no place left to hide. "Well, I've met him already, actually, and once was enough."

I said that we really must go and nudged Jamie out the door, imagining errant golf balls falling like apocalyptic hail onto the bonnet of our fleeing station wagon.

Chapter 18

The great thing about dreaming up a regional magazine is that it creates excuses for explorations without end. Cork is the largest county in Ireland, running about 110 by 60 miles at its longest and widest reaches, though about as regular in dimensions as a cloud. It has arthritic long fingers of stone probing the wild Atlantic to the west, knobby formations poking toward Kerry and Tipperary's mountains to the north, while to the south scalloped bays and craggy promontories undulate and switch directions and moods in a slow sojourn east toward County Waterford. In short, the place is such an improbable land mass that a precisely drawn map of it looks like the work of a drunk.

West Cork alone offers a nearly inexhaustible feast for the traveler: out of sight lie hollows where potato whiskey (*poteen* – the little pot) is made; high lakes and primal Gaelic-speaking mountains; tractor-shaved farm valleys; fishing villages; holiday havens; biker paradises; hippie colonies; curious offshore islands (one of them reachable only by cable car). All of these, and more, polka dot the endlessly fascinating region. Being fairly thorough in our weekend tours of our new land, we'd about covered two-thirds of West Cork by now. But Mid-Cork, with its market town of Macroom, which is populated by Macrumpians, and its tiny overlooked encampments with names like Drohideenaclochduff and Inchigeelagh, beckoned, precisely because they were off the tourist charts.

A typical January Saturday or Sunday ran as follows: "C'mon boys, it's time to hit the road."

"Where are we going this time? Why don't we just stay here? Can Connor come? Scott? Feidhlim? No? Well, I want to stay here and play. Why not? I'm not going!"

"But Mommy's packed lunch."

Hands on her head, Laura, a finalist at this point in the slowest-dresser-in-Ireland competition, would stare in disbelief as I loaded the car with fishing gear, bicycles, baseball mitts, skateboards, cameras, slickers, Wellington boots, and why not a sketch pad. "Laura! Would you grab the binoculars please?"

"Aren't you forgetting the pole vaults and trampoline?" Jamie would ask.

So off we sallied for a while to the megaliths, woodland walks, and backwaters of Mid Cork, until the family had its fill there.

After a week's pause, there dawned a troubling realization that our little ingrates knew nothing about North Cork. This seemed unforgivable, because here waited another exploration, and perhaps even a cover story for the new *Cork Magazine*.

So we set our sights on a region that boasts the gorgeous River Blackwater, running through a valley of verdure and great houses, and attracts aristocrats the world over to this day, with British toffs champions of the social set.

At the ungodly hour of noon, our daughter rubbed sleep from her eyes. "North Cork? Why?"

Hadn't I stayed overnight, Laura, with foxhunting Anglo-Irish holdovers on a sprawling estate outside Mallow, still measuring about eight thousand acres? Hadn't I helped them muck out their stables, because we shared a dear mutual friend? Hadn't I savored fine whiskey at their kitchen table afterward?

"Why didn't you ever mention this before, Dad? Why don't you ever talk about some of the fabulous people you have met?" asked Laura, finally grasping the depths of her father's Irish connections.

Cough. "Because they charged me for that drink."

"You're a regular lord of the manor," said Laura.

Winding through the back roads outside Kanturk about an hour later, I slowed before an ivy-entangled plaque asserting that seven thousand Irishmen had died in the next field during the mother of all battles in the Williamite wars. A quick check with the mental calculator confirmed that this amounted to more fatalities than were suffered in about every other battle in Irish history combined, even including the exploits of that most supreme warrior,

Cuchulainn, hound of Ulster, who could lop off as many heads as the day is long, park his chariot, down a quaff of mead, and disembowel a few captives while he blathered around the campfire to a circle of obsequious bards.

Harris, lifting his eyes from the dementia of some electronic game, suddenly got picky.

"Wait. We just learned in school about the battle of Kilmichael. My teacher said maybe twenty-one British soldiers died there, but that this was the most important battle in the history of Ireland."

"Right."

"But that doesn't make sense," the ten-year-old said, peering at stupefying rows of cabbage without so much as a commemorative spear sticking up between their green heads.

"Well, nobody in the entire world understands the Williamite wars, and the good and bad guys are impossible to sort out, so I guess they're easy to forget."

The sun meandered higher for another week and at last we arrived at Firbolg, which is (very) nominally regarded as the beginning of spring in Ireland, although it is but the first day of February.

"Where are we going now?" whined Laura, as I began ferrying the Wellies, cameras, binoculars, and the rest toward the miserably claustrophobic car.

"East Cork," I muttered with a "don't defy me" look back over my shoulder.

And, of course, the entire family snickered.

"Dad, you've got to stop trying to provide for our every second over here," said Laura.

For a man with a hurling stick, remote-controlled toy car, and skateboard under one arm, an eight-foot salmon net under the other, and a map in his mouth, this little chorus of know-it-alls took the biscuit.

At least the scoundrels climbed into their appointed seats without protest, and toned down their ridicule as the Opel, the "estate" car, for the Lord's sake, coughed onto the open road. The first stop was Midleton, a bustling market town with decent restaurants, a splendid farmer's market, and some very oddly named enterprises.

The sign over Wallis' Bar, for example, said "Auctioneers, Valuers, Monumental Sculptors, Undertakers," while at the other end of the decorous main street there was Hyde's ("Funeral Services, Children's Ware"). In Midleton, they can take your money coming and going. But then again, in Fermoy, a half-hour's drive north, one can comparison shop at Jackie O'Brien's ("Lounge Bar, Undertakers") and idle away one's final hours after a last supper at the local ersatz McDonald's – Supermacs – whose sign says "100 percent Gaelic" and "*mainstir fhear mai*" (perhaps meaning "special sauce"). "Are you okay?" the clerks in these places may ask waiting customers in the customary Cork way. "Yes, thanks, I'm dead."

Midleton, as Laura well knew, boasts another venerable Protestant secondary school, an arch rival of Bandon Grammar. The chief building there proved to be a three-story affair shored up with enough finely cut stone to fit out a castle for a British earl, though the satellite buildings are a mishmash of thrown-together cubby holes and bright new classrooms. The gentry not enjoying the same clout they once did, the place also holds forlorn, cramped dormitories that Irish kids nonetheless accept more or less cheerfully.

On the other hand, Midleton College happens to boast the only outdoor school swimming pool in Cork and expansive green playing fields dotted with interesting sculptures. These are dwarfed into inconsequence by a ring of nearby exhaust towers wafting peculiarly attention-getting fumes over the tranquil campus. Their job, I explained to the boys, is to vent the by-products of pastoral Erin's most potent industry – distilling whiskey. Gargantuan aluminum tanks holding that stuff – Paddy's, Power's, Jameson's, even Cork Gin (all owned now by the French Pernod Ricard conglomerate) – loom over the campus like a brace of Apollo moon rockets. Irish tourist brochures tout other awe-inspiring sights like the Cliffs of Moher and Giant's Causeway, but not one of those inspires the imagination like the eighty-proof firepower arrayed beside Midleton College's Jameson Hall of Science. "What did you study in chemistry class today, Finbarr?" asks a local father. Young eyes roll dreamily. "Cripes, dad, how could I remember, yerrah?"

Flann O'Brien had further thoughts on this subject, suggesting that his newspaper columns be printed in a special alcoholic ink, to be called Trink, in order to mesmerize the wandering populace into more attentive reading.

Drive five miles in any direction in East Cork and one encounters shocking contrasts between the garishness of modernity and the timelessness of the past. The imagination can barely square the scenes the English writer William Cobbett described two hundred years ago:

> I went to a hamlet near to the town of Midleton. It contained about 40 or 50 hovels . . . They all consisted of mud walls, with a covering of rafters and straw. None of them so good as the place where you keep your little horse . . . The floor, the bare ground. No fire-place, no chimney, the fire (made of Potato haulm) made on one side against the wall, and the smoke going out a hole in the roof. No table, no chair . . . There was a mud wall about 4 feet high to separate off the end of the shed for the family to sleep, lest the hog should kill and eat the little children when the father and mother were both out, and when the hog was shut in. No bed: no mattress; some large flat stones laid on other stones, to keep the bodies from the damp ground; some dirty straw and a bundle of rags were all the bedding . . . There is a nasty dunghill (no privy) to each hovel. The dung that the hog makes *in the hovel* is carefully put into a heap by itself, as being the most precious. This dung and the pig are the main thing to raise the rent [for absentee English landlords] and get fuel with. The poor creatures sometimes keep the dung in the hovel, when their hard-hearted tyrants will not suffer to let it be at the door!

Just a couple of miles south of Midleton now lies one of the ghastly modern housing developments springing up across Ireland with the vengeance of mushrooms after an autumn rain. Invariably, they are called something like Celtic Woods, though a prospective resident would have to execute one of Cuchulainn's gravity-defying salmon leaps to land in the nearest copse. Every dwelling is inevitably an identical stucco and polyvinyl-chloride affair with a prissy front sitting room, a television-dominated entertainment room, and a mod-con happy kitchen in the back. Under the eaves will run the inevitable plastic dipsy-doodle molding, the notion being to add an infantile Hansel and Gretel touch of "character," often reinforced by a few would-be Tudor boards and gaudy stained-glass Dutch tulips flowering in the front door. The tiny lawn in front of the tenth-of-an-acre lot – soon to be enchanted with insidious prefab leprechauns – will undoubtedly be dressed with a mean concrete wall, and capped by a pair of four-foot columns fronting a tiled drive, with this touch meant to suggest a great house of grandeur. The cost: a quarter of a million pounds, or about enough to buy an eighteenth-century château surrounded by olive groves in the south of France.

Prospective purchasers will not utter a word of complaint about this crass homogenization. Somehow, the mod-con Irish are strangely inured to their physical surroundings, perhaps due to a collective memory of the deprivations described by Cobbett and of the eighteenth-century days when Catholics weren't allowed to buy property at all, and owned only 5 percent of their native land, while paying 98.5 percent of the country's rents.

How a people with such visionary powers could be so architecturally blind nonetheless remains one of Ireland's abiding mysteries. Despite being rooted in one of the most beautiful landscapes on earth, the Irish do not fret much about blighting jaw-dropping panoramas with phoney, slapped-together haciendas. Of course, until recently people didn't have the money to worry much about the niceties of aesthetics, and the Irish government perniciously proffers substantial tax deductions to anyone who invests in a horrid concrete-block rental scheme by the sea.

An architect friend put it this way: "This country creates some of the most ungodly building horrors on earth, and the only way I can explain it is that people were so poor and oppressed for so long that they put all their imagination into other things – like ballads, hurling, and horse racing – because a good house was the one thing they knew could never be theirs. Yes, we as a people therefore remain architecturally blind."

One bitter anomaly amidst the gaudy new developments is that haunting reminders of the past will inevitably lie in the next field – because in Ireland ancient mysteries lurk everywhere. So some abomination of a faux-Mediterranean bungalow will sprout beside a four-thousand-year-old circle of standing stones. Outside Clonakilty, a come-hither hotel advertisement lists against the edge of one such mystic circle. Another unspeakably ugly development has been flung together beside one of the thousands of "mass rocks" that epitomized the oppression of yore. These were crude fieldstone altars from which priests offered the Eucharist to secret assemblies after the English, during the Penal Law period in the seventeenth and eighteenth centuries, bolted Papist churches shut, banned the speaking of Irish, and forbade natives from owning horses worth more than five pounds.

Incongruity is forever Ireland's magic card. Only minutes down the road from the gleaming Celtic Woods slumbers the village of Cloyne, seemingly eternally gloaming in the mist and haunted by a vast underground cave with its only access through a wishing-glass hole in the gardens of the local big house. Cloyne's bungalows huddle together as if praying for warmth, and the place whispers of an earlier Ireland – closed in, with no hint of the hectic pace that has taken over the remote metropolis of, say, Midleton.

The first of its resident bishops was one St. Colman, who was persuaded to give up his pagan ways by St. Brendan the Navigator, the famous sixth-century voyager who is said to have waved good-bye as he sailed across a sea strewn with flowers. In searching for the Isles of the Happy, Brendan purportedly reached Iceland and perhaps Newfoundland, then pointed his animal-skin boat back to his happier homeland. In 1976, the explorer Tim Severin successfully reenacted the Newfoundland voyage from Dingle, County Kerry, in a similar craft. Not to be outdone, in 1998 a team of Rastafarian-styled dreamers from Toronto raided their local dump for salvage timbers and discarded tarpaulins and set off for Ireland in a vessel that looked like a floating squatters' camp. Transatlantic freighters circled in disbelief at the sight of this outlandish junkheap bobbing its merry way toward Cork. Ireland being a place where the make-believe can easily pass for truth, the crew announced after arriving in Cork that they would soon circumnavigate the rest of the globe in a hot-air balloon constructed out of "found" scrap objects in the surrealist tradition of Marcel Duchamp.

As Charles Smith related in 1774, East Cork's strangeness has been obvious for a long time:

> In the winter of 1695, and a good part of the following spring, there fell, in several places, of this province, a kind of thick dew, which the country people called butter, from its colour and consistence, being soft, clammy, and of a dark yellow, as doctor St. George Ash, then local bishop of Cloyne, has recorded in the Philosophical Transactions; it fell in the night, and chiefly in marshy low grounds, on the top of the grass, and on the thatch of the cabins, seldom twice in the same place; it commonly lay a fortnight without changing colour, but then dried, and turned black; cattle fed as well where it lay, as in other fields; it often fell in lumps, as big as the end of one's finger, thin and scatteringly; it had strong ill scent, somewhat like that of churchyards and graves; and there were most of the season very stinking fogs, some sediment of which the bishop thought might possibly have occasioned this stinking dew; it was not kept long, nor did it breed worms or other insects; yet the country people who had scald or sore heads, rubbed them with this substance, and said it healed them.

Smith, like most of the other exotic blood in East Cork then, came from England. Throughout the region, the planters built their stately houses with finely arched doorways, imposing stone facades, and meandering drives through manicured pastures leading to the gated entrances in their omnipresent walls. Some treated the natives under their employ with steadfast benevolence, but others, including a local branch of the Wilkinson clan, exacted brutal tithes while blithely spending most of their days in still grander residences in England. During the War of Independence, IRA Flying Columns enjoyed some pay-back time by burning many such big houses to ruination, sending their owners fleeing back to Mother England in an exodus that quickly reduced the Protestant class from 10 to 3 percent of Ireland's citizenry. This has recently been recounted with exquisite poignancy in William Trevor's *The Story of Lucy Gault.*

Many who hung on watched their estates list into rainy oblivion, with the roofs leaking, the timbers rotting, the brocaded paper peeling away from weeping walls, while the bulbs in the crystal chandeliers went dim one by one. The inexorable decline produced some of the most potted eccentrics in the world. In a Cork village called Castlefreke, one unraveling scion spent his twilight years quaffing port and pumping bullets into dining room portraits of his ancestors. Up in Westmeath, the late Adolphus Cooke became so obsessed with hot-air balloons that he had miniature versions of them attached to his dining room chairs, perhaps hoping his guests could join him for nonstop flights to St. Brendan's Isles of the Happy. Alas, this peculiar romantic became terrified of the idea that vindictive foxes were eyeballing him from the hedges. More unnerving, he believed he would be reincarnated as one of those fretful creatures – after all, his father had come back as a dog – and forsook his dreams of blithely ballooning to the ends of this earth in order to devote his remaining energies to fighting off the sly bastards who were watching his every move.

Despite such marvelously eccentric histories, the great Irish country houses eventually could be bought for a song, provided one possessed a fortune for subsequent restoration. Over the last few decades, rock idols, celebrities, financiers, and the Irish nouveau riche have been doing that with a vengeance. One tranquil East Cork inlet features a turreted mock castle that was inhabited in the 1990s by a family of German teenage pop stars called, for some reason, the Kellys. The great lawns and walled gardens used to be patrolled by Prussian security guards yelping into their walkie-talkies, but now an erstwhile Wall Street fat cat named Glucksman (meaning "lucky man!") has moved in with his Irish-American wife. The new earl has spread his philanthropy freely enough to become wined and dined by the powers that be in Dublin, and pocketed an overnight honorary doctoral degree from Trinity College there.

So, in observance of the honored tradition of what is called "the touch," this couple became my first target to back the new *Cork Magazine*. Alas, the appeal fell on deaf ears. "I don't know you, Mr. Monagan, and I am not interested in hearing your presentation," growled the keeper of the castle after one phone call. Maybe he had more Cork blood than I realized.

As it happened, we were soon treated to a far more gracious taste of East Cork "big house" living, at a place that embodies the potential of the old manors to become reintegrated into Ireland's evolving modern fabric. This transpired at Ballymaloe Country House, which has become world famous for its exquisite restaurant and gourmet cooking school looking out over peacock-infested island gardens and flowing green fields.

The lady in charge is named Darina Allen, and she is a champion of the Irish culinary renaissance now being supplied by a new artisan class of local growers, herdsmen, cheese-makers, bakers, and butchers. Meanwhile, her mandolin-playing brother-in-law, Rory, is seeking to expand the place's spirit with regular sessions of Irish traditional music. Better yet, he likes to fill the dining room with a sprinkling of guests whose sole function is to contribute laughter and talk – not a bad job assignment, I reasoned after an invitation popped up. So we sidled inside, not quite sure what entertainment we could contribute. Perhaps Jamie would have to trot out her "looking for a noodle" song.

Elizabeth Rush, an American friend with a house nearby, was the intermediary, but she proved to be Elizabeth Slow in appearing herself. No bother. All one has to do to get comfortable at any Irish table is start talking – about anything – and the interweaving circles fall into place, the conversation spreading as easily as mist. Here was a charming accordion, or "box," player who proved to be a close friend of a friend; here a pretty Australian flautist fresh from a decade in Vienna. So the talk flowed and the wine was poured. It felt like balloons were lifting every conversation and elevating our own identities into the free-floating ether that sometimes surrounds a person who has changed countries. Far from home, the relentless ordinariness of life can, on certain magic nights, be transposed into moments of endless charm, provided the right balloon power is arrayed at every neighboring chair, so that you yourself no longer feel as humdrum as you once were. So in a brief shining moment of forbearance and grace, one is allowed to recount the campaigns that got you to where you are tonight, like a dottering retired British colonel reliving his glory days with Lord Gordon in Khartoum.

Now, for some chamber music in the drawing room.

But naturally.

Let me just adjust my balloon.

Of course, this wasn't our first indulgence in the Big House fantasy. Once, Jamie and I stayed in a vast home in Sligo called Temple House, with its own lake, thirteenth-century Knights Templar castle, working farm, endless walled gardens, and rooms filled with priceless heirlooms. Ancestors of the owner, Sandy Perceval, who had been grievously afflicted with chronic fatigue syndrome by the toxic baths that are used to rid sheep of worms, had been looking after this pile since 1665.

After dinner at Temple House our host offered me a cigar, which I dumbly declined. "There are hundreds of these in the basement. In fact, the maids used to dry them in the sun so they could start fires with them when I was a boy. But they've managed to retain a decent taste," Sandy offered from the wheelchair he resorts to of an evening. A year later, the *Wall Street Journal* reported the discovery of a million dollars worth of the oldest Cuban cigars in the world in a perfect humidor of a Sligo basement in a place called ... Temple House. An infusion of desperately needed funds could now be put into bolstering the farm and renovating some of the house's crumbling derelict rooms. Fair play to that, for the grand country estates are an intrinsic part of the island's history, and the reality of gawking foreign tourists having to keep them alive is sad, when the most industrious farm operations can rarely do so.

Still, modern Ireland produces some bizarre juxtapositions of its own. Some of our other East Cork trips brought us to a spot just past Ballymaloe where Seamus Wilkinson was transforming a huge stone barn for himself and his wife, Mary, whose family had once suffered grievously in the troubles in the North. Seamus, in contrast, had it made – and why not? Every detail of the work in progress was being executed with attention to the aesthetics of the land, just as Bun Wilkinson had done on a much smaller scale at the end of the Dingle Peninsula a quarter of a century earlier. We saw grand rooms in various states of completion, and climbed half-finished stairs to look out at the orchards, duck ponds, and vegetable gardens presently being laid out in Seamus's visions. Green fields rolled off to the distant lighthouse blinking just beyond the fishing village of Ballycottton.

Yet one couldn't help look at this spread and wonder – what if the Celtic Tiger comes to a halt? What will become of the thousands of Irish families racing after a prosperity they themselves – let alone their parents – could not imagine even twenty years ago?

Seamus, who must ask himself that question often, quietly interposed, "We will walk there now beside the cliffs, and ye will see how lovely it is out here. But I want ye to know that I have not yet brought anyone else to see this place. I think that tells ye something of my feelings for ye," he said, leaving me humbled, but also scratching my head, once again.

I kept pressing on with the magazine, at one point borrowing a photograph of Brian O'Donnell beaming in strange transport from the Hi-B's bar as he stood before a crew of the usual eccentrics. A graphic designer transformed this into a mock-up of the magazine's cover and added a priceless headline: "The Maddest Man in the Whole Damn Town."

A week later, I returned to show this off, along with a more conventional alternative.

"How are you, love?" asked Esther.

"Not too bad. And yourself?"

"Fabulous," Esther said, despite looking somber. "But Brian's not been well. He says he was mugged."

"By his fecking shadow, more than likely," cackled John Burke.

"Ah stop. Maybe that was in his own head, but he's lost enough color to paint a house," Esther protested.

Soon, Brian was consigned to hospital. The official complaint was of a nosebleed that would not stop. "Well, they don't seem to ever end, like. He's had one after another for days. He calls me in the middle of the night. 'Ah Esther,' he says, 'you better come here now as I am not feeling myself.' He was needy, like. So I got him signed in. I'm telling the truth now – the man looks weak.'"

Having written a bit about medicine, I was instantly concerned. Despite his mad whims and "talent to abuse," Brian had been nothing but kind in my direction, and always interested in my family's well-being. I saw a larger soul than some of his regular customers took in, and Brian was grateful for my respect. His love of music and drawing, and impatience for dimness of all kinds, spoke of frustrated dreams for some higher calling, and his wife, occasionally glimpsed in the bar now, was a figure of startling elegance. I wanted Brian to be well, to carry on with his peculiar magic theater of a disappearing Ireland. But there was change in the air, for him and for me, and, if a person looked at all behind the scenes, for the entire country. Some kind of curtain was obviously drawing closed, perhaps on my own fantasies.

Chapter 19

One cannot know Ireland without understanding its relationship to the sea, for the ocean's moody fickleness pervades the country's soul – from the ever-changing weather to the wistfulness of the Irish people's apprehension of the present, which is never to be taken for granted. More concretely, the surrounding Atlantic has through the ages dispensed endless bounties, mellow currents, and countless freak deaths. In the last few months alone, twenty-eight commercial fishermen had been swept off into eternity; children collecting cockles, anglers casting amiably into the surf, they too had drowned; and several despairing teenagers had walked to the edge of Ireland's picture-postcard cliffs, stared into the dark water below, and jumped.

In March I landed a magazine assignment to look into the remarkable confraternity of volunteers who man Ireland's search-and-rescue lifeboats, and whose grim duty it is to pluck the imperiled, and often bloated corpses, from the unforgiving ocean. Arrangements were made to participate in a training exercise with the crew of the oldest lifeboat service in Ireland, in an out-of-the-way West Cork village called Courtmacsherry. As luck would have it, the appointed day proved gale-tossed, cold, and menacing. There was no choice but to proceed.

Trees shuddered and bent in the howling winds as I followed the winding country road from Bandon to a kind of time-warp settlement called Timoleague, which is crammed like a tourniquet at the end of a huge lagoon, spreading west toward the Old Head of Kinsale. Listing over the place and the ever-shifting waters of that mournful bay lies a crumbling eight-hundred-year-old Cistercian abbey, with every inch of its grounds stuffed with skeletons. A large portion of the gravestones that are not rain-battered beyond recognition bear the names of Hurley, O'Neill, and Deasy. My mother's Deasy ancestors, *my* ancestors, could well be lying beneath my feet, I thought, as I picked my way through the creepy ruins, wondering just how many of the dead had perished at the ocean's whims.

A pretty stone causeway turned from Timoleague to the western shore of the estuary, which was now roiled with a wicked chop. After a few miles, I reached my destination – a village with a single street filing under the lee of a pasture-strewn hill. Across the darkening bay, I could see the odd distant house looking about as significant as a sheep grazing in the dreamy blue-green distance. Sidewalk eyes met mine every hundred feet, taking measure.

Courtmacsherry has hosted a volunteer sea-rescue service since 1824, a time when every family's survival was linked more to the beneficence of the ocean than the hopelessness of the region's thin soil. Untimely death was the epitaph of many a villager here. Even just a few decades ago, shopkeepers, fishermen, and farmers would come running from nearby hovels whenever a ship foundered, and braved wicked gales with a ten-oared rowboat – because the great monster at their door, the pitiless ocean, could seize their kin or the next clan's any time it chose. All that has mostly changed, what with progress. Now, sleek as a Ferrari, a powerful modern rescue vessel bobbed just offshore, its orange superstructure and deep blue hull gleaming as it sunk and rose in the chop – this was one of the classic boats of the RNLI, or Royal National Lifeboat Institute, an all-volunteer coast guard that rings the coasts of Ireland and Great Britain.

The vessel spoke. One look and you could tell that its presence out here at the edge of creation loomed as large as the Space Shuttle at Cape Canaveral.

I parked beside the Travera Lodge, a nineteenth-century guest-house on the main street.

"You're going out in this?" asked my host, himself a Dublin landlubber newly moved to the village, yet instantly accepted in this radically transformed new Ireland. "I'd have a double brandy first, if I were you."

I instead sought a soothing pint at a waterside pub called

the Pier Inn. A few souls sat silently soaking up the gloom like shrouds pondering through the timeless shadows that are, in the end, Ireland as it was and shall be. After some long pauses, one of these revealed himself to be Alan Locke, a portly candy salesman by day but passionate lifeboat volunteer whenever trouble erupted.

"Have you eaten?" he asked solicitously, once I explained that I was joining the evening's training exercise.

"Not much."

"Going out on a night like this, it's better to have a full stomach," Alan advised.

About two minutes later, I was welcomed into his comfortable, suburban-styled house, the ample windows of which offered sweeping views of the ever-more-frothing and angry-looking bay. His wife, Liz, laid forth heaping plates of roasted potatoes, garden carrots, and gravy-sweetened pork.

Alan, now three years from the RNLI's mandatory retirement age of fifty-five, gazed wistfully upon the lifeboat, its orange superstructure casting luminous reflections upon the darkening water. "I look out there and think about my service ending and it makes my heart sag," he said quietly. "I've loved every minute of it."

Alan, who has a son volunteering on the lifeboat too, explained how, whenever an emergency call sounds on his beeper (which the Irish call "bleeper"), he runs three hundred feet down the hill from where we were sitting and jumps the neighbor's hedge to save precious seconds. He talked of harrowing recent rescues, including a dismasted French yacht that was mortally foundering in hellacious seas after being slammed by a Norwegian freighter in the predawn darkness of St. Stephen's Day, the day after the Christmas just passed.

Tonight it was not necessary to jump any hedges. Instead we walked the short distance to the stone-clad lifeboat station, the hissing wind tearing at our cheeks. I felt excitement and embarrassment as the door opened to the locker room inside and I was introduced to Dan Dwyer, the wiry, balding forty-seven-year-old first coxswain, or skipper of the crew – embarrassment because it felt like I was merely hitching a ride into Ireland's soul.

"So you want to write something about the lifeboat service, is it?" Dwyer, a primary school teacher by trade, sized me up with a witheringly intense gaze.

I gave a speech, a testimony of my interest and respect, while feeling very small, and very foreign.

"If there's a movie to come of this, I want the lead role," said the station's mechanic, Mícheál (pronounced Me-hall) Hurley, breaking the ice.

"And you'll sink that project too," rejoined a ruddy-faced fellow named Martin, one of the village's last three commercial fishermen, whose wife is also a lifeboat volunteer.

Oilskins and a life jacket were proffered, and I soon clambered with seven volunteers onto the *Frederick Storey Cockburn*, a five-year-old, £1.4 million vessel whose twin 865-horsepower engines rumbled to life with stomach-rattling potency.

And we took off. Dan Dwyer barked out commands with the same fervor I had once glimpsed among the friends of my deceased fighter pilot brother, as the vessel charged at a speed of twenty-five knots – a pace that one-third of the rescue vessels belonging to the mighty United States Coast Guard still cannot equal – through the inner harbor to the riled ocean beyond. On the flying bridge, sixteen feet above the swells that had been whipped across three thousand miles of open water, it felt like a crazed bronco ride. The innards churned and the legs buckled with every surge, but Dwyer exuded invincible confidence. It was an Irish spring evening after all, with stinging sleet flying laterally into our faces and winds now surging to forty knots and licking foam off the breakers. And it was strangely thrilling.

A wan light arced from the lighthouse at the distant craw of the Old Head of Kinsale, where this search-and-rescue team had recently helped retrieve the remains of a mangled suicide jumper. To our right lay the ghostly, sinuous shapes called the Seven Heads, where Algerian pirates, British traders, a German submarine, and countless yachts have all been swallowed – a small fraction of the nine thousand or so wrecks that have smashed into Ireland's shores.

Dwyer spoke of more recent history. Two years earlier, essentially the same crew as on board now braced thirty-five-foot swells and eighty-mile-an-hour winds in one of the more daring rescues in the annals of the lifeboat service. A young Courtmacsherry farmer named Colin Bateman, who would have been married the following week had his fiancée not suddenly died in a car crash, pulled himself together and was among the first to respond.

The volunteers soon confronted what would have been termed a hurricane elsewhere, although the Irish have too much experience with the sea to give its whims names. Plowing through the maelstrom, they neared a dismembered yacht staffed by a nearly senseless, wounded crew. The bereaved Colin clambered into a raft to deliver a lifeline so that the imperiled sailors could be winched away from imminent death.

Tonight, the nearby outcroppings offered a protective shore and we began the training exercise under their lee. A couple of volunteers were dropped overboard in an inflatable dinghy and promptly abandoned.

As the engines throttled, Dwyer gazed out toward the scene of one of the most epochal disasters in maritime history, the U-boat rending of the *Lusitania* only a half-dozen miles farther out in the now howling Atlantic Ocean. "People up and down these hills heard the explosion and came running and riding bicycles and horses to the lifeboat that was then kept just a mite back from where we are now. Fifteen men took turns pulling on the oars for three hours because the day was so calm that their sail was useless. They found nothing but a mass of floating dead bodies, because even in May the coldness of these waters will kill a person in about ninety minutes. If they had the boat we are in now, people would have been saved in minutes."

"Human flesh gets very squid-like in no time around here," assured Alan.

Somewhere behind us, two volunteers were bobbing like lost seal pups in the swells. Dwyer explained his various means for locating them – sonar and computerized global positioning systems, searchlights, and flares, if necessary. "What happens if none of that works?" I asked.

"They have a pair of oars and if they're very good at rowing, they'll get to shore. If not, they won't," he said with deadpan Cork wit.

Of course they were found, and swiftly. A variety of other exercises followed – steering this formidable vessel with nothing but a heave-ho on guy ropes around the rudder, working the fire hoses, tricks of navigation, and the like. Finally, I was put at the controls, and the feeling was like commanding the raw power of an F-16, as my brother once did every day, flying over these same waters from NATO bases in England.

It was heartening to share a pint with these stalwart souls afterward. "These boats are tough as steel," Seán O'Farrell, the second coxswain, said as we settled into an eccentric pub called the Anchor Bar, whose owners were so blasé about technological progress that they not only have no cash registers but throw months worth of change into a pirate's larder of a wooden drawer. "The hulls are a three-inch-thick sandwich of fiberglass and Kevlar, and even sledgehammers can't dent them. A lot of people say that 1700 horsepower is overkill for a boat of this size, but we are asked to go out where danger is real."

The mechanic, Mícheál Hurley, picked up the thread. A born storyteller, the man was a portrait of wide-shouldered mirth and had oversized white teeth that clamped down as he coltishly bit, sometimes with a little snort, into his point. "You'd be a fool to believe all the jargon the technical fellows would be giving that the boat's self-righting and all singing and dancing," he replied when asked about the risks involved in the service. "That's all very fine, but if you're off on a lee shore and have one or two engines stall, and these things can happen, all the power in the world is no good. Machines are just machines and you can get sucked in by the euphoria of their being invincible. A boat is a boat, and all boats have engines and they can break down. If you hit a submerged container or a log, or a freak wave, and the boat caterwauls, the end can come at any time."

Seán O'Farrell returned to the village's history. He lives above Courtmacsherry's only remaining shop, run by his wife and naturally called O'Farrell's. But he explained that a few decades past, when cars were scarce, there were eighteen shops in the village, which then had a population three times its current size, most of whom rarely even ventured to nearby Timoleague. Now there is just O'Farrell's. The railway that was a lifeline for imported coal and outgoing salted mackerel is forty years gone, as are a dozen other spurs that once stitched together the fabric of Cork County's life. The village's formerly substantial fleet of trawlers has shrunk to but three or, on a good day, four. Only thirteen of Courtmacsherry's two hundred residents were actually born there, as the blood relations of the past have been replaced with holidaymakers and newcomers with no ties to the sea, along with the to-and-fro of transient Dutch, Germans, and Brits seeking Irish redemption. Rather than tending near fields, Courtmacsherry's residents often drive an hour to their work, and unlike their desperately emigrating forebears, think nothing of jetting off for the weekend to Dublin or even Paris, which is little more than an hour's flight from Cork City's airport. But somehow, the lifeboat remains an icon burned into the village's soul.

Mícheál Hurley, proffering another dark sculpture of a pint, spoke of the vessel's power. "When I was a boy they'd launch a walloper of a rocket – it was called a maroon – whenever the lifeboat was heading out. It would shake the house and we'd stop our playing and run up to the pier, and the old lifeboat men would shout, 'Keep back, you!' as if it was the secret service. You'd see them hauling out to that boat gleaming offshore. You could not get that vision out of your eyes."

I stepped aside, marveling once again at the conversational magic land that is Ireland, and looked around amiably – well, in fact, dumbly. Suddenly, it became clear that everyone in this pub and in this village had been constantly watching me. One of the three Fleming brothers, who acted as pub managers, gave a nudge. "You're a writer, aren't you?" asked Padraig Fleming.

"Well, I guess."

"I read your last piece in the *Irish Independent*. Wasn't bad. But c'mere to me." He pointed to some back wall black-and-white photographs of an earlier generation of lifeboat men, boasting worn overcoats and threadbare ties for the ceremonial portrait.

"Do you see how these lads are all touching each others' shoulders as they stand there? Could you ever imagine the modern crews doing the same thing, sharing the same camaraderie?"

"The boys back there seem like good fellows to me."

"They're grand and all that, but listen to me now. The lifeboat men today are a softer breed than was seen in my father's day. Ah sure, they have all their high tech and self-righting compartments, and sonar finders and all the fiddle-faddle they could whistle for, and they love the press notices they collect whenever they haul somebody in and shout for attention. But they don't know half of the danger or sacrifice that used to come with being a volunteer."

So, here in a village whose spirit still revolved around an icon of extraordinary constancy, I confronted one of the oldest Irish values – begrudgery. The man had his rights, being among the thirteen natives actually left in Courtmac, and was such a self-possessed individual that he cared not a whit about his outspokenness. Courtmacsherry seemed the more vibrant for his openness, a village that easily welcomed it new gay innkeepers, graciously accepted crusties and foreign "blow-ins" (a name for newcomers of only, say, twenty years), while mustering one out of every eight citizens to volunteer for life-risking duty on the lifeboat any time a stranger became imperiled at sea. I fell in love with the place.

The next morning I drove to the Seven Heads to gaze over the waters traversed in darkness the night before. But nearly every back lane was capped by warning signs about the foot-and-mouth disease menace that had recently worked up a froth of national alarm. What a stupid nonevent, it seemed to me. Farms had become no-go areas, and disinfectant-soaked mats had been stretched across nearly every rural juncture.

The Republic of Ireland responded with laudable rigor, con-cerned that infiltration of the disease within its borders could make the multibillion-pound tourist industry and crucial agricultural exports disappear with a fairy's poof. Hundreds of *gardaí* were therefore dispatched to prevent the smuggling of infected ani-mals across the border with the North by rogue livestock traders, and livestock were vigilantly tested after evidencing the slightest symptoms. Yet some of the more extreme measures seemed more wishful than scientific, especially the disinfectant-soaked mats that made me instinctively feel that I should not roll across them and perhaps spread the spores of disease.

Nearly every turn was blocked by ratty old rugs. The things had lately been placed before schools, churches, chlorine-reeking leisure centers, and inner-city pubs – even the bottom landing of the Hi-B's eternally contaminated stairs, where few cows grazed, sported its own squishy mat.

Picking my way forward, I finally found a matless path toward an abandoned pier, where I gazed off toward the spectacular Old Head of Kinsale. The ocean gleamed and gulls screamed. I imagined the 1200 bodies from the *Lusitania* floating on the swells; the fleets of seventeenth-century British sailing ships heading off for the West Indies; the prehistoric Celts offering animal sacrifices in the ring forts and magical stone circles that haunt every other hill in Ireland's southwest. There was no stage of Irish history that could not be envisioned if one stared long enough into the silver fire dancing on the sea. It was the history of my blood, and my children's.

Deasy.

Kirby.

Butler.

Monaghan.

Donnelly.

McDermott.

McKeon.

How many of these ancestors had been swallowed by the smiling predations of the Atlantic? How many had been wrestled from the pummeling surf by some fellow peasant who risked all, long before there were any rocketing modern lifeboats or any scribes to take a record of the everyday heroism on Irish shores. Foot-and-mouth disease, this meant next to nothing to me before the ballads of mortality now being whispered out of the sea.

Chapter 20

True spring was approaching and it felt as if our Irish lives were progressing on all cylinders. Jamie kept busy publicizing plays for the Cork Opera House, and raising funds for the looming Picasso do, all the while meeting an ever-expanding cast of Corkonians. When not working on article assignments, I kept laying building blocks for the magazine. Cutting back on the weekend expeditions, we let the kids enjoy their own rhythms of school, study, and play as the days lengthened. The garden rang with cheerful voices, and the mendicant teenagers seemed to have moved off to meaner pastures. Under the watchful eye of an appreciative teacher, Harris, meanwhile, appeared to be prospering. Near the end of March, Jamie departed across the Atlantic to visit her mother. Even that separation had its bright side, as Laura, less fang-toothed than at the dawning of her adolescence, pitched in to help with the household chores, and the boys gathered close for bedtime readings.

The night Jamie was winging back toward Ireland, I awoke around 2 a.m., descended the stairs for a glass of juice, then gazed over several items from my coat pockets that seemed oddly littered about on the kitchen table and floor. Half-asleep, I assumed that one of the children had briefly arisen earlier and trashed the room in their usual style. So what else is new, I thought. Just before dawn, a ringing phone had me lurching out of bed again, immediately alarmed about my wife's passage.

"This is the Gurranabraher *gardaí*."

"Yes?" Not having a clue that Cork, or anywhere in this world, held such an unlikely sounding police precinct, which was roughly pronounced "go on and bra her," this call sounded like a joke to me.

"Do you know that your car – an Opel Astra, is it? – was stolen last night?"

At this point I was more or less naked and fully confused. "What are you saying?"

"Well, we have recovered it in a housing estate nearby. It appears to be drivable and you can come and get it at any time," the voice said.

Down the stairs I shambled to make both tea and sense of this news in the light of dawn. In every room, cabinet drawers hung open and papers and clothing lay strewn wildly. A sickening realization took hold that someone had climbed in the kitchen window while I slept, while my innocent children were curled in their beds, and perhaps even stood lurking behind a door while I drank my juice. They had rifled pockets, stolen the car keys, and fled.

That I knew where the car had been found – a dismal northside neighborhood called Knocknaheeny – helped not at all. Sure, I'd heard stories about that place, about a pub dubbed "The Flying Bottle," where visitors who ask whether their parked cars will be safe receive the joking response, "Why would that matter, when you'll have every stolen car in Cork available to choose from by the time you leave?"

At the police station, I was handed the keys, which had inexplicably been found in the ignition, and a life-like silver toy pistol that Owen had left in the back seat.

"Ye can drive it away now, but we would like to take fingerprints later in the morning, if leaving it here can be managed," said the desk officer.

"Let me just have a quick look inside," I replied. A stink of gasoline sent me reeling upon opening the car door. Clearly, the thieves had intended to torch the vehicle after reaching their destination, a place full of dismal "county council," or welfare, housing where life is generally spent on the dole. The torching of stolen cars has become a nightly ritual in Irish inner cities, ostensibly to prevent the recovery of fingerprints, but possibly in pursuit of satisfying more primal urges. Our kindly neighbor Pat O'Neill had recently had his van broken into one night; and after stealing £2000 worth of tools, the vandals burned his car fifty feet from our own door.

I'd seen plenty of charred metal hulks in my morning walks for the newspaper, but this one was close. In January, the windows of five cars parked in our cul-de-sac had been smashed without a single vehicle being driven away.

After taking a taxi back to our house, I pieced together what had happened. My disgust deepened once it became clear that the creeps had even stolen the boys' soccer balls, indicating that they were either so kited on drugs, or otherwise so *Clockwork Orange* senseless, that they would risk a potentially violent encounter for the most juvenile of loot.

A pair of *gardaí* soon showed up from some outpost about five miles away, scribbled notes in little pads, then disappeared with a poof. Another officer from a different station made a brief appearance, followed later on by another from a third substation half a mile down the hill at the edge of town – closed inexplicably on weekends and every night between 6 p.m. and 8 a.m. when their presence might matter most. It was apparent that each wave of well-meaning coppers had received no crime report from their predecessors, but all blithely jotted away in their notebooks none-theless, like wacky characters from Flann O'Brien's *The Third Policeman*. A detective from Cork's headquarters appeared out of nowhere and tried to lift fingerprints here and there, scribbling furiously. Over tea, he explained that he was the only fingerprint expert working in Cork on this day and had just come from a rape scene, plus three burglaries.

"I might have gotten a nice print off one of your bowls by the window," he allowed. "We'll send it off to Dublin for a computer check."

"How long will that take?"

"About four weeks," he replied, which was not reassuring.

"But this house is very secluded and couldn't these robbers, now knowing how easy it is to get inside, come back?"

The detective worked his spoon. "It's not likely. On the other hand, it's not impossible. I would investigate a good security sys-tem, if I were you."

Jamie returned from the airport safely, and I revisited the *gardaí* station where our car still sulked. A talk with another desk clerk resulted in further scribbling and I began to wonder when any of this shorthand was ever read again. Every shop in Cork had some sort of computer system, but apparently not Ireland's police.

The car wouldn't start, so I called a tow truck. "You're lucky you didn't confront those bastards, that I can tell you. They would have been only too glad to smash in your head," the driver consoled me in the cab.

We neared a garage that had done our repairs and I suggested that our Opel be dropped off there. This made the driver wheeze with laughter.

"You're joking?"

The place was at the rear of a big petrol station. "What's the matter with it?"

"The punks around here will burn any car left here for the sheer joy of it, that's what."

Let us say that I was by now thoroughly rattled. The exploding crime rate in Ireland, so often discussed in the newspapers, had become personal. My fundamental ability to protect my wife and children had been violated, and it now felt like the threat of further intrusions by the same culprits was being shrugged off with a "good luck to ye," system-wide indifference. In the pubs, people constantly complained that the rule of law in Ireland was finished, that the *gardaí* were stretched thin and demoralized, thanks to parsimonious funding, overcrowded prisons, and turnstile courts dispensing absurdly lenient sentences. Murderers and serial rapists who received "life sentences" served at most the statutory minimum of seven years, while perpetrators of vicious street assaults inevitably got off with a £100 fine.

Deep into each night, I began patrolling the house with a base-ball bat. I slept like an insomniac, jolting awake at the slightest sound. The rising menace that is the underbelly of Ireland's great leap forward now gnawed deep and personal. It had long been obvious that the police were fleeting presences after dark, but only now had the consequences struck home. A neighbor appeared with a shattered elbow in a sling, having been savagely assaulted for no reason other than some sadistic hoodlums' pleasure upon finding him strolling home from his late-night restaurant job. The brother of another friend had a different drunken pack stomp on his head for sport, detaching a retina. Unlike two university students who received similar late-night greetings in successive weeks some months later, he was fortunate not to end up on a permanent life-support system.

Obviously, urban lawlessness is pervasive in many western countries and comes with the territory wherever old values disintegrate. But Ireland's problem was especially disturbing because at times the random violent assaults had no apparent motive, not even robbery. A nationwide obsession with intoxication, as depicted in the tale told by the nasty cab driver about the transformations of the peacock into monkey and pig, was the only cause many commentators could attribute to the rising savagery. Almost equally troubling was the general fecklessness – perhaps the word the Irish most despise hearing about themselves – being brought to bear on this crisis. Stupendous piles of capital were being poured into the country's infrastructure, such as new roundabouts and a showy sports stadium in Dublin. But less glamorous concerns, such as health care, public safety, and the horrendous fatality rates on the roads, were receiving scant attention from Irish politicians, world masters at speaking obliquely and doing as little as possible about anything problematic, a pursuit in which they are not alone. "A Lot Done, More to Do," ran the pitiful, don't-rock-the-boat bugle cry of the ruling political party (Fianna Fail) some months later. Meanwhile, a survey of 1250 Irish crime victims by a group called Victim Support showed that more than three-quarters received zero police contact after reporting their burglary or assault.

In Connecticut, we left our doors unlocked, trusting in the vigilance of the police. At times, the reach of American law seemed heavy-handed, but to live in a country where even unruly adolescents could not be controlled felt scarier by far – it was like a reincarnation of the every-man-for-himself Wild West.

What was so different about Ireland? It was obvious that the *gardaí* were understaffed and that Irish prisons were bursting at the seams. In fact, Cork's jail was a laughing stock, what with all the drug-filled tennis balls flung over the walls into the exercise yard. The wardens responded by stretching protective netting overhead; so the inmates' friends started chucking over light bulbs that smashed upon impact and showered intoxicating chemicals upon their beloveds.

The Irish Minister for Justice, Equality, and Law Reform, Michael McDowell, orated one day that wanton violence, thuggery, and destructiveness were obvious symptoms of a society whose sense of civility and public order had run amuck.

"They undermine our collective sense of security; they decrease our sense of freedom from fear; they degrade our amenity of life, especially in urban areas. Indeed, one of the most disturbing developments in recent years is the mindless but vicious behavior of young men who carry out random 'run-by' assaults consisting of a blow to the face of completely innocent and inoffensive strangers," McDowell said, laying the blame on rampant alcohol abuse.

Some profound transformation seemed to be occurring before our eyes. A letter to the *Irish Times* pointed out that in 1958, a year of horrendous poverty and miserable unemployment, Ireland and Spain had the lowest serious crime rates in the world, with four murders committed in the Republic, 10 rapes, 79 sexual assaults, 267 violent assaults, 61 robberies, and 3315 cases of burglary and/or breaking and entering.

Forty years later, the country was booming with record employment levels, high living standards, free university education, and unprecedented economic, personal, and sexual freedom. But in 1998, despite a modest growth in population (to 3.7 from 2.9 million in 1958), there were 38 murders, 292 rapes, 598 sexual assaults, 691 violent assaults (a more liberal definition put the number at 8664 in 1999), 2500 robberies, and 25,730 burglaries (which the *gardaí* liked to celebrate as a major decrease from a couple of years back).

The Irish police also have another omnibus crime category called "public order offences," which embrace everything from street brawling to vandalism, public drunkenness and abusiveness. From 1995 to 1999, they counted 111,286 of these everyday acts of social mayhem all told, but in the first eight months of 2000 the number shot up to 50,984, a number that would reach more than 400,000 if projected over the next few years. The columnist Louis

Power thoughtfully asked how crime rates could have exploded in the midst of the sweeping new affluence when compared to those of a destitute, but much more law-abiding, Ireland of four decades earlier.

The answer, the writer suggested, was that Ireland had made a Faustian bargain in tossing aside its age-old religious beliefs and deeply rooted, community-based social norms for the gratification of unfettered modern indulgence. Personally, I didn't want my children to be beaten into adherence to the old Irish ways, as happened in too many schools a generation back. But Louis Power certainly had a point.

Concerned about my ability to protect my family in the face of such lawlessness, I brushed aside past warnings about direct speaking and mentioned in an opinion column in a national newspaper, without naming names, some of the problems we had encountered in this rapidly changing Ireland.

Perhaps it was a coincidence, but the menacing local teenagers, with new recruits, soon resurfaced in our lane, with one snickering, "You got your car stolen and too bad it wasn't burned." One friend suggested that "we sort them," which at certain levels of Irish society means assembling a vigilante pack to appear at a "messer's" doorstep in the night to exact either psychological or physical intimidation. Those weren't my methods, and I struggled to hold my peace, even if it was intensely unnerving to feel that our family had become another one of xenophobic modern Ireland's punching bags. One April afternoon, the young pack assembled outside our door shouting "Fuck Americans!" with no provocation whatsoever, unless they heard the curses I'd been hurling their way in my dreams. This ugliness wouldn't have even qualified as a public order offence, but it was too much.

With another recently victimized neighbor and supporting phone calls from a third, we finally filed a formal complaint with the *gardaí*. Action must have been discreetly taken, because the pests once more crawled out of our lives – this time, we hoped, for good. Our burglars were reportedly also caught, so there was progress. But too often lately, Ireland, this country of the welcomes to which we had moved with such hope, had been breaking our hearts.

Chapter 21

We cinched our belts and resolved not to let such brushes with unpleasantness crush our dreams. The teenage miscreants were no more than that after all, and the burglars had been "sorted." The street crime problem could be avoided by keeping out of town late at night and taking various other precautions. So we carried on.

Possibilities beckoned. I contacted the managing director of Ulster Television in Belfast, whose company had made £30 million in profits the year before and had just paid £6 million for a pair of Cork radio stations that had a fast-talking American DJ as their signature "fifty-second state" voice.

"Would you be interested in backing a brilliant new Cork magazine concept as well?" was the basic pitch to one John McCann.

It seemed like he might be, and we began having regular phone chats, conducted as easily as between old friends. No freelance writer in New York or London could ring up the head of a huge media empire without being frozen out by a phalanx of impenetrable secretaries. But this Irish magnate offered instant access.

"Have they caught the hoodlums who broke into your house yet?" the personable McCann would begin our conversations. "Are your wife and kids sleeping okay?"

We had never even met. But that didn't stop him from being welcoming and decent, and plans were made for a formal presentation of the magazine's prospectus, business plan, and design prototypes – the whole pack of cards. Ireland of the welcomes was back.

Jamie, meanwhile, was making more tangible progress, meeting with the movers and shakers of Cork society and garnering more work than she could handle. She felt like she was connecting with the hum of local cultural and commercial life. And she loved it.

Easter approached and the countryside, even the neglected garden beside our house, rioted with fresh growth. The easy saunter and ebullient busker music returned to downtown Cork's streets. Neighbors emerged from their hibernations and invited us in for the cups of coffee and tea that, in Ireland, typically take an hour to finish.

Finally, we came to the twenty-four hours of national atonement known as Good Friday. This was the one day, besides Christmas, that the entire country and every one of its eight thousand pubs (Scotland and Wales have only six thousand combined) shuts down in a national rite of penance. The night before, I passed an off-licence and witnessed a line of supplicants stretching clear out the door and onto the sidewalk. Stocking up on the Scrumpy Jack with a vengeance, no doubt.

The soulful morning was itself so beautiful that I joined Seamus Wilkinson for a drive to West Cork. His new Mercedes was chugging beside the Bandon River, by now undoubtedly streaked with returning salmon, when Seamus mused, "Isn't the story of Jesus amazing? To think the life of one individual could have such a vast influence that 2000 years later every single pub would be shut down in his honor for an entire day?"

"An interesting point," I said, never having imagined the impact of Christianity in exactly the same terms.

"Of course, you could get a pint if you really wanted one."

"Really?"

"Yes, if you are an official traveler holding an official ticket, you could get one at the railway station. I've known fellas who've bought a round-trip ticket for ten miles or so, just to get a Good Friday pint."

And glory to Christ, I could imagine them all praying silently as they hoisted frothy glasses to their lips.

The next day, about eighteen children combed our garden for hidden Easter eggs and jelly beans in a ritual Jamie transferred from across the seas. Easter Sunday broke bright, with heavenly singing from the choir at the exquisitely renovated St. Mary's of the Dominicans, whose doors we were darkening with increasing, if spotty, frequency.

Jamie produced another one of her feasts, and in the evening we invited a few of our closest friends over for a drink. Ten people in all piled into our kitchen, and even Paddy and Anne Wilkinson, who had been visiting their cousins, paid us a surprise visit. Once again, it felt like we had found a place of embracing belonging, where laughter and wild stories were tossed around like bouquets. Eventually, the evening wound down, and only Shaun Higgins was left at the kitchen table. It was time for a "drop," which in Ireland means whiskey. The inspired Shaun, who is an operatic-quality tenor, burst into a wrenching old ballad known as "Maggie."

"I wandered today to the hill, Maggie; To watch the scene below; The creek and the old rusty mill, Maggie; Where we sat in the long, long ago," he began, eyes rapt, hands outstretched to take in my presence and the stars outside, the entire mad Celtic universe with the risen Christ somewhere at the top bestowing a glorious night on just the two of us now. Ireland was speaking and Shaun was its oracle, illuminating with each rising octave why we had left our enviably secure former lives and stepped through the looking glass into a richer, if more unpredictable, life.

I wanted my far-off mother to share this moment, to just possibly understand our past yearnings and present lives. So I dialed Connecticut, heard her voice quake hello, and, without saying a word, softly placed the receiver before Shaun's impassioned singing – thinking my dear mom, so Irish to her soul, so Cork in her conjoined Kirby-Deasy blood, would experience a revelation from her ancestral land. I blinked away tears, thinking how moved she would be.

"And now we are aged and gray, Maggie; The trials of life nearly done."

Unable to carry off the ruse any longer, I grabbed the receiver. "Isn't Ireland beautiful?" I exclaimed.

The telephone was stone dead. Repeated calls back produced only busy signals. On the final try, my mother answered.

"Wasn't that amazing?" I asked.

"Who is this?" she demanded.

"Your son. Remember, the one in Ireland? Did you hear that singing?"

"Oh dear me. I thought it was a crank call. So I hung up and took the phone off the hook."

Ah well, yet another experience never predicted in the Guidebook to Loopy Midlife Migrations. But of course surprises had become our daily staple by now.

One of the biggest worries any married man can have – and especially a somewhat exiled one – is that his wife will suddenly walk off in the arms of an unsuspected rival. As Easter approached Jamie began to do this every day with a man who gave new meaning to the word "distinguished" in that he looked hundreds of years old, what with his foot-long beard spilling down into his wizard's sackcloth topped by a necklace of crystals. Worse, he spoke in nothing but riddles, being a professional impersonator of Gandalf from *The Hobbit*. The wife's new freelance assignment was to usher this druid to media appearances while promoting the upcoming Tolkien dramatization at the Cork Opera House. The two were a swell pair.

One night I proudly watched as Jamie prepared to address a group of teachers who might help coax more school kids into the theater. She had lobbied to make this kind of work her permanent responsibility. And lo, her wish came true. "We've just got a substantial new grant and it would be wonderful if you could work here permanently," whispered one of the Opera House's administrators, minutes before the reception began.

With that, the gate Jamie had been waiting for swung open. After the usual Irish series of follow-up and "what did we say before?" meetings, she was asked to create a new education outreach program. She had netted a dream.

A conversation with her new boss later in the evening revealed that this relationship came with its own circle, once I told him some personal history. "You were a friend of Bun Wilkinson? Extraordinary. I spent two months helping him with that cottage in Dingle later that same winter!"

April sped along, and we resumed our weekend expeditions to places like Courtmacsherry, for walks by the sea, and ruined four-hundred-year-old Kanturk castle in North Cork, whose towering walls we adopted as a home-run fence for our family baseball games. Meanwhile, I sallied off to research and write about more lifeboat excursions, meeting up with new crews in County Kerry, on both the island of Valentia and at Fenit on the end of a peninsula jutting into the Atlantic just north of Tralee. Further compelling tales were revealed and fresh excitement came with more sea voyages, one with a helicopter roaring twenty feet overhead and winching volunteers off the deck in a mock rehearsal of the life-and-death retrievals that so commonly occur far out in the Atlantic. Valentia, between Ballinskelligs and Dingle, provided the European landing point for the first transatlantic cable, laid in 1866, and was also littered with five-thousand-year-old remnants of the earliest Celtic civilization to inhabit Ireland. A fantasy "work" destination, in other words. So I was reeling in some dreams myself, being paid to travel and write about the country I'd loved for so long.

The lifeboat crew in Fenit even took Harris on board and, to his thrill, let him handle the controls as we headed far out to sea. The magic of Kerry's surrounding headlands and mountains breathed over us as he steered forward, and the scene felt like a lifelong memory in the making. Despite assertions otherwise by W.B. Yeats, romantic Ireland was not yet dead and gone. No, it lived on in my family.

Chapter 22

Some of the most delightful rites of the Irish spring come in the form of all-amateur hurling matches between rival counties. Played with slender sticks with heads flanged like tomahawks, hurling began as a kind of semicontrolled warfare between rival clans, just as did the North American Indian game of lacrosse. The Irish being a fierce lot, they used skulls as balls in the early days, which helped inspire epic poems regarding the more memorable contests. Eventually, a hard leather-wrapped ball (called a *sliotar*) began to be whacked instead, with about a hundred or so Gaels on each side trying to belt the thing across bogs toward the homeland of the other bunch. Damage was inevitably done to certain pates in the course of the melee, but rowdy celebrations afterward helped dull the pain.

The cricket-playing British didn't like hurling's inherent wildness, so they banned the playing of this glorious sport, just as they had banned Catholicism, the speaking of the Irish language, and the presence of the shoeless natives in their walled towns after dark. The wily Irish responded by moving the game to the hinterlands, finally organizing the mayhem in the late nineteenth century under a national body called the Gaelic Athletic Association, or GAA, whose local clubs became breeding grounds for a variety of insurrectionary activities against the Crown.

Knowing such things, I jumped at the opportunity to attend a game between Cork and Tipperary when John Burke, the gravel-voiced eccentric and resident sculptor of the Hi-B, invited me to join him. The fact that Burkie's father was a notorious IRA man in Tipp added a certain aura of authenticity, because a proper hurling match has intensely nationalistic undertones to this day. No Irish native can ever forget the fact that in 1921 the Brits, knowing exactly what the GAA (often called the "gah") represented, drove an armored vehicle into the middle of a Tipperary-Dublin hurling match in Ireland's national stadium of Croke Park. Without warning, they raked the horrified crowd with bullets, killing eighteen innocent fans and maiming four times as many. This infamous "Bloody Sunday" payback was provoked by the fact that Michael Collins had orchestrated a killing spree against a dozen British intelligence agents the night before.

Today's pre-game warm-up, in contrast, featured a more amicable chat over pints in a little downtown bar named Corrigan's, which for some reason boasts side-by-side photographs of Small Dennis beside Michael Jackson, perhaps indicating a future cultural exchange project.

"Like I keep telling you, Ireland is not half as strange as your country," Burkie wheezed. "I mean your place is so big, like. I went to Las Vegas one time with my girlfriend, Frances, and we did feck all on the slot machines and thought we were hurting bad. Then this Texan in cowboy boots came up and I told him I'd just lost eighty dollars. He says, 'Well, I just lost eighty thousand.' Your man lights his cigar and laughs, 'It's Vegas.'"

The hurling match began to seem like a doubtful destination. "So we went off to Phoenix the next night because Frances knew somebody in this rich suburb there. Every tree was bursting with oranges. So I said, 'Stop the car, Frances, I'm going to pick some oranges.' 'Hee, hee,' said she. But I climbed this tree and was shaking the branches and there were oranges falling everywhere, when suddenly a cop car appears.

"Here I am like some capuchin monkey rooting around in the branches when the cops draw their guns and shout, 'What are you doing up there?' I say, 'I'm Irish. I just wanted to get an orange.' The one says, 'Do you have alcohol taken, sir?' I said, 'Look idjeet, I'm pissed as a parrot. Why else would I be in a tree?' and they just started laughing. Why, they even escorted us home."

Cork's hurling stadium proved to be conveniently located at the end of a narrow dead-end roadway with parking facilities for about two hundred of the ten thousand or more cars that attend every match. My sculptor tour guide, dressed in an absurdly heavy dark overcoat on a glorious April Sunday, solved that problem, in the way any anarchic Irish person might, by tossing aside plastic police no-parking pylons so we could nose into an illegal spot close by the gate.

"You're in Ireland now, boy!" said he.

The vast crowd at the ticket windows irritated Burkie, so he affected an old man's limp to cut ahead. Following sheepishly, I imagined the scene inside would be one of sheer loutishness, full of the kind of excess that ruins so many American athletic spectacles and hooligan-ridden British soccer games. Wrong.

The only misbehavior I witnessed was exhibited by Burkie. "Follow me," he barked as we pressed in invalid fashion ahead of hundreds of less preposterous fans.

Inside, we beheld a huge field bronzed in sun. No one therein was drinking, because the only beer taps in the place were situated in a remote bar that required circumventing the entire stadium in a twenty-minute stroll with a twenty-minute queue at the end, and because this is not the tradition when watching hallowed GAA games. In a U.S. arena of equivalent size, there would be spigots every two hundred feet and menacing clusters of obscene chanters emerging by the time the game had barely begun.

As the fifteen contestants on either side trotted out in their bright jerseys and dark shorts, I asked Burkie about the meaning of the park's peculiar name – Pairc Ui Caoimh. "Nobody bothers to think about that, for Christ's sake," he wheezed. "They're all named after some fecking bishop or IRA man."

Pairs of men in long white butchers' coats assembled at the sides of the goalposts at either end of the field. Their job was to decide whether the *sliotar* had been whacked cleanly between the uprights for one point or whizzed between the roughly ten-foot-high by twenty-foot-long rectangle below for three. A small window opened in the distant scoreboard at one end of the stadium and another white-coated man, evidently the scorekeeper, leaned his bald head forward, took in the sun, and either toted the point or unloaded some pork chops. The crowd rose for the national anthem, a whistle was blown, and without further fanfare there commenced a nonstop stampeding and whaling of hurley sticks at a hot potato never allowed to sit still for two seconds. The players picked the bouncing demon up with their hands, lobbed it to tennis-serve level, and slammed it on a high windhover arc that flew like a gravity-defying baseball home run hundreds of feet up and down the field. As the *sliotar* descended, three, four, and five would leap to stupendous heights for another whack, sometimes spinning backward and driving it at impossible angles through the goalposts eyed by the imitation butchers. At each score, the little bald man in the middle of the scoreboard would open his window, confirm the point with his fellow off-duty butchers below, and chalk up the fresh tote.

It looked like bedlam to me, a magnificent display of amateur athleticism with the ball being kicked, lobbed, whacked, pursued, retrieved, cradled, and raced forward on the end of stick – then, without any apparent pause for aim, launched in another gorgeous arc toward the rival team's goal. The players wore no protective padding, and only a scattering had helmets, yet somehow they escaped maiming as rivals' sticks crashed down on every side, like blows from the swords of murderous samurai. Players scored, collided, crumpled, and suffered god-awful wallops, but never exhibited the attention-seeking histrionics of jubilation and pain so repulsive and ubiquitous in European soccer or American football. The action was breathless – a physical equivalent to Irish talking.

"This is fantastic, like ice hockey on grass," I said.

"It's a low-rent ballet today," Burkie cackled. "They should be wearing pouffy white dresses."

For seventy minutes the hurlers raced and whacked without cease (other than a half-time break that featured a bagpipe performance of "The Rose of Tralee"), and the score flipped and flopped before Tipperary staged a final victorious rally. The action was stupendous.

"You better like it," Burkie said, "because hurling is part of Ireland's soul."

At the end of the afternoon, we stopped at the Hi-B. Some of the usual types were holding forth: a poet called "The Ancient Mariner;" the first mate on a replica Famine ship that never seemed to get out of dry dock; and a witheringly funny electrical contractor who refused to ever open the proverbial gate to his self. Kieran O'Connor was there too, and he revealed that playing hurling as a youth had rewarded his scalp with two hundred stitches. "It toughened me, like, and you should have seen the other guys," he laughed. That's Kieran, that's the pluck of the Irish who are so fabled for responding, when cornered in a dark alley with odds that are ten to one, "I got them where I want them."

But the resident Oisín, Brian O'Donnell, was nowhere in sight, and was in fact rarely apparent on the premises anymore. Noisy, vulgar fools were sloshing drinks in the background, the kind of dullards Brian would only yesterday have driven away at a glance, without even bothering to cut up their ties. I took a wary look around as a local character wandered in, sporting a face like a gargoyle's. His left eye was nearly swollen shut and his cheeks offered a florid show of blue, black, and purple.

"What happened to you?" I asked curiously.

"I got in the way of myself the other night."

"Oh, I see."

One could imagine tables crashing, a whiskey bottle toppling, a lamp falling on his head as he polished off his final nightcap and lurched forward – an indoor hurling match conducted by a team of one. Another barroom denizen appeared hanging onto a cane. No puzzle there – I had seen him reach his arm out to emphasize a point to someone a few evenings before, only to mysteriously crumple on the floor. "Drink taken," as they say in Ireland.

The talk was lively, but I grew quiet. The Irish love affair with alcohol, which had seemed like such fun in our early going, was revealing its darker side. One study indicated that the country's citizens had officially topped the Luxembourgians as the top quaffers in the world. Some pundits beat their chests, calling drink "the spiritual disease of the Irish," but mostly everybody laughed, and why wouldn't they with newspaper advertisements featuring twelve twenty-ounce pints lined up in rows above a slogan saying "Live life to the power of Guinness." God knows increasing numbers were doing their best, now that Ireland's former legions of "pioneer" adherents to the Father Mathew message of abstemiousness had largely disappeared. The Irish understandably despise the stereotype of being regarded as a nation riddled with alcoholics, and the fact is the vast majority use the drink as moderately as any other people.

But tonight there were far too many riffraff in sight, vacant-eyed and menacing, while acting as if a bright afternoon was all the excuse needed for going bananas after dark. Statistics say that in the last decade the country's per capita consumption of wine has risen by 300 percent, hard cider by 500 percent, and beer by 26 percent, the latter growth sounding modest possibly because it couldn't get much higher. The average intake of the hops, barley, and malt has reached 150 liters for every citizen over fifteen, despite the fact Irish women generally eschew the stuff, and the very young and senior citizens drag down the national statistics. Even the suds-loving Germans manage to swill only an average of 127 liters, although the Czechs still rule at 163 liters of beer per head. In terms of the pure alcohol equivalent, Ireland's per capita intake has risen from five liters in 1960 to 12.3 liters today, double the U.S. rate of 6.6, and well ahead of the boisterous Aussies, who down but 7.5 liters. Various souls behind Burkie now looked as if they were making a beer push to leave the Czechs in the dust.

A month or so later during the World Cup appearance by the lads in green, the Irish were clocked drinking *twenty million* more pints than on the equivalent weekend the year before – not bad for a country of 3.8 million citizens.

There are of course hilarious sides to all this, as evidenced by a recent 3:30 a.m. search of a County Mayo pub where the *gardaí* learned much after-hours singing and raucousness had been in progress. The owner protested that he was merely cleaning up, but he could not explain the presence of his daughter, two bar staff, and five customers huddled together in the toilet. His solicitor explained everything in short order: "My client advises me that he was giving a lift to some of the people and some were waiting for taxis. He normally runs a good house."

"There was nobody driving, as such," added the publican from Knock, a place normally known for the tens of thousands of pilgrims who annually trudge barefoot up the local mountain to commune with the hallowed spot where St. Patrick, with a foot on a viper, had his Moses-like tryst with God.

A lot of Irish people saw no humor, however, in a report a couple of days later about a drunken twenty-one-year-old Cobh mother being arrested after her two-year-old son was found with a glass of wine in one hand and a cigarette in the other. Archbishop Sean Brady, the Roman Catholic Primate of All Ireland, put it thus:

> It is not just the social and the sporting events – religious occasions are involved. From baptism to confirmation, marriage to funerals, we have developed a culture of drinking that is sometimes shocking.
>
> Sometimes I fear that we may be witnessing another lost generation – a generation of young people who, instead of emigrating abroad, are leaving the shores of moderation, responsibility, and spirituality.

I was beginning to worry that this particular rising tide could lift all boats, including my own . . . and for that matter, my children's a few years down the road. Sometimes when driving Laura to the bus station at dawn we saw disheveled teenagers only a few years older than herself staggering in the streets, the girls' low-cut party dresses askew, the boyfriends looking deranged after an all-night binge in celebration of some major examination just passed or failed. Oscar Wilde humorously labeled such rituals "the first tottering steps in the dance of the damned." But not funny, as the Archbish observed, is the fact that as many as 20 percent of Irish children have taken their first drink by the age of nine, and that the country has the highest rate of teenage binge-drinking in Europe, which undoubtedly has much to do with the appalling rate of road fatalities among the young.

One eye-opening statistic would be a tally of the number of stupid and abusive rants that occur in pubs after heavy swilling – the scary second Janus face of the Irish drinker. Experts at this sport develop invisible, hydraulically activated gauges in their heads that keep them upright when those of other nationalities would topple over hours earlier.

A couple of decades ago, these gauges came imprinted with the get-even word "British." Whisper the B-word in the evening's declining hours and you would immediately witness gears turning in slack faces and vacant eyes burning with fresh life – chugga-chugga bang went the internal hydraulics and out came a tirade about the last eight hundred years. It was hard to argue with some of the underlying notions; but then again, no refinement or elaboration was ever sought to temper these outpourings, whose main point was to demonstrate the super-human flush of brilliance and virtue that had suddenly erupted in the speech gearbox of the elocutionist.

Float the word "Nigerian" to the wrong person some night in an Irish pub, and you will see a similar display of astonishing nonstop vitriol, so passionately do a few misbegotten souls despise this particular group of impoverished immigrants, a small minority of whom, it must be said, are not always model citizens. The Irish have had so little prior exposure to people of color on their shores that one can almost fathom the mental flailings the subject induces – until receiving the same treatment.

Irish-Americans have long thought of themselves as being blood brothers with their forebears across the seas, like Jews come home to Israel. Unfortunately, many visitors will soon confront the unpleasant surprise that, in contrast to Burkie, certain ornery swillers with those hydraulic gauges in their heads no longer like Americans much at all.

"Are you American, is it?" begins a typical conversation.

"Why, yes," responds the visitor proudly, not suspecting in the least that he is walking into a trap.

"What part?"

"The northeast."

"Aye, it's a big country ye hail from." Bleary eyes is buying time now, sizing up his target, rehearsing his rant, honing his verbal razors, assuring himself of his supreme cleverness.

"Ever been there?"

From this type, you will not be getting a disquisition about his six successful butcher, baker and lawyer cousins and an uncle working "the high steel," as the Irish sometimes call construction jobs on skyscrapers, on foreign shores. Instead you might be asked: "Tell me, what do ye think of Cambodia?"

The wise would do well at this point to race for the door.

"I don't really ponder the place frequently."

"Oh no?" Behold now a bemused but dangerous smile. "Well, what about Vietnam then?"

Responses like "Fortunately, I never served," will not save you; nothing will.

"Nicaragua?"

"Granada?"

"Guatemala?"

"Panama?"

"Palestine?"

"Chile?"

Your swiller has the whole world in his pocket and wants nothing more than to drop all of it, every shard of his superior, lord-of-history knowledge at your feet. And fool that you are, you could try to say something mollifying back. Don't.

"I'm telling ye now, ye come from a nation of bullies. Ye have bullied the entire world but ye will never bully us, because we are a proud and independent people and we do not need you. Ye bullied the blacks and the Indians and the Mexicans, and ye even put your flag on the moon."

Don't dare mention that "ye" are being bullied now – although you will pay for the silent tactic as well.

"Why, you're very smug, drinking your pint on our soil, and saying nothing like you're very clever indeed. Ye are a very arrogant people."

This class of booze-hound by now will be convinced that he has boxed you into a masterful corner. But he's not done.

"Would you like another pint?"

That is when you leave.

Having been through this two dozen times before, I was not nearly so offended as the man wished. Ten to one, he'd be grinning at me on the street the next morning, Janus head rearranged as if we were best of friends. I wasn't thrilled with a lot of my homeland's recent gunboat diplomacy myself, and of course had no vision of how far it would eventually head. By the time the Iraq war started, I might have had a rant or two to offer myself. But still.

Chapter 23

In America, our lives had been overwhelmingly focused upon raising the children. But changing adult tangents and diversions had taken hold in Ireland, and sometimes it felt as if the kids were getting short shrift. In Connecticut, we would rise at dawn from October to April to ferry all three to Saturday morning ice-hockey games where every participant's progress was closely admired by their parents, despite the fact that excursions to practice also ate up two evenings each week. After-school skiing and family sledding on our snowy driveway in the woods further enriched the children's life. The spring brought baseball and tennis; the summer, swimming competitions, fishing, and canoeing at the lake two minutes from our door. But Ireland had no ice, no snow, no baseball, and waters so cold bathers jumped out of them screaming "fecking hell!"

Jamie and I had more than enough to occupy ourselves – the start of my magazine venture lay as close as locating one believing benefactor with a pot of gold, and Ulster Television's John McCann still seemed close to biting. Jamie, meanwhile, was enamored with the bright challenge of introducing sometimes deprived kids to the magic of live theater. But we had occasional misgivings about our kids' unrelieved city living, where the boys, at least, spent so much of their free time booting balls about the hard pavement of our treeless street. The only sport Christian Brothers offered was rugby, and Harris and Owen were still coming to terms with these Saturday morning contests, which few parents bothered attending, perhaps because they were often drowned in epochal torrents of rain. The contrast between the wholesome, if often over-organized, pastimes that our kids had been offered in the U.S. and the more fend-for-oneself Irish way of rearing sometimes seemed stark.

Obviously, Irish children – and our own street-living offspring –

seemed basically as well adjusted as kids anywhere. Laura, having faraway school friends, waxed a bit lonely some weekends but was always happy when roping in a classmate for a crisps- and cookie-strewn sleepover. But there were scarcely any nearby fields for the boys to play in, save those owned by the local GAA clubs with their offerings of hurling, rugby, and Gaelic football. The problem was that the ones near us seemed a tad rough.

One Saturday the Christian Brothers rugby teams had their games scheduled at a "gah" club about four miles from our house. Upon arrival, the boys were exhorted to scurry off to the club's locker room.

"The what?" Owen asked in confusion.

"In there," his coach said, pointing at what looked like a steel container fallen off the stern of an ocean-going freighter.

Meanwhile, a prodigious deluge commenced.

"I don't want to change in there, Dad," Owen remonstrated.

"Go on, you're a rugby player," I urged.

"It looks like somebody's chopped the place up with an axe. And the rain is pouring through the roof."

Well, Owen was right. The "changing room" appeared to have been attacked by a pike-wielding maniac, with holes in the gaping roof and long gashes in the walls baring jagged twists of rusted, tetanus-breeding shrapnel. Empty Scrumpy Jack cans glowered from beneath the graffiti-scarred benches.

The congenitally muddy playing fields outside oozed like a pig wallow. Then somebody blew a whistle and the kids set to throwing each other head first into the muck. I tried chatting with another father, but neither of us could see the other through the rain streaming down our wiper-less eyeglasses.

Gradually it became clear that Irish parents compensate for some of the weaknesses of organized kids' activities in their culture through a variety of inventive alternatives, some of these involving their on-again, off-again affection for the Catholic Church. Young Owen's upcoming First Holy Communion, for which Christian Brothers had been prepping its little angels for months, provided an object lesson there. Little did we know what a national rite of passage awaited. The occasion is at heart a festival of hope. But the rub is that First Communion must duly be preceded by the cleansing of First Confession, in which parents, even very sinful ones, are expected to lift their duffs off the pews and step forward as proper models of penitence. The prospect was petrifying.

The church nonetheless resonated with song and pageantry on the First Penance day. Owen looked to be in deep conversation with the Lord as he and his classmates stepped up to the altar and expressed their sanctified contrition, as did little girls from neighboring schools. A forty-something priest stood at the lectern, beaming at the assemblage of innocence. A much older one stared out from stage left. The first looked kind, the second stern, and it felt as if they had worked out some kind of spiritual balancing act. Father Kind gently invited the parents to come forward to vouchsafe their stature as proper role models. "I realize many of you will not be regular confessants, but it would be helpful for you to demonstrate the power of your own redemptive faith to your children. All you have to say is, "I am sorry for my sins" – nothing more."

"This is a good deal," I thought. As a boy I had regularly cringed in murky confessionals before opaque screens behind which invisible beings threatened eternal damnation. If no sins could be remembered, you made them up in order to be done fast with whatever string of "Hail Marys" and "Our Fathers" were demanded. When the voice cracked with puberty, it got worse.

So this new confession-lite sounded nifty. The only problem was that Father Stern did not look happy.

The liturgy proceeded, and the seven- and eight-year-olds advanced to whisper their offences against their families, teachers, and the Lord. Touching it was to behold.

Now it was the adults' turn. A mass inertia seized the congregation, as if this were Lourdes in reverse – instead of the lame miraculously walking, parents in the prime of life seemed to undergo a collective paralysis. Father Kind smiled patiently, but Father Stern scowled. After a lengthy pause, a few adults inched forward. Muttering soon broke out in the next pew.

"Don't go to the older priest. He's changed the terms," an attractive brunette whispered to her husband. "I said 'I'm sorry for my sins,' but that wasn't good enough for him. 'You'll have to tell me something more specific," he insisted.

Forewarned, I veered toward Father Kind and got off easy.

The real First Communion followed a couple of weeks later. The children were enthralled, the boys sporting rosettes on their pressed blazers, the elaborately coiffed girls wearing immaculate white dresses and veils, like little brides of the Lord. Four priests in brocaded vestments presided, and the dolled-up mothers betrayed moist, doting gazes. Goodness shined. Jamie's mother and wheel-chair-bound sister, freshly arrived from the States, cooed.

We certainly felt some reverence ourselves. Children need faith; we all do – at least in something more elevated than our own selfishness. Our little boy had been beaming for weeks, clasping his uplifted hands in prayer at every church service, announcing that on Tuesdays, for some reason, he was making an effort to be especially good. I asked Owen about what private prayers he had offered before receiving his First Holy Communion. "That Aunt Martha will be able to walk again," he whispered.

And what could be wrong with that? In America, the pendulum of individual entitlement had swung so harshly that mentioning the very notion of God in school was a cardinal sin, and in fact a potential firing offence for teachers. American schools have lost so much common purpose that they breed another kind of anarchy, a spiritual one, perhaps more disruptive than the unraveling apparent on Ireland's streets. Self-direction is the rule in dress, behavior, and belief. One of Laura's third-grade classmates announced that he recognized no obligation to recite the Pledge of Allegiance to the Flag – a thirty-second reflective pause employed to settle American kids down for the beginning of the school day. Then again, the father's benediction to his boy's teachers was to announce – "My son will show you respect when you have earned it."

So we were happy to see Owen enjoying his moment of untarnished devotion. His neat little uniform helped set a tone of order to his school day, and that was fine, too. American teachers were struggling to control classrooms with fifteen ten-year-olds inside – half the size of many pin-drop quiet Irish ones. Never once in Ireland did we see any of the widespread "public order" offences in the classroom. It wasn't screaming or corporal punishment that achieved the workable peace – the banshee in the boys' school had been sacked in a few weeks, after all – it was parentally supported respect for the educational process. So the reverie with which the First Communicants embraced their sacrament seemed uplifting, an expression of able stewardship and loving concern.

How long this young piety would endure was another question. Henry Sidney, a sixteenth-century lord deputy of Ireland and father of the poet Philip Sidney, dismissed Irish Catholicism as but a veneer with which the natives dressed up their essential evilness.

"Thei regarde no other, thei blaspheme, thei murder, commit whoredome, hold no wedlocke, ravish, steal and commit all abomination without scruple of conscience," he reported home. "You would rather think them atheists or infidels."

His contemporary Barnaby Rich chipped in with the comment that the Irish lived "like beastes, voide of all lawe and all good order" and were "more uncivil, more uncleanly, more barbarous and more brutish in their customs and demeanures, than in any other part of the world that is known."

The legacy of oppression that resulted from such bigotry was enough to make me sign my kids up for Catholicism on political grounds alone. But the inherent contradictions of Irish life always have their twists. Once our little Owen's sacrament of First Communion was done, the "wantone," if still loving, secular aspects of this day became manifest. In Ireland, the Catholic rites of childhood – both First Communion and Confirmation – produce a stupendous outpouring of beneficence, which is spelled C-A-S-H. The kids lift their hands to God with fervor, then keep them outstretched afterward.

No sooner did Owen unite with God than the money envelopes started fluttering into his palms from kindly neighbors and friends. Within two hours, the boy had over £400 in his pocket. Burkie chuckled at this haul as being pitiful, however. "Is that all? One of my friend's kids picked up £1500."

The first twenty guests at our celebration party said their goodbyes by seven o'clock. Very civilized. But then the next dozen hit the doorbell and Shaun Higgins sang his "Maggie," and we shoved some heretofore well-behaved neighbors out the door sometime after 3 a.m.

"Getting to be one of us, for better or worse," the ever-watchful Shaun chortled devilishly the next afternoon.

We had the threads of something wonderful in our fingers. We were having the time of our lives whenever we paused to think about it. Every day had patterns of easy belonging, serendipity, and surprise that our over-earnest friends in the U.S. would pay thousands of dollars for on a summer holiday and talk about for the rest of their years. *Craic*, as the natives call great fun, was so readily available that one had to hide from it during the week, lest one's whole life become a burst of laughter. People at every turn said that they were starting to forget that we didn't actually hail from Cork. Frightening was that notion. We had executed the most dangerous of midlife casts and caught something live and quicksilver.

But . . . the guilt was always nipping. We kept picking at the slightest knots in our routines and worrying the skeins, trying to re-create the happy routines our children enjoyed back at home. We would fret about them and our distant families so much that we occasionally lost sight of the fact that this Irish safari had made us all larger than we'd been just a year earlier. The seasons had turned and it was time to make plans.

"It sounds like you're having a great life there, no matter what hardships you've weathered. I'd dwell upon that if I were you, because you both were complaining before you left. If you as parents aren't happy together, your children will pay a price that is heavier than whatever geographic dislocation they are suffering," a friend from the States sagely wrote.

Hmmh. And our kids scarcely looked like they were hurting, what with the boys dragging four friends into the house or garden every day, and Laura consorting every other weekend with the daughters of yacht designers and horse breeders, of sherry-soaked Brit ambassadors and New Zealand and American romantics and executives who had all ended up in Cork for one reason – they were fishing for dreams themselves.

Our lives were full. So what was there to lament? I went fishing for trout when I could and kept writing, while Jamie threw herself into her expanding responsibilities.

In mid-May, I went to Dublin to present my magazine proposal to the courtly John McCann of Ulster Television. A few years previously, that outfit wouldn't have had a prayer of flexing its muscles in the Republic, where any enterprise doing business with the Brits was despised. But these were new days. John McCann decided to run the proposal by UTV's new Cork office with all its resident Corkonians – an idea akin to sending a bee back into an incestuously gossiping hive.

The feet kept moving to the sunny side of the street. A couple of weeks later, the manager of UTV's Cork operations called to say that he admired the proposal, but was not in a position to back the magazine. Ouch.

The consultants organized another meeting, then called a second to cap the first one off, and set up a third for the hell of it – as tick, tick went their hourly meter. After a few days, they arranged a presentation before the managing director of one of the biggest newspaper conglomerates in Ireland, the Cork-based Thomas Crosbie Holdings. Once again, the headman there expressed keen interest, though he used few words and held a poker face. He would get back to us on Monday – though which Monday was not immediately clear.

Chapter 24

The Mondays passed, the mellow evenings lengthened, and the kids' schools were all closed at the very beginning of June. Collecting children on their last day of classes is always a touching rite of passage, especially when it serves as a benchmark of a year on foreign shores. Our three were scarcely the same kids we had dropped off in the eagerness of early September, countless uniform stains ago. They were inches taller, their accents had altered, and their presences were larger as they stood in their schoolyards surrounded by beaming friends who were no longer foreign but as familiar as those left behind in Connecticut. The eyes moistened at the thought of all this, and the fact that they would be on our hands nonstop – *for three months.*

A wonderful sailing camp near Kinsale launched their summer happily, and we proudly watched Laura tack across the jeweled bay, handling this challenge as if it were an easy metaphor for the much larger voyage upon which she and her brothers had embarked. In the evenings we played chess, the kids having gotten quite shrewd at that pastime, as phenomenal numbers of children do in Ireland, what with the country's affinity for caginess of all kinds.

Eventually, the time came for a follow-up meeting with another exec at Thomas Crosbie Holdings. In most places, an interview of similar importance would be fraught with straightforward probes to challenge and inspire personal revelations about why one felt qualified for a particular job. But nothing about this session and this individual squared with my expectations. His longish hair was parted in the middle, his spectacles horn-rimmed, his fingers worrying at the knot of a stylish silk tie knotted above an academically plaid shirt – as if the point of the meeting was to discuss Joyce or Yeats. Adding to the confusion was the fact the man was formerly the editor of the town's afternoon tabloid newspaper, the *Evening Echo*, whose paperboys sing the name through Cork's streets with a skip in their voices that is meant to, well, echo and echo. "I imagine you're quite well versed in Cork culture by now," he feinted. This wasn't phrased as a question, yet I wondered whether I was supposed to recite some list of bona fides, or perhaps launch into a personal rendition of "Maggie."

"I've met a tremendous number of people here," I started. "I love Cork, and this magazine will be a tribute to the town and county's dynamism."

"Your enthusiasm is apparent. But how do you envision the ownership structure being formulated?"

Hold on there, I hadn't finished responding to the opening gambit, and already we were galloping off on a new tangent.

I just smiled and laid out my plans for the great publishing venture. The paid consultants nodded and settled into their chairs while their billing meters whirled.

"We think the idea is worthy of further consideration," the interviewer concluded, disappearing before my elaborate portfolio of sample covers and articles could be presented.

Attempts to arrange a casual follow-up lunch failed. Phone calls and emails were not returned. So there was no surprise when June ended with a runic note indicating that, for reasons unexplained, windfalls of investment capital, sometimes called "dosh" in Ireland, would not be blowing my way. The subtext seemed to say that I was not yet long enough in Cork to be considered bankable. It felt as if my shiny new Irish identity was still painfully tentative. Back in the U.S. I could walk into a business presentation and confidently anticipate every nuance. But in Ireland there remained a slipperiness underfoot, as if some part of myself had still not arrived across the sea. The question nagged as to whether I could provide for my family, with this or any project here. Had I perhaps been pursuing a fantasy all the Irish while? Was our excursion nothing more than a lark now needing to be curtailed so that we could return to the stability of our previous lives? Night after night, Jamie and I pondered and talked. I fretted that Ireland was doing to us what it had done to every invader, seafarer, and planter who had landed over the centuries – dizzying our bearings, and confusing our direction.

"There are other fish in the sea. You've got to give this thing more time," Jamie said. "We've only played half our hand here."

She was right.

We made plans for a holiday in the U.S., while in the meantime squeezing in various lunches and get-togethers with Irish friends who might offer words of wisdom. "You absolutely must stay; we're only just getting to know you, and look, you're all doing beautifully," said the raven-haired Mary Lynch, whose warm sentiments were seconded by many others.

To add fresh italics to our lives, the Courtmacsherry lifeboat crew took the family out for a voyage far along the coast of West Cork – past the Seven Heads where starving locals used to race to the stony shore to retrieve the barrels of maize and rum that washed in from Famine-era shipwrecks, but now blithely lolled about in the summer sun; past Galley Head with its gleaming cliffs topped by timeless pastures and newly hatched holiday haciendas; past Glandore with its spectacular yacht-dotted bay where a few commercial fishermen still plied their ancient trade. The light on the water was heaven-sent, the journey a reverie of Ireland old and new.

That evening a great throng materialized on Courtmac's main street. It was time for the village's annual horse race on the mud-flats exposed by the ebbing tide. Shafts of silver flooded through the clouds as the riders in green-and-gold jackets walked their steeds forward. As if out of nowhere, country men with tweed caps and rugged, time-worn faces gathered in clumps, while gnomic bookmakers unfolded slate tote boards on which to offer their odds. Freckled children wheeled about with fistfuls of sweets, and suddenly it looked as if Ireland had never changed. The first contestants gathered beside a huge oval that a tractor had traced in the wet sand, and Laura shouted, "That's Gavin! He's from my school!"

So we wagered a fiver on the young jockey just before the starter's pistol fired. What unfolded was spellbinding, the galloping steeds hurtling beside incandescent waters, the sand flying at their heels, a rainbow exploding overhead to create the aura of a dream. We lost our dosh, but won something else.

As the sun set and the moon rolled on high, I walked along the strand, reflecting back over our year now finished. Inevitably I thought of Bun, and could almost feel his presence, like a shade, keeping a brisk stride beside me in the twilight, pointing toward discoveries large and small. "Good man yourself, you haven't done a bad job, not at all," I could almost hear him whisper. Without Bun I would never have embraced Ireland so long ago, would never have been so mesmerized by this island and pursued our improbable adventure. I stepped down that lonely Irish beach and suddenly began to rejoice, thinking my transplanted family had completed a great circle of becoming on these shores, with profound indebtedness to my old friend.

"Every person I meet makes me larger," Bun once said to me. Well, I was immeasurably larger for having known him, and now thanks to so many new friends in Ireland, my wife and kids were too. When each of us befriended another person here, when we were astonished by the outpourings of imagination and mirth that this society of storytellers tossed around like goblets of inspiration – well, we were passing on gifts first presented from Bun to myself, and in some not insignificant way passed ineluctably forward.

"Only enough to kill a hardened sinner," Bun had said of his magic carrot elixir, but of course he was speaking of the incarnate spirit of Ireland, which by now seemed to be our element, too.

I wandered back to the village and found my family caught up in a sidewalk conversation with Gavin and his parents and many siblings. Looking back over everything that had happened, I could only conclude that we had done the right thing. But our departure to revisit the States loomed.

Our return to the U.S. in late July brought many reckonings, some salutary and some not. True, certain accents encountered on our first stop in Jamie's New Jersey turf were grating enough to send one running for the nearest earplugs, if only the heat wasn't so hellishly torpid as to discourage walking to the next room. "It's a scorcher," they say in Cork when the temperature is about as mild as an April breeze. An American "scorcher" could reduce an Irishman to a puddle, and I was gasping for the more moderate, albeit fickle, weather of our adopted land. But the ocean in New Jersey, while not remotely as beautiful as the coast of Cork, can be swum in for as long as one likes, without shrieking for the warmth of terra firma. The grilled hamburgers and steaks, the clams, sweet corn, ice cream, pizza, bagels, nachos, and junk food beyond naming were all much more indulgently satisfying, even if the strip developments that purveyed the stuff looked more nightmarishly ugly than anything Ireland has yet produced. Jamie's family surrounded us with warmth, and even our young German shepherd, whom the in-laws had nurtured during our absence, responded as if we had only left the week before.

Our house in Connecticut, the next stop, seemed like a haven only fools could have ever left. By day, the kids swam in the lake, and in the evenings we had a string of those leisurely, mosquito-ridden barbecues that are the hallmark of an American summer – sixteen nights in a row featured visits by friends close and far, and my side of the family. Young Owen, who seemed to never eat in Ireland, suddenly wouldn't stop. "I only grow in America," he explained.

Yet many aspects of life there remained disenchanting. At the beach, the different cliques assembled in their usual spots, with invisible lines drawn in the sand around each one, and hardly a smile passed between the locals and the New York weekenders. Things work like that in present-day America, where people can let you know with one turn of the head that your conversation will be a burden, rather than joining together in the free-flowing exchange that is Irish life. I myself grew introspective.

One night we drove thirteen miles to the nearest watering hole in a chintz-bedecked New England inn – a distance that anywhere in Cork would offer a dozen talk-filled pubs. Several people inside well knew that we had returned from an unusual experience, but studiously paid little heed, indifference being one way to show superiority in our part of the States. A great Irish-American talker who had made a killing on Wall Street cast a wan smile our way before mouthing, "How ya doing?"

"Great. We're just back from a year in Ireland."

"Really? Must have been interesting," he perfunctorily muttered before retreating to his table of fancy friends.

"Book the next flight," I said to Jamie. In Ireland, people with whom one has only passing familiarity scuttle forward with enthusiastic salutations and earnest questions after an absence of mere weeks. The climate is not remotely as chilly as in New England, at any season. I got scolded for parking at the wrong angle *at the dump*, of all places. In Ireland, there is no such angle.

Children, at least, are free of such adult games. Ours rejoiced in the kids' amenities that flourish in America – miniature golf and mighty amusement parks, frog-jumping contests, swimming races, and bicycle parades around the town green; so many indulgences of childhood that the Irish have not yet organized. So we worried about a potential insurrection as our return to Cork neared. But our young travelers barely complained when we headed off for Year Two. After such a huge summer, they actually pined to return to the other half of their dual lives.

Chapter 25

"It's my go," screeched Owen as Feidhlim booted a ball down the street toward Harris. The boys had been back on their Cork pavement for mere minutes but the thread was effortlessly rejoined. Laura, meanwhile, had her beak in a phone – excitedly calling her scattered West Cork friends.

A lovely neighbor named Lorraine came by with welcome "home" gifts, and so did Shaun and Breda. The next days brought friendly greetings from even the most casual acquaintances. The stringy-haired musician bowing the bent saw was making his magic off Patrick Street; saucer-eyed crusties beamed over their bongos; and young and old stood at the corners collecting coins for some worthy cause, as they do every single day in Cork. On the pavement beside Brown Thomas, the *Titanic* was being repainted for the thousandth time, just as one would expect.

Nearby stood a new petitioner for attention, this one standing beside placards that read:

Family Lawyers = Child-Trading Association

These Incompetent, Inept, Bungling Bloodsuckers are the Gene Pool of Tomorrow's Judges

Family Law is a Killer

To the carnival of life we had returned. But hints arose that our second year in Ireland would be different, beginning the first time I walked into the Hi-B. The eccentric Brian O'Donnell remained absent, and the customers did not look quite so carefree as I'd remembered. A photograph hung ominously on the mirror of the fellow who had offered a soliloquy a year before about the way Corkonians cherish spontaneity, and who we had put up in our house one spring day after he returned from a long hiatus back in his native Scotland. The photo, I soon learned, was a testament to his recent suicide.

The children returned agreeably to their schools, Jamie to her job at the Cork Opera House, and an international magazine celebrating Ireland's riches asked for a regular column concerning life in Cork, even as a literary agent in Dublin suggested a meeting there. Meanwhile, I began to devise fresh strategies for launching my *Cork Magazine*. All this seemed to augur well, and I decided to have a haircut in preparation for my trip to "the big smoke," calling into the Turkish barber on MacCurtain Street. Past sessions had featured no Turks, but rather a Kosovan, Tunisian, Italian, and Glaswegian, all testifying nonetheless to the ever-increasing diversity of modern Cork life.

This time, Ahmad, the swarthy fellow with the black ponytail and gold neck-chains, was waiting.

He didn't like Americans so grew fierce with the razor, burning Q-Tips, and the follicle-yanking noose, but he couldn't have foreseen the imminent clash of our nations any more than I might have myself.

"Saddam a great man," Ahmad said. History will tell whether Saddam's nemesis in Washington was a hero, fool, or tyrant himself, but the Barber of Baghdad definitely gave me a tongue-lashing along with the trim. A lot more of those would come our way soon.

Whoosh went the hair, and ouch went the ear, and I got out of there. The newspaper joke piece I started about that encounter was never finished. The next day I traveled to Dublin for my meeting in the lobby of a hotel and was puzzled by an open-mouthed crowd gathered before a television screen. September 11, 2001, was the date – the time in New York about 9 a.m. In minutes I, too, confronted the newly minted images of what appeared to be the beginning of the end of the world – the apocalyptic flights into the World Trade Center and the Pentagon with all their certainty of unimaginable carnage and military retaliations to follow. Our meeting ended abruptly. Even three thousand miles from New York, the televised pictures seared the soul. Every viewer looked devastated, but the Americans stood out by their weeping.

On the streets, some pedestrians stood blithely yakking into mobile phones, while others shuffled along beside me, looking haunted. It was obvious who knew and who didn't.

Heading for Heuston Station, I ran into a passionate, troubled songwriter I had met a number of times in Cork. Noel Brazil's eyes filled with grief and he grabbed my hand. "This is awful. I am so sorry. I am speechless." His photograph, too, would be pasted on the Hi-B's mirror a couple of months later – an aneurysm, not a hijacked plane, abruptly felled this anguished talent at the age of forty-four. I phoned Jamie from the train station and we wept. The ride back to Cork took an eternity.

It felt like there was no haven anywhere anymore, not even in Ireland.

The children all waited up, tossing in their beds, processing their own waking nightmares. Owen, that former filament of sunniness, threw his arms around me and asked, "Will they attack us here, Dad?"

"No, of course not. We're perfectly safe."

What else could I say? I did not let him see my tears.

Jamie and I struggled on as if we had lost our next of kin in the distant infernos – and indeed a niece and cousin-in-law had had narrow escapes (a delayed flight here, a prolonged chore there) from personal dates with immolation at the World Trade Center. The only course forward was to wrap the children in the everyday rhythms of their Irish lives, while tucking some extra sweets into their lunch boxes and taking them on a slow walk through that waterfall-replenished glade I'd found a year ago. Some ancient standing stones, resolute through the millennia, arose from nearby fields, but whatever solace they offered was short-lived. I looked at the young beings who mattered more than anything else I knew, whose lives I had tried so hard to enrich in the course of our great adventure abroad, and had the sickening feeling I could no longer protect them or provide for their futures, not in Ireland, not in America, not anywhere.

There was no going back to Connecticut, not now. No planes were flying, and who in their right mind would put their family on board one of those, unless bereft of all choice? Normally, it is all too easy to spot American tourists abroad, by their naive gazes and hapless clothing first of all. But the Yanks were unmistakable for different reasons on the streets of Cork now, shuffling like aimless ghosts as they blankly stared at what would have otherwise been pleasing sights. Across the country, kind souls began putting these stranded visitors up for free.

Our own Irish friends surrounded us with unstinting compassion, because they grieved and were wounded themselves. One put it simply, "None of us will ever be the same again now." Neighbors came by to ask what they could do for the children; we had invitations to dinner, where everyone tried to make sense of the certifiably mad world. As gratified as I was by these outpourings of kindness, I kept searching the nation's media for chaffs of meaning. Alas, there arose an overnight torrent of that Irish penchant for snap answers and sniping analysis. Before the first bodies were removed from New York's rubble, numerous television and newspaper commentators floated instant geopolitical rationalizations for the unspeakable atrocities, and scoldings about America's place in the world. The timing of these diatribes felt all wrong. The message between certain pundits' lines seemed to be that Ireland, more than ever, must keep resolutely neutral even in its sympathies, and back in those raw days, this was hard to take. Suddenly, I felt Irish no more. The idea that we were still somehow blessed by Bun's guiding spirit seemed like a sentimental indulgence. Of course, my old friend would have cringed at the heartless punditry, too.

In the anguished days following September 11, the blather from certain sorry corners of the country's citizenry grew deplorable. In the pubs, I heard various diatribes from star members of the "you had it coming to you" brigade, who offered ad hoc epistles about how America itself was the culprit, provoking extreme actions by earnest people who had no other means of making their case heard. However, larger spirits took me by the arm and pointed out that such blowhards scarcely expressed the sentiments of the overwhelming majority of Irish people.

In fact, a gifted Cork writer named Gerry McCarthy summed up the crumbling of the Twin Towers better than any commentator I ever heard. "It was like watching the *Apollo* moon rocket, with all the world's hopes on board, going in reverse," he told me. His perspective wasn't Irish or American – it was human.

On September 14, every single business enterprise in the Republic of Ireland shut down for a national day of mourning, an exercise in shared compassion that was replicated in no other country, not even America itself, and one that would mean a very personal sacrifice for countless Irish people. We attended a commemorative Mass in a church that was packed with more parishioners than had been seen inside in fifty years. The mood was shattering.

However, the eve of this day of mourning had an undercurrent of tension. We walked about town then with some friends and witnessed packs of young people celebrating an unexpected midweek break with gusto. For them, the connection with what had happened in the U.S. was obviously remote. I felt a massive disjoint between my adopted country and my true self. Certain voices in the press kept wishing terrorism away. Opinion polls soon suggested that more than half of Ireland's citizens did not want their airports used for as little as a stopover by American planes en route to Afghanistan, and fewer than 10 percent favored Irish participation of any kind in the global coalition assembling against Osama bin Laden's nest of terror.

Small packs of protestors occasionally gathered on Cork's Patrick Street, waving banners saying, "The U.S. and U.K. are Terrorists!" and even in one inane instance, "Make Love Not War." Laura cried at the sight.

To stake out some sense of identity for my anguished children, and to mourn for our country's dead, I hung an American flag before my home office window. This act quickly incited our teenage minders to gather before our door and shout, "Yeah Osama, Palestine rules!" whatever that meant. Fortunately, the father of one of these teenagers made him deliver a message of apology the next day, and the parents of the rest of that crowd finally succeeded in putting an end to their sprees of mischief, once and for all.

"I want to go home," Harris would weep into his pillow at night, and I myself sometimes sat disconsolately for hours, saying nothing. Somehow, Jamie held the family together.

We discovered that we were scarcely the only Irish-American expatriates suffering from personal abuse. A Boston-born Cork woman called us sobbing about the taunting her thirteen-year-old daughter had endured at school; a Pennsylvanian twenty miles distant said that after more than a decade of contented life in Ireland, he had been so wounded by daily anti-American harangues that he wanted to vacate the country for good. A letter to the *Irish Voice* in the U.S. bitterly observed, "What fools we Irish-Americans have been. Why did we keep the tradition alive here all these years? We must have been laughing stocks going to Ireland, sending money … My mother-in-law who scrubbed floors at night to support five kids always sent clothes and more home when she needed help herself . . . This has really put an end to anything I will ever have to do with Ireland."

For months afterward, Irish newspapers hosted heartbroken letters from Americans who had chased personal dreams to the land of their forebears and were now feeling bereft and alienated. Quite often, these would excite a torrent of "go away" missives from poison-pen correspondents who did not wish to hear such complaints.

Still, this bitter cross fire scarcely represented the Ireland that had welcomed us with such warmth for more than a year. And many other Irish-Americans penned their own missives of gratitude for the great compassion that had been shown them, while other prominent Irish columnists mocked the equivocations of some of their colleagues.

For a long time, the to-and-fro numbed us. In our hearts we were injured, spiritually and, yes, materially. With advertising plummeting in the global economic crash following September 11, publications on both sides of the Atlantic stopped commissioning freelance articles, beginning with my regular feature on life in Cork. And a silly humor book I had started – to be called *Ireland for the Unwary* – now felt like a waste of time. Advancing the *Cork Magazine* fantasy, targeted partly at the flight-terrified tourist market, seemed ridiculous. Dreams died. Many mornings, I'd lift my head from sleep and crave the idea of shepherding the kids and Jamie back to the United States, the country of our birth, to be with our grieving families and friends. I felt, for the first time, exiled. Every one of us did.

Chapter 26

Endless rain blackened the weeks after September 11, and the Irish had their own struggle with the changed terms of the world. The tourist industry and foreign investment, both critical to the country's fortunes, plummeted; layoffs occurred by the thousands; and the overheated property and construction markets ominously stalled. A fear spread through the land that the Celtic Tiger might be tottering on its last legs. But the Irish know as much about economic travail as perhaps any people on earth, and they simply soldiered on.

We tried to do the same, concentrating on the children and our work, while slowly regaining our day-to-day direction and resolve. In time, the rhythms of life began to provide their healing, as did the invigoration of fresh experience one gets from living abroad, once one turns a deaf ear to fools. And what had all our Irish struggles amounted to in the end, compared to the suffering of families directly affected by September 11? Friends from the U.S. kept saying how fortunate we were to be far from the malaise that had settled over our homeland, that there would be no profit in trudging back there. In time, we began to take a larger stock. It was obvious that malaise had not yet conquered Cork. The life force of the place was too resilient for that, and, considering the gloom elsewhere, we resumed thinking that this was the best place to call home, at least for now.

Jamie's brother Dave and his wife returned for Christmas, and, escaping the monsoons this time, were treated to a grand tour of the places we had come to love. "You should just stay here, you know that?" advised the ever-supportive Gayle.

We sampled the cornucopia of Cork's gifts – the theater, the music, the laughter, all combined one night in a marvelous candlelit performance by three local tenors in white dinner jackets at a pub called Pa Johnson's – and counted our Irish blessings. A memorable trip followed to the haunting Burren in County Clare, that lunar landscape of endless rock shelves and rubble where nature still finds a way to spring tendrils of fresh life through the smallest crevice. The even more treeless and gale-wracked Aran Islands floated in the hazy distance, where survival, until recently, required that garden soil be conjured out of seaweed and sand. All one needed to learn about fortitude and perseverance lay right there.

Harris had his twelfth birthday in January and received the one thing that our household still sorely lacked – a pet snake. This he named "Roberto Boa," after his best friend and former snake-hunting partner in the U.S. Mr. Boa was in fact a four-inch-long baby corn snake that a St. Patrick-defying Cork entrepreneur had flogged for seventy euros (the insufferable new money having taken over on New Year's Day). The creature, the very species Harris used to pluck out of woodpiles for free any summer day he chose, soon shed his old skin, and we began to do the same.

The despair of autumn receded further as the seasons changed and spring approached again. Many of our problems had faded: the diatribes disappeared as the world spun forward; Harris prospered under the nurturing of a single, unchanging teacher; the teenagers who had harassed us had mercifully continued their hiatus; and no night raiders crept back through our kitchen window. Meanwhile, certain positive developments began to emerge from the society at large. The *gardaí* finally made sporadic efforts to curtail the late-night violence on Cork's streets, and Irish motorways started being policed with a new, radar-equipped vigilance. The country also started tackling some of its mounting environmental problems, pushing recycling and even instituting the simple innovation of levying a fee on every plastic bag that heretofore had been mindlessly left to blow off onto the beaches and streams where I fished.

And despite the economic setback after September 11, Ireland, so long accustomed to adversity, seemed determined to keep growing. Diminutive Cork, the little metropolis that could, was appointed European Capital of Culture for 2005, meaning that more than ten million of Brussels' euros would be poured into the city's coffers for the realization of grand visions for its streets and public squares and arts of every kind. Meanwhile, shops were being spiffed-up on every street, even as certain venerable pubs, more sadly, underwent ghastly face lifts.

Americans tend to think that they live in a land of unique opportunity, energy, and can-do spirit. Yet a vastly smaller country like Ireland has in many ways more-fixable problems, while remaining largely innocent of threats from abroad. The pace of its changes and breadth of its contradictions kept amazing us. The call of piety remained strong enough that over a million people visited the touring relics of St. Theresa, often standing in queues for hours to get their seconds-long chance for veneration. Meanwhile, Ireland's holy wells were still attracting supplicants in great numbers, the visitors draping ribbons and fragments of the clothing of departed loved ones on nearby trees as they prayed that God would speed the souls of the deceased on to eternal life, or work miracles for the infirm.

Yet as April 2002 unfolded, frosted glass "adult stores" and slick new lap-dancing clubs spread throughout downtown Cork – this in a city that would have all but banished a young lass in a halter top a generation ago. A flagship of such establishments, Dublin's Club Lapello, was recently hauled into court for not having a license to facilitate patrons dancing with their hostesses. The defense solicitor argued, "There is no practice within the club of people dancing *with* people rather than *at* them."

One personal change was to limit visiting hours to a certain establishment where two more newly deceased regulars had their photographs taped to the mirror. The place was becoming bad luck. But the curious old Lee-side town and the inspiring county that surrounds it continued to amuse and engage us with its plucky celebration of life. You never knew when people would break out singing, in your home, on the street, or in the pub – or when the ever-improbable Irish would dart onto the center of the world's troubled stage. Bono, the illustrious Dublin rock star with two seaside homes about to be connected by an aerial walkway, was busy touring Africa with the straight-arrow American Secretary of Commerce; the weird duo explored schemes for eliminating poverty, while draped in black-and-white striped robes and clown-ishly floppy hats that made them look like prison escapees in a vaudeville act.

"I still haven't found what I'm looking fo-oor," Bono sang from under his omnipresent wraparound blue shades to African children who did not understand a word. But neither had I, and Ireland still had room for grand dreams. I even wondered if one day I might yet launch that long-planned *Cork Magazine*, my small testament to all the brightest things we had come to know in our new land. The post-September 11 world had settled into some kind of new equilibrium after all, and so, it felt, had our lives in Ireland.

One weekend, we journeyed for a lunch in Inchigeelagh, an exqui-sitely tranquil nook in the hidden folds of Mid-Cork. "Now!" said a slightly shriveled, bob-haired waitress as she made a flurry of activity out of setting five paper napkins around a table in a cosy, hearth-warmed room in Creedon's Hotel. Something about her was pure cat.

Out she came with the forks and knives. The cutlery descended, and our very pleased waitress repeated "Now!"

Tea came with a "Now!" Saucers: "Now!" A bowl of sugar: "Now!"

Surprisingly strong portraits of time-weathered country people and rugged hills stared down at us over discreetly displayed bits of sculpture. Serious books lined nearby shelves. And here came our soup – "veg" naturally, but steaming and spiced true to some prescient soul's fine sense of taste. "Now!"

Was the server blipping monosyllables because she was daft?

Or perhaps she was a native Irish-speaker who knew no other English word?

Baskets of sandwiches appeared with a fresh "Now!"

Laura had her eyes cocked in amusement. No McDonald's could have provoked the same sly smile.

"Now!" The woman repeated it perhaps five times more before we were done with that meal, never uttering a single other word.

Perhaps the waitress was an oracle.

"Now." What a ring that little word held. We had fretted so often about the past and the future and probably the pluperfect, too. But there was the message – *carpe diem*. Cork was our "now," and the spirit and rhythms of the place were in our bones; perhaps this "now," right here before us, was where we belonged, not on an extended lark, but for good.

So it was that we contemplated buying a house in Cork, and at last putting down roots. This quest proved frustrating, however. Unless one has Bono's riches, purchasing property is not an easy process in Ireland; in fact, commissioning seven thousand slaves to erect a desert pyramid could be less daunting. Thinking back on the beneficence of small-town living for raising kids, we first explored possibilities in Kinsale. But it became apparent that one would get better value in Beverly Hills or the toniest enclaves of London. So we pointed our Irish dreaming to Clonakilty, that charming, bustling gateway to West Cork.

Perhaps I felt some ancestral pull toward the place owing to the Deasy blood on my mother's side. That versatile Timoleague and Clonakilty clan had once distinguished itself by smuggling contraband along the West Cork coast; it then graduated into running rum from the West Indies, before finally creating a great brewery in the nineteenth century. The resultant stout was so thick and faculty dimming, locals dubbed it "the wrastler." One wag remarked that across a pewter pot of the stuff "you could trot a mouse."

So it was Deasy Land here we come. The first inspection was of a Georgian behemoth on an exquisite town square. Never mind that it had twelve bedrooms and we had only three children – Michael Collins had boarded inside as a youth, and there was no telling what we were capable of while in the process of remaking our lives inside out. Running a hotel? No problem. That would be a piece of cake compared to some of our more capriciously discussed alternatives to the magazine: starting a miniature golf course, a slick coffee shop, an art gallery, or perhaps pushing a hot-dog cart outside Cork's hurling park. A hotel seemed doable, and wouldn't it be wonderful to give the kids access to the playing fields at the edge of town, and the great beaches and fishing spots at a stone's throw, when not insinuating ourselves into the talkative company at De Barra's to quaff a few "wrastlers"? The only catch was that the particular abode had no heating, the walls festered with rot, and it carried a price tag high enough to cover the cost of every property in the village two decades before. Drive on coachman, drive on.

Next we settled upon a house that had been owned by Michael Collins's nephew. This one had fantastic gardens and an orchard, hefty spaciousness, nice views, kids nearby, and a cracked and noseless figure of the Blessed Virgin that looked as if it had been thrown down the stairs in a tantrum. Up and down the hillside rose newly built homes, many done with a stone-facaded tastefulness that Clonakilty's civic planners, God bless them, encourage. The local school seemed a model of bright stewardship. Perfect. We would live here and flourish.

However, the Collins house had a certain price. Little did we know that this signified nothing. The prices listed for Irish properties proved to be no more real than a free-drink ticket slapped into one's hands by a shill outside a New York City strip joint.

"We like this place. We'll buy it," I told the auctioneer, which Irish real-estate agents are tellingly called.

"You want to make a bid, is it?" he asked, poker-faced.

"Yes, we'll pay the full asking price."

We knew Clonakilty's history, and thought the offer more than fair.

"Well, there is a higher bid on offer already actually."

"How much higher?"

"Thirty thousand."

Back when the town was devastated by the Famine, they used to say, "Clonakilty, God help us," for other reasons.

"Who else exactly is interested?"

"I am not at liberty to say that. I am sure you will understand."

"But of course." Now here we were, talking like tut-tutting Brits – a gentlemanly, if cute, former West Cork horse-trader in Michael Collins land (on Michael Collins's family turf, for Christ's sake) and a displaced Yank considering pushing a hot-dog cart through his post-fifty years.

Would things in Ireland ever be simple?

"We'll give you thirty-two more," I said, wheeling and dealing away.

Night fell. "We have your offer and it is a handsome offer indeed, but there has just been a fax to our office indicating that the other bidders will now go to thirty-five thousand more," explained the man's boss the next morning.

Gasp. Reflection. Delay. Then a call back: "We'll go to forty."

So went our days, and our next two weeks – consultations, hair-pulling, ever-higher bids against unknown beings, a process everyone reassured us was routine when buying Irish property and officially called "gazumping." Clonakilty seemed ideal, full of friendly people starting businesses of various descriptions – one astute soul was even launching a scaled-down newsprint version of the local magazine concept I had so fervently pursued, and it occurred to me that I might hook up with him. But there were limits, and when the negotiations reached fifty thousand above the original asking price, we backed out. The phantom bidders evidently went poof as well, because that fine, fine house is still available as I write.

Ultimately we reset our homesteading sights upon Cork City. An interesting nineteenth-century house with a walled garden was available at the end of a shockingly narrow road in the desirable Montenotte area up the next hill from where we were living. This had increasingly familiar ingredients – mortar walls crumbling with the infernal Irish damp, and this time, not one but two separate rival bidders appearing from the Irish ether that is so chock-full of reposed saints and panting house purchasers. Up and up went the asking price, and down, down went our resolve.

We tried one of Cork's southside suburbs. The modest dwelling had four other potential purchasers poking and prying inside when I arrived for an inspection. In many countries, a potential buyer of a $1000 diamond ring would be ushered into a back room for a respectful, private viewing. But a prospective plonker for a commodity worth three hundred times more will be treated with no such respect in the isle of ancient horse-traders. The gazumping of course started right on cue. Goodbye to all that, I said. Ireland had simply gotten too expensive, too modern, and too complicated, and I was topped out. Having walked to the very end of the gangplank, I feared I could not earn enough money to pay the Irish piper for the rest of our years.

So, with sadness in our hearts, we would go back to America after all. The O'Neills, Hans and Lourdes, Owen and Maria, and all the rest were told. We had a wonderful home there for raising children, and, when the truth was weighed, a sound school and good community, even if the latter needed to lighten up. I missed the beauty of the New England countryside intensely. Our Irish adventure had been rich, and would never be regretted, but the stars signaled that it must end.

Stupid me. I had altogether forgotten about Irish circles. One day in May, Shaun Higgins banged on our door, saying that he had convinced a neighbor across the street to sell his house to us at a very reasonable price with no auctioneer or phantom bidder on the hustings. "Don't ye see? Ye won't have to move anywhere at all? Ye can stay right here among all the friends you and the children have already made," said Shaun. "This is where you belong. Don't you understand that this is your home now?"

The Victorian, ivy-clad terrace house had superbly high ceilings, grand fireplaces, and a foyer archway leading to winding staircases, but it cried out for renovation at every turn. It could have had banshees, for all I could tell. But Jamie was convinced that it was a project equal to our dreams.

An aged German woman in the Hi-B listened to our plan and said, "I first came to Ireland with my husband twenty years ago, and thought it was the most beautiful country with the friendliest people in the world."

I smiled. "And?"

"We bought an old house to renovate, just like you're considering."

"And?"

"My husband had *three* heart attacks. It was a nightmare, what the builders did to us, and now he's dead," she said and burst out crying. Esther whispered that I should pay no mind, because the woman was called "Waterfall" for this teary penchant.

A few days later I went to a hidden stream to reflect. Some beautiful trout were hooked and released, but I barely admired them, so intensely was I assessing our time in Ireland. Bubbles suddenly began rising from the lip of a long adamantine pool, as if a fat salmon had swum in from the sea. I half-seriously thought of lying down in that dark water with a stone on my belly in order to breathe in those bubbles until I could reason clearly. But memories floated past in the river's swirls, producing illusions of clarity, one by one. So very much had fallen into our hands in return for what we had risked and I could not walk away yet: it was that simple.

That old, incredibly cluttered, unheated terrace house across the street took on a sheen of promise. We talked and we thought; and, with our Cork friends promising they would pitch in at every stage of the work ahead, we bought it. Whether this meant committing to a third Irish year or forever, only time could tell. But mark this, ye adventurers, and mark this well – no man who has dipped his feet in Cork's dreams will ever leave easily.

Epilogue

"It's only enough to kill a hardened sinner," Bun had said about his homemade magic potion, the carrot whiskey.

The renovations that consumed the first half of our third year in Ireland had a similar impact upon our equilibrium.

Oh, we thrilled alright to the pulsating dance of the "kango" – this being the Irish term for jackhammer. Often, I was tapped on the elbow as the things were trained, like grenade launchers, upon little G-spots of sensitivity within our prized acquisition.

"Ah, do you have a minute?"

"Of course."

"This bulge in the wall here. Ah, I hope you don't mind my saying so, now, but it has some problems with the plaster. The sag is fulsome. It seems to be very, very old plaster. You would be advised to clear this whole area away."

"Is it a big job, Mick?"

"Not at all; no."

"Ah, just a moment there, Dave?" – a fresh tap on the sleeve, this time from another workman – "I hate to say this, but the wall in the front hallway, there is a touch of trouble there."

"And?"

"The whole thing really should go."

The doorway itself had to go; and of course the electricians, deciding that new wiring was called for in every room, needed massive channels bored through every two-foot-thick, 120-year-old facade that caught their eye. The plumbers, who seemed to be a particularly disgruntled and multitudinous lot, developed a yen to shove pipes through this barrier and that, and while they were at it, blast floors into oblivion.

On the curiously sunny mornings of that autumn of 2002, I

would stride hopefully across Bellevue Park, throw open the front door to our new home – back when a doorway existed – and . . . gag. The entire house was forever enveloped in a post-nuclear-bomb-like cloud of plaster dust and pulverized wall fallout, while the kangos roared and workers in masks slipped like shrouds through the haze.

One day, my old friend Paddy Wilkinson paid a surprise visit to see our "progress." He found me with my eyes bulging dementedly, my face and every inch of exposed skin filmed in white powder like the cracked Marlon Brando's aboriginal friends in *Apocalypse Now*, while I heaved a choking wheelbarrow down our hallway of personal renovation hell. A particularly fine demolition party was in full swing. The kangos were symphonic and had never rang prouder.

"It's going to be a fine house," Paddy, the master renovator, reassured. Like phantoms in the fallout, a couple of fellas with breathing masks at their chins sat at a surviving table placidly sipping tea, and watching to see whether I would finally lose it. Paddy and I examined the scene, caught each other's eyes, and suddenly started laughing like madmen. That sound, quickly louder than even the wildest decibels of the kangos, ricocheted down the halls and up the stairs, where it was picked up and amplified by only God knows how many Irishmen who were presently tearing my family's life apart. It may have even reached the heavens, that chorus of the blessed and the damned.

In time, after heartbreak and at amazing expense, Paddy's prediction proved true. We had in the end a beautifully restored house and a firm foot now planted in our adopted land, while we all began to recover from yet another escapade not advised for the fainthearted. Any number of friends had shown what they were made of and showered grace upon our progress – working for nothing, and giving us carpets, cutlery, beds, meals, help of every kind. That was more than something.

But then people started dying and growing ill back in the States.

A beloved uncle, a brother-in-law, another uncle gone, and now an aunt and my mother in trouble. I was making journeys home for the worst reasons.

In June of 2003, the whole family flew back across the pond to reconnect and sort out, yet again, our imperatives. The truth was that Harris, now thirteen, had struggled painfully through his first year at Christian Brothers' big secondary school. And with household mayhem prevailing through that sensitive transition, we had done a poor job of organizing a better option for him the next year. All through the summer we struggled to solve issues large and small, among them the fact that the most recent renter had blithely walked out on our Connecticut house.

In more than a little confusion, we began packing our bags for the mid-August flight back to Cork – we loved the place so much still. But we had just buried our saintly Aunt Seena, and questions nagged. What about our mothers, what about Harris, what about this, and on and on? One day we told our kids we would stay on in America for a while after all, then another afternoon we pronounced no, we would leave, that the rest of our lives hung in the balance, and Cork was it as far as we were concerned.

Then, as the flight back loomed but thirty-six hours off, Jamie and I looked in each other's eyes and knew the truth. We could not just blithely wave goodbye to my dying mother, to all these people who made up the very fabric of our lives.

Alone and numbed, I flew back to Cork to take care of our affairs.

There on Wellington Road, I met a house painter who had practically moved in with us for a few weeks, before walking off the job and leaving his brushes, radio, and painting overalls behind for some better assignment. In time, we would understand that this was fairly routine.

He was Tony, but I called him Professor.

"Professor," I said, always liking this ponderous soul, who sometimes made a point of undercharging us. "I have bad news: we are moving back to America."

"Jesus Christ, tell me you are not serious?" Tony responded, his eyes instantly moistening. "You can't be leaving us."

And there I was, not knowing how to explain my confusion, wiping away tears as I talked with a painter who had left his trousers in our closet and vanished. That I had taken this, too, in my stride was perhaps a measure of how Corked or uncorked I myself had become.

I would soon go through the same anguished routine with innumerable closer friends.

"I am shocked," said Pat O'Neill.

"But you are one of us," said Hugh McPhillips.

It felt as if we were committing some betrayal. We had been tested and scalded but ultimately accepted with open arms in this strangely interconnected little world; we had survived a rite of passage reserved for very few from points afar – and now we were just packing off and leaving.

I hid behind curtains and answering machines, not wanting to tell our story anymore. What a remarkable thing it had been to move across the seas with such caprice and find that you belonged in your adopted town, at your stab at the end of the rainbow, more fully than anywhere you had lived since childhood. How remarkable that you had discovered your heart's home at fifty, but now were abandoning it.

Jamie flew back to Cork to help with the final, rending packing. The banger of a car was sold at the last minute, and renters were found for the year ahead, though turning over the keys to them was not easy. I couldn't look at the towering brick hearth without seeing Pat Lynch applying an evil goo to strip off ages of encrusted paint; way up on the dangerously steep roof there still reigned the smiling face of Hans, the friend who would placidly risk his life for us without charge. Renovated and polished to perfection, this house was filled with spirits. And they were ours.

That night the doorbell began buzzing, with the word out that we wanted to say some goodbyes. In they came, people from every aspect of our Cork lives – the neighbors from our Bellevue Park village, the school parents who had looked so lovingly after our kids, the marvelous pub originals, the crowd from Jamie's Cork Opera House, and, a bit later, Paddy Wilkinson. They showered us with gifts, they brought laughter, they filled our house with warmth.

There was dancing until, oh, around midnight. Some then had to leave.

Those remaining drew close. Somebody speechified about how deeply we would be missed; I grabbed a marvelous Australian transplant and said, forget that, Amy is carrying our spirit forward now. Too serious, Diarmuid said, and started a little song. The pause at the end was touching – for maybe three seconds. Time for another. So someone else closed her eyes, and delivered a ballad no one knew was in her. This was followed by about seventy more songs, never with a moment's surcease, many delivered in rousing choral fashion, many with the Opera House ladies stepping forward for dance routines in the night that promised to go on forever.

Close to dawn, the first soldier fell and was helped away; the canary in the coal mine. Jamie and I, now alone in the silence, held each other's hands. We were more happy than sad. We had been loved, for God's sake.

Is there any wonder that as I write these words we are scheming and dreaming to one day return to our house in Cork?

Acknowledgements

The encounter with Ireland that this book describes was made possible by many beneficent spirits. First of all, our families, whose astounding selflessness blessed our passage; Mick and Hylda Buckley, who opened some of the first gates to Cork; the hearty souls of Bellevue Park, who accepted us with every Irish blessing; and Paddy and Anne Wilkson, who kept the link alive for decades. Gratitude is in fact owed to more Corkonians than can be mentioned here – to people like Peter Murray and John McMonigle, who nearly lifted the Cork magazine idea into being; to Gerry Barnes and the damsels at the Opera House.

Special thanks are in order for those who helped refine the book through its growth pains: Jonathan Williams, Owen McIntyre, and the gentleman and poet Tom McCarthy in the earlier going; and the gifted Lonely Planet editors Janet Austin and Meaghan Amor through the many stops and starts to the home stretch. But Jamie – here was the muse, the partner in jaywalking who turned dream to reality.

A number of texts were also helpful in writing of this book, particularly *The Cork Anthology* (Cork University Press, 1993), edited by Sean Dunne; *Discovering Cork* (Brandon Book Publishers Ltd., 1991) by Daphne D. C. Pochin Mould; and *The Lie of the Land: Journeys through Literary Cork* (Cork University Press, 1999) by Mary Leland. Other historical background came from *The Coast of West Cork* (Appletree Press Ltd., 1972) by Peter Sommerville-Large; *Sneem, The Knot in the Ring* (Sneem Tourist Association, 1986) by T. E. Stoakley; *The Secret Places of West Cork* (Royal Carbery Books, 1990) by John M. Feehan; *Irish Country Towns* (Mercier Press, Cork, 1994), edited by Anngret Sims and J. H. Andrews; *Narrative of a Journey from Oxford to Skibbereen During the Year of the Famine* (Oxford, 1847, reprinted by Cork Corporation 1996) by Lord Duferin and the Hon. G. F. Boyle; and *Clonakility, a History* (Litho Press, Midleton, Cork, 1999) by Michael J. Collins.